Preface

We wrote *Smart Cooking 1* primarily to steer students
premade foods and to encourage them to create deli
right ingredients for a better, healthier future. In our
environment where processed and convenience fooc
and readily available, but often expensive and unhealthy, becoming food literate is a life skill that will serve to enhance resilience, especially among the young.

Food literacy enables consumers to make informed choices about food. **Food Literacy** is defined as understanding the impact of food choices on one's health, including its influence on the environment and the economy. It is a set of skills and attributes which help people to sustain the daily preparation of healthy, tasty, affordable meals for themselves and their families. It builds resilience because it includes the food skills, techniques, knowledge and confidence to problem solve, modify and improvise to suit each individual, including special diets. This includes an understanding of how food is produced and prepared from farm to fork.

The psychosocial factors experienced in planning, preparing, cooking and eating food together cannot be overestimated. Self-reliance, self-efficiency, self-confidence, self-control, household food security and wellbeing are all enhanced by the ability to produce and consume good, healthy food.

At a practical level, *Smart Cooking 1* has been revised with emphasis on wellbeing, see new 'Chapter 8'. This compact, practical student-friendly book is laid out to create interest and build confidence in student cooks. It includes organisation skills for planning, buying and storing foods, and the selection and use of Irish produced foods is emphasised throughout. This book is designed to empower young people to meet the objectives of the new specification for the Junior Cycle Food Literacy Skills Brief and Practical Food Skills Examination. Revised examination guidelines for briefs and all practical cookery aspects have been included.

This book aims to nurture skills in researching food and in creating and using recipes by following instructions in a clear, organised way. The Key Words, Food Facts, Healthy Hints and Chef's Tips which appear throughout the book help to integrate good practice, food safety and practical knowledge with sound nutrition and life skills. *Smart Cooking 1* contains timed, basic recipes, followed by variations to give choice for creation, improvisation and also modifications to cater for special dietary needs.

Smart Cooking 1 provides a bridge to the Senior Cycle syllabus including research skills, self-resilience, resource management, consumer education and kitchen safety. The long-term goal for the student is to recognise that knowledge is power and to continue to be passionate about cooking appetising food, while enjoying the rewards of healthy eating. To that end we hope *Smart Cooking 1* will be shared in many homes and be there for future homemakers and families.

ACKNOWLEDGEMENTS

The authors would like to extend their thanks to Mary Martin for her vision and enthusiasm and to all those teachers who helped with this book, especially Miriam O'Brien, Deirdre Healy, Mary Anglim, Mary Hyland, Grace Linehan, Yvonne Cooney, Ann Cunningham, Leonie Byrne, Geraldine Timlin, Bairbre Ní Loideain, Kathleen Geaney, Fionnuala Casey, Jane Morgan, Coleman O'Reilly and Jenny Halliday.

Thanks also to the following: Fiona Cribben, Ivor Cribben, Niall Cribben, Ann Mealy, Orla Sweeney and Ita Dockery; Pamela De Bri, Graeme Syme, Peter Murphy, Shíofra Murphy and Robert Murphy for assistance with photographic material; Clodagh Murphy, Rachel Davies, Andrew and David McGeady, Kate Gilbride, Catherine Kelly and family, Helen MacGoey, Fiona Brady, Emer Fitzgerald, Eithne Murray, Ruth Farragher, Tracy McDonagh and Eimear Cassidy for recipe testing and tasting.

Published by
CJ Fallon
Ground Floor – Block B, Liffey Valley Office Campus, Dublin 22.

ISBN: 978-0-7144-2761-4

First Edition July 2019

Printed In Ireland by
W&G Baird Limited
Caulside Drive
Antrim BT41 2RS

Glossary of Icons

The following glossary and explanation of icons will help you navigate the hints, tips and ideas that appear throughout *Smart Cooking 1*.

Chef's Tip! Icon
Indicates general tips on how to choose ingredients and cook food in practical and efficient ways.

Food Fact! Icon
Provides information about the recipe's ingredients. The *Food Fact!* icon defines an ingredient and explains the nutritional advantages, disadvantages or concerns of certain foods.

Healthy Hint! Icon
Highlights how certain foods can impact on one's health, eating habits and digestibility.

In a hurry! Icon
Practical recommendations on how to speed up or adjust the preparation of a meal.

Idea! Icon
Simple suggestions on how to resourcefully modify recipes for specific diets or special occasions.

Watch Out! Icon
Indicates warning or caution in order to avoid injury or hazard in your kitchen.

Resource Management Icon
This icon shows how natural resources can be managed to encourage sustainability, prevent waste, store ingredients safely, upcycle leftover dishes, save energy and dispose of waste correctly.

Look Up! Icon
Advising students to conduct further research is very important. This icon acts as a reminder to learn more about cooking and food literacy outside the classroom.

Buy Local, Buy Irish! Icon
Emphasises the importance of purchasing and using fresh, local, Irish ingredients and produce.

Key Recipes! Icon
The key symbol highlights basic, essential recipes. A variation recipe often follows these key recipes, where ingredients have been altered in order to make a new dish.

Cooking Time Icon
Indicates the expected cooking time for a dish. As ovens and hobs can vary, the time is an approximation. It is advised to get to know your oven and adjust the time accordingly.

Serves/Makes Icon
Suggests the average number of servings a recipe produces based on the quantities of ingredients indicated. Some people will eat more or less food, depending on age, height, weight and diet.

Evaluation! Icon
This icon appears at the start of every chapter and acts as a reminder to evaluate their task or dish/dishes as soon as possible. All aspects of the task or dish/dishes should be evaluated from planning, preparation and costing, through to cooking and tasting. See pages 223 and 224.

Icons for Special Dietary Requirements
These icons appear on recipes that are suitable for individuals with special dietary requirements or where modifications can be made to suit specific diets. They can be found under the recipes as variations, Chef's Tips or Ideas.

vegan **vegetarian** **gluten-free** **dairy-free**

Many recipes can be easily modified and become gluten-free by using gluten-free pasta, Tamari instead of soy sauce and cornflour instead of flour. Certain recipes can become dairy-free by using non-dairy milks and oil instead of butter. Vegans can use non-dairy milks and oil instead of butter.

CONTENTS

Organisation: Getting Ready for Cooking

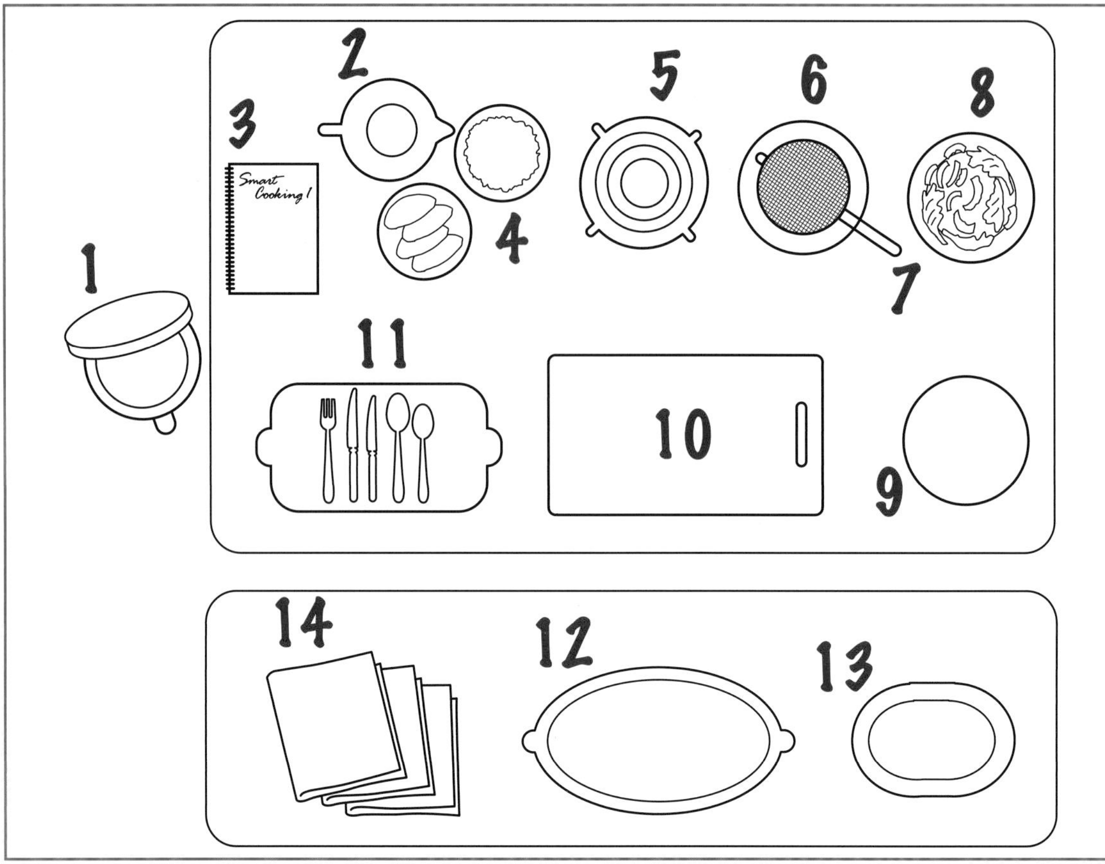

1. bin, *2.* jug, *3.* recipe book, *4.* plates and bowls for ingredients, *5.* pot stand, *6.* bowl, *7.* sieve, *8.* compost bowl, *9.* empty plate, *10.* chopping board, *11.* cutlery, *12.* serving dishes, *13.* pie dish, *14.* cloths.

Hygiene in the Kitchen/Good Practice while Cooking

Personal Hygiene

Before cooking, you should do the following:

1 Tie back hair, roll up your sleeves and remove jewellery.
2 Wash your hands thoroughly. Cover any cuts.
3 Put on a clean apron.
4 Disinfect the worktop.
5 Collect all necessary equipment and set the worktop as indicated in the diagram above.
6 Weigh and measure all ingredients accurately.
7 Prepare baking tins and preheat the oven if required.

Resource Management: Don't waste ingredients. Peel fruit and vegetables thinly. Turn off heat when finished. Avoid wasting water.

Hygiene in the Kitchen/Good Practice while Cooking

Kitchen Cloths

All cloths should be spotlessly clean. You should have the following cloths:

- **Dish cloth or J-cloth** For washing up, wiping tables and cookers.
- **Tea towels or drying cloth** (one for class, two for exams) Use only for drying clean dishes. **Never** wipe cookers or tables with these cloths.
- **Hand towel** Use for drying hands only.
- **Oven gloves or mitts** Use for taking hot dishes from the oven.

Recycling

REDUCE, REUSE, RECYCLE, REPAIR

Think before you buy, think before you throw.

- **Organic Waste**, e.g. food waste and paper are biodegradable. Organic waste composts or breaks down naturally over time.
- **Inorganic Waste**, e.g. metal, glass and some plastics are not biodegradable. Inorganic waste will not break down but can be recycled into new products. Wash and dry before putting into the correct recycling bin.
- **Do not throw out food** that can be used. Put it into a clean container and refrigerate if necessary.
- **Compost** vegetable peelings. Do not compost meat, fish, eggs, cooked foods or egg shells.
- **Water plants** with used water. Never wash fruit or vegetables under a running tap.

Washing Up Made Easy

SCRAPE, STACK, WIPE, WASH, DRAIN, DRY, INSPECTION

- **SCRAPE:** Scrape food and scraps from utensils into the food waste bin.
- **STACK:** Stack utensils neatly beside sink or on table.
- **WIPE:** Wipe down table and counter top.
- **WASH:** Wash the cleanest things first in hot water with a little washing-up liquid. Use a brush or cloth to get things really clean. Avoid using a dishwasher unless you have a full load.
- **DRAIN:** Turn things upside down on the draining board.
- **DRY:** Dry everything thoroughly using a tea towel.
- **INSPECTION:** Call teacher for inspection of utensils and equipment before putting away.
- **GENERAL TIDY UP:** Wipe cooker and counters. Clean out sink and wipe area all around it. Brush the floor in your area and then do your special duty.

Good Practices while Cooking – Beware of Cross-Contamination

Food Safety and Hygiene

- When finished with one food, **wash knife and chopping board carefully** before preparing another food. **Be especially careful to scrub the board after cutting raw meat or fish.**
- **Wash** any cutlery that has fallen on the floor.
- **When tasting food with a spoon**, wash it after each use.
- **Use kitchen paper, and not your fingers, to grease** pie dishes or tins.
- **Avoid touching your face or hair** while cooking.

General Safety

Organisation

- **Remove peelings from chopping board** before cutting food. Clean after each use.
- **Remove prepared foods from chopping board** before cutting something else.
- **Do not leave spoons in saucepans** while cooking food; place on a plate beside cooker.
- **Do not use a knife or fork to stir food** in a saucepan.
- **Choose correct-sized saucepan.**

Cooking

- **Always heat oil** before sautéing or frying food. Use a high temperature for sautéing.
- **Browning food develops flavour.** Allow food to brown before turning or stirring.
- **Taste the food to check for flavour**, and season if necessary during cooking.
- **Allow food to simmer** or cook long enough to allow flavours to develop.
- **Test food** to see if it is properly cooked before serving, especially chicken and burgers.
- **Do not fill casserole dishes too full** as they could overflow in the oven.

Resource Management

- **Use labour-saving equipment** where possible.
- **Always use an electric kettle to boil water** for stocks, vegetables, pasta, etc.
- **Put lids on saucepans** while cooking when possible, except for pasta.
- **Avoid opening oven door** during cooking as it cools the oven and delays cooking time.
- **Do not waste ingredients** – peel thinly, use all edible parts.
- **Store unused ingredients** correctly – clean, cold and covered.

General Safety

- **Be careful** with **freshly sharpened knives**.
- **Turn the handles of pots and saucepans** to the side while cooking.
- **Use oven mitts** instead of tea towels for hot dishes.
- **Use pot stands** for hot dishes.
- **Be careful when moving hot liquids or dishes** from place to place.
- **Wipe up any spills** from the floor as soon as they occur.
- **Do not overfill** a chip pan with oil.
- **Do not leave cooking oil** in saucepans, woks, frying pans or deep fat fryers **unattended**.
- **Have matches or lighter ready** before turning on a gas cooker if it isn't automatic.
- **Wear oven gloves** when opening the oven door.
- **Keep your face back** from fan ovens or microwave ovens when opening the door.
- **Turn off** cookers, rings and ovens after use.
- **Use a timer** if available to time the oven.
- **In cases of breakage** sweep up broken item carefully, wrap in newspaper and put safely in a bin.
- **If you smell gas**, turn off the supply as quickly as possible and tell somebody in charge. Open a window if you can, and leave the room. Telephone the gas company if you suspect a leak. Do not light a match or switch on anything.
- **Avoid trailing electrical flexes**.
- **Do not handle electrical equipment with wet hands.**
- **Use electrical equipment according to instructions.**
- **Do not** overfill a liquidiser.
- **Never put hands or knives** into liquidiser.
- **Be careful when washing and drying the blades of processors.**
- **Familiarise yourself** with use of the **fire blanket and equipment**.
- **If your clothes catch fire**, you must **DROP** and **ROLL**. **That means drop to the ground and roll over to quench the flames.**

Weighing and Measuring

Measuring Liquids

Use a measuring jug, and place it on a level surface.
There are 1,000ml in 1 litre (l).

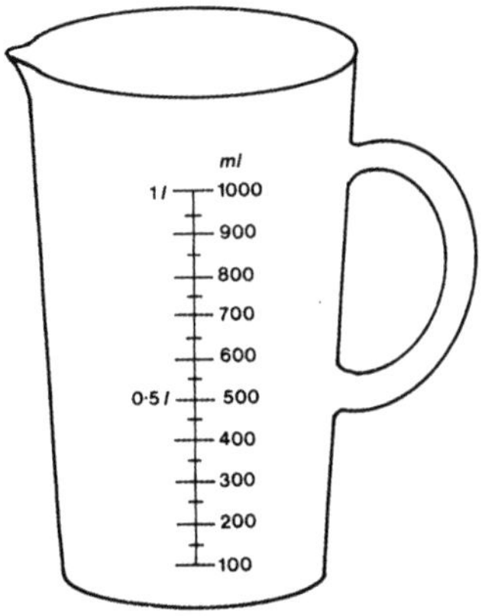

Spoons

Liquids or dry ingredients are often measured in spoons.

1 teaspoon = 5ml (the small spoon used in a sugar bowl).

1 dessertspoon = 10ml (the spoon used when eating morning cereal).

1 tablespoon = 15ml (the spoon used for serving from a serving dish).

1 rounded spoon = 1 spoon

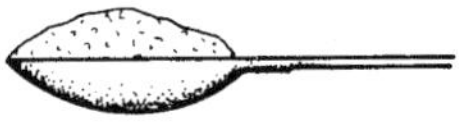

1 level spoon = ½ spoon

¼ spoon = ½ a level spoon

1 heaped spoon looks like this

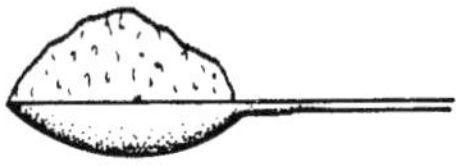

Weighing Meat, Dry Ingredients

Use a weighing scales if possible (see page 6 for approximate weights).

There are 1,000g in 1 kilo.

Look carefully at your scales. It will be divided up into smaller **20g or 25g** sections and larger **100g** sections.

Electronic scales usually weigh **5g** at a time.

Conversion Tables (approximate)

Grams	Ounces
25g	1oz
50g	2oz
75g	3oz
100g	4oz
200g	8oz
300g	12oz
400g	16oz (1lb)

Approximate Measurements

A **250g block of butter** can be sectioned off into 9 x 25g portions (approximate weight only). Use **two sections as 50g** and **one section as 25g**.

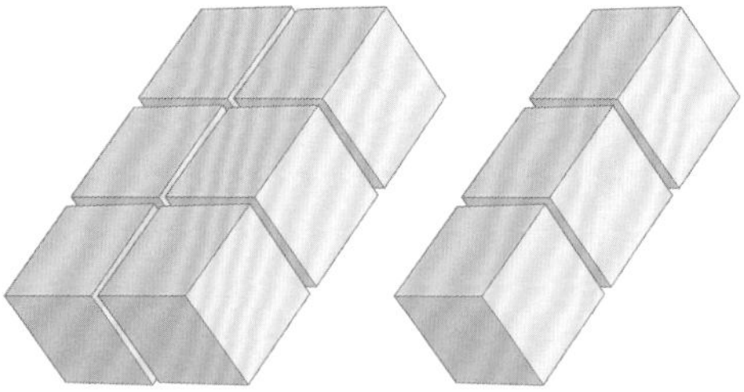

A 250g block of butter divided into 9 x 25g pieces

To obtain 25g (approximately) of the following foods, use the number of **level tablespoons** given below.

Breadcrumbs, fresh – 6	Cornflour – 2¾	Sugar, caster, granulated – 2
Butter – 2	Flour, white – 3	Sugar, demerara – 2
Grated Cheddar cheese – 3	Flour, brown – 3½	Sugar, icing – 3
Cocoa – 3	Rice, uncooked – 2	Syrup and honey – 2

Other Useful Measurements

125g pot of yoghurt = 100ml yoghurt	1 x 400g tin beans, drained = 230g to 260g beans
1 standard can chopped tomatoes = 400g	Single cream = 170ml carton
4 fresh medium chopped tomatoes = 1 tin	Sweetcorn, drained = 165g small or 280g large
Cream cheese = 200g or 225g packs	Crème fraîche = 200g carton
Cottage cheese = 225g tub	Small packs of fruit juice = 200ml

Choice and Selection of Ingredients

- The best chefs and cooks source their ingredients locally and often grow their own herbs and vegetables. The fewer kilometres travelled, the better the flavour.
- **Always choose foods in season, buy locally grown produce, source farmers' markets, buy organic and buy Irish.**
- **Look out for:** quality and freshness, Fair Trade logo, long date stamps, traceability, lists of ingredients, additives, allergens, etc. Compare quantities and weights. Take advantage of special offers but buy exactly what you need to avoid waste. Food in season is cheaper, fresher, the enzymes are still alive and the vitamins are intact.
- **Avoid pre-packaged fruit and vegetables**, buy loose where possible. This is often cheaper and reduces excess packaging.

Using your cooker: the cook should always be in control

Get to Know Your Cooker

Every oven is different. It may be slightly slower (cooler) or faster (hotter) than this book requires. **Cooking times** may vary slightly depending on the individual oven. Dishes can be placed on any shelf in a fan oven, but they are best placed on the top shelf of a conventional or gas oven unless otherwise stated. Always use your oven mitts/gloves.

The Correct Temperature

It is important that the oven is preheated to the correct temperature before starting to cook.

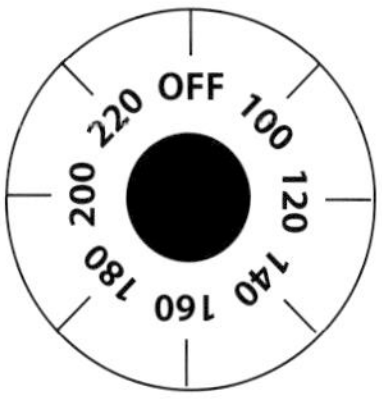

Electric Oven

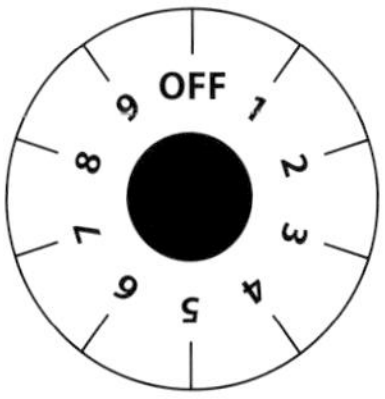

Gas Oven

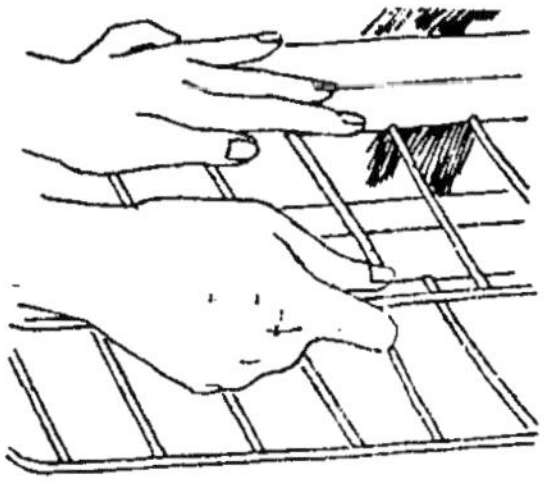

Chef's Tip!
Always place oven shelves in position before turning on/lighting the oven as they expand when hot and are then often difficult to move.

Oven temperatures may vary so get to know your own cooker!

Electric	Fan	Gas Mark
140° C	130° C	1 Cool
150° C	140° C	2 Cool
160° C	150° C	3 Warm
170° C	160° C	4 Moderate
180° C	170° C	5 Moderate
190° C	180° C	6 Fairly hot
200° C	190° C	7 Fairly hot
220° C	210° C	8 Hot
230° C	220° C	9 Very hot

If you smell gas, turn off the supply as quickly as possible and tell someone in charge. Open a window if you can and leave the room. Telephone the gas company if you suspect a leak. Do not light a match or switch anything electrical on or off.

If your clothes catch fire, you must **STOP, DROP** and **ROLL**. That means drop to the ground and roll over to quench the flames.

Setting Tables

Clean and polish the table. Polish all cutlery, plates and glasses to be used. Each place setting is called a 'cover'. Space all covers evenly when setting a table.

To **set a cover**, you must do the following:

1. Place a table-mat at each place needed. Place cutlery beside each mat as in the diagram, i.e. knife on the right, fork on the left. Each item should be 1.5cm from the edge of the table. Use your thumb nail as a rough guide.
2. Place the dessertspoon and fork, if using, above the table-mat as shown in the diagram. The dessertspoon should be above the dessert fork.
3. Put the side plate in place on the left of the fork. Place the small knife on the side plate.
4. Put the napkin in place. See serviette fold on page 9.
5. Place the glass just above the large dinner knife.
6. Add other items, e.g. pepper and salt, water jug, flowers, etc.
7. Place a table-mat for the main course dish and a tablespoon near this mat for serving.
8. Line up a chair evenly with each cover.

Lunch Table Setting

Formal Dinner Setting (four courses)

Buffet Table

1. Arrange the table so that guests can serve themselves easily.
2. Place cutlery and serviettes at one end of the table to be collected by guests.
3. Arrange table-mats for hot dishes in neat order – main dishes first followed by accompaniments and salads. Place serving spoons beside each mat.
4. Arrange additional items, e.g. salt and pepper, sauces, flowers, etc.
5. Glasses and drinks, water jugs, etc. are usually served at a side table.
6. Place hot foods on the table at the last minute.
7. Keep cold food covered and chilled until 30 minutes before serving.

Trays and Decorative Touches

Setting a Tray

1 When setting a breakfast, afternoon tea or supper tray make sure that the tray, delph, cutlery, etc. is clean and polished.
2 Use a tray cloth or paper if the tray is very slippy or very plain.
3 Use very small dishes for butter, marmalade, jam, milk, sugar, etc.
4 Place things in logical order, e.g. the teapot, milk and sugar should be together.
5 Use a very tiny flower vase if possible. Choose a serviette to complement the colour scheme.

Breakfast Tray

Decorative Touches: flowers, serviettes and candles

- Candles or floating candles make a lovely centrepiece. However, you must be very careful when using candles. **'Think Safety'** and blow them out before they burn too low. Never put a candle on a tray.
- For special occasions, match the colours of the flowers, candles and serviettes for good effect.
- A low vase of fresh flowers with some greenery looks good. One bloom is enough on a tray.
- Serviettes and napkins must be clean. They can be folded and put on the side plate or on the table mat. They look great when given an interesting fold or placed decoratively in a glass.
- For special occasions, tie each napkin in a ribbon. Plan the colours to co-ordinate.

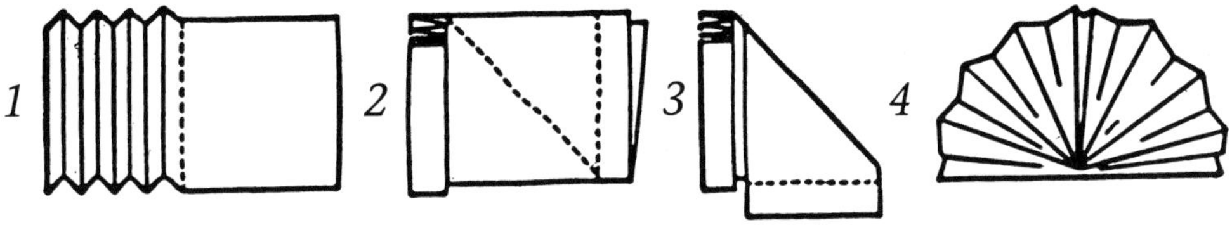

1 Fold napkin in half towards you. Make concertina pleats to halfway point with the last fold under the napkin.
2 Fold in half again, away from you.
3 Make a diagonal fold towards you, leaving a flap at the bottom for the support. Fold the flap under the triangle.
4 Open up the fan.

Garnishing and Decorating

- You **garnish** savoury foods, whereas you **decorate** sweet dishes.
- Take care with the arrangement of food on the plate. Choose a plate or dish that is neither too big nor too small for the amount of food you have prepared. Keep the food away from the very edge of the plate. If the dish is too small, serve the excess on a separate dish.
- Clean the edges of the dish with dampened kitchen paper if necessary.
- Choose a garnish/decoration to complement and contrast with the colour and texture of food. The garnish or decoration should have some link with the ingredients used in the dish itself.
- It is a mistake to disguise the food completely. Don't overdo it!
- Choose good-quality garnishes as blemishes tend to show.
- Foods used in garnishes should be washed and dried. Slicing should be very even and finely done. Use a sharp knife.
- Prepare the garnish beforehand so that hot foods don't get cold.
- Cakes should be served on a doyley – a fancy paper disc with a lacy finish (see page 226).

Spring Onion Tassel

Fresh Herbs

Leek/Carrot Julienne

Lemon/Lime Twist

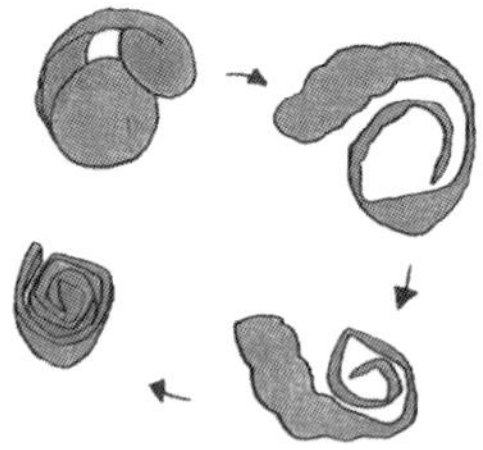

Tomato Rose

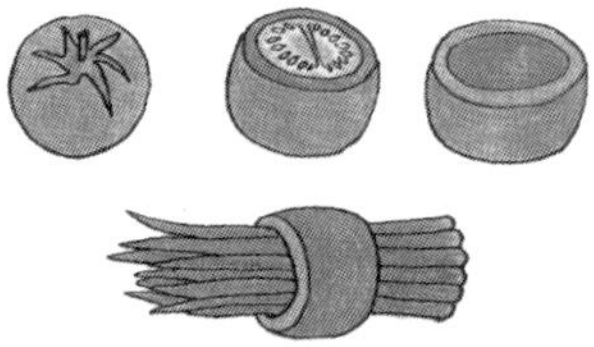

Tomato Hoops

Gherkin Fans

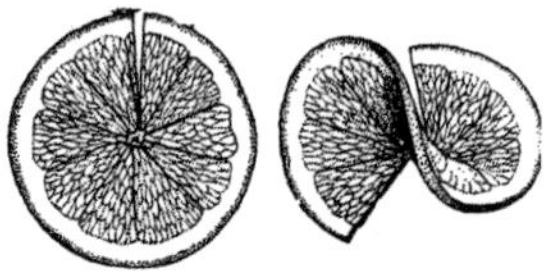

Twists and Butterflies
(lemon, lime or orange)

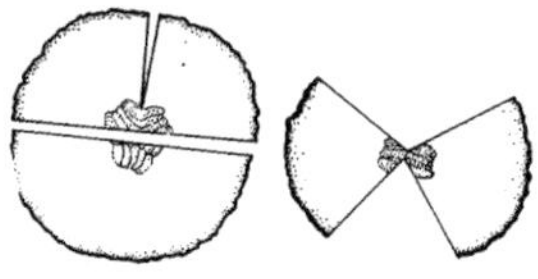

Cucumber

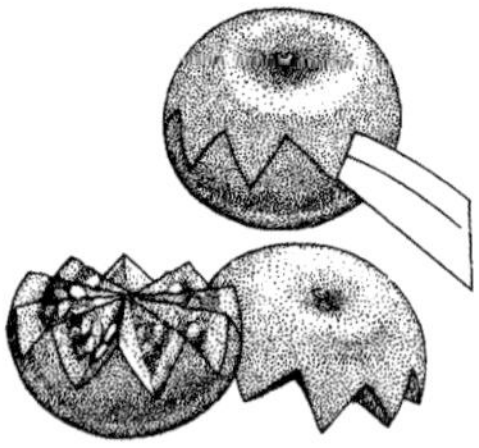

Tomatoes

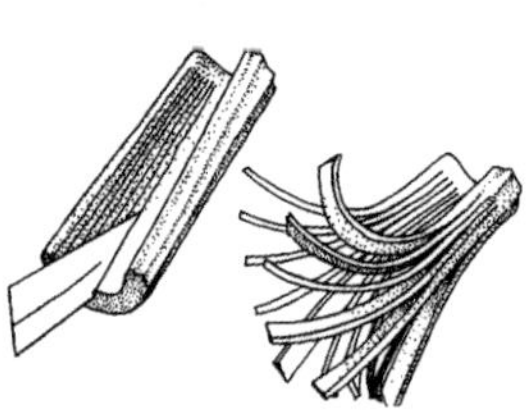

Celery tassels: cut them and put them into iced water to curl.

Radish Roses

Smart Culinary Skills

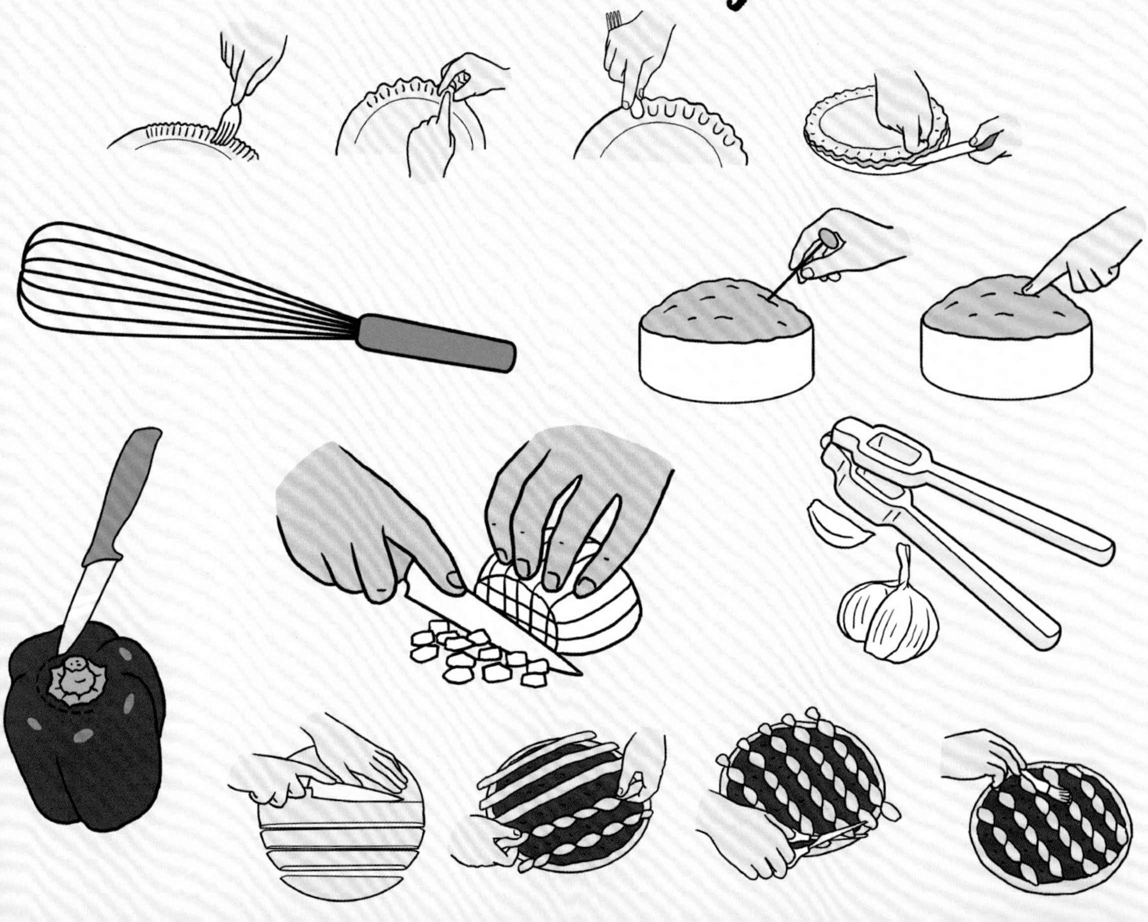

Sample Menus

Menu

Family

Leek and Potato Soup

. . .

Meatballs in Tomato Sauce with Rice

. . .

Eve's Pudding and Custard

Menu

Students on a Budget

Smashed Avocado on Toast

. . .

Spaghetti Bolognese

. . .

Chia Pots

Menu

Anaemia

Garlicky Greens

. . .

Chilli Stuffed Peppers

. . .

Beetroot and Walnut Tray Bake

Menu

High Fibre

Waldorf Salad

. . .

Cottage Pie

. . .

High-Fibre Fruit Crumble

Chapter 1

Smoothies, Starters, Dips, Stocks, Soups and Sandwiches

Starters are small, tasty dishes served as a first course at the beginning of a meal. They should be fresh and colourful, hot in winter and cold in summer. Aim to have nutritious, healthy dishes that complement the main course. Irish-produced foods are among the best in the world. Most of the recipes in *Smart Cooking 1* use ingredients that are produced in Ireland, such as yoghurt, milk, cheese, butter, cream and vegetables.

Key Words and Skills

- ❖ enzymic browning
- ❖ consistency
- ❖ julienne strips
- ❖ stock cubes
- ❖ bouquet garni
- ❖ spatula

Other suitable recipes:

Avocado, Apple and Walnut Salad (page 51), Cocktail Fish Bites (page 110), Chickpea Patties (page 138).

Evaluation! See pages 223 and 224.

- ❖ Did you meet the brief and did you refer to the specific requirements of the task or dish/dishes?
- ❖ Discuss the results of your finished dish/dishes including the presentation, colour, taste and texture.
- ❖ What aspects were done well and what aspects could be improved?
- ❖ Did you correctly cost and budget for all ingredients?

Healthy Smoothies

Serves: 2

HEALTHY BERRY SMOOTHIE

Ingredients

8 strawberries, 8 raspberries
200ml water or milk
1 banana, ½ cup ice cubes
1 dessertspoon oats

Equipment

liquidiser or food processor, measuring jug, teaspoon, 2 tall glasses, 2 paper straws, 1 dessertspoon, spatula.

AVOCADO SMOOTH DUDE

½ avocado, 1 sweet apple
50g spinach or kale
1 tablespoon almond butter
200ml unsweetened milk
1 peeled banana, frozen or fresh

SUPER SEVEN ENERGISER

50g blueberries, 1 banana
1 teaspoon cocoa nibs
1 teaspoon chia seeds
1 apple, 200ml milk
1 small tub natural yoghurt

SERIOUSLY HEALTHY STARTER

1 cooked beetroot
50g fresh spinach or kale
1 apple or pear
1 tablespoon nut butter
1 teaspoon cocoa nibs
1 teaspoon chia seeds
1 teaspoon linseeds
½ teaspoon cinnamon
200ml almond or rice milk

WINTER WINNER

1 apple, 1 orange
2 tablespoons muesli
1 teaspoon nut butter
½ teaspoon cinnamon
300ml warm milk

Steps **Method**

Gather equipment, collect/weigh ingredients, set worktop.

1 Blend all the ingredients at medium speed until the mixture becomes smooth. (See page 15 for help using blenders.)

2 Use a spatula to clean down the sides of the container.

Serve in two tall glasses with a paper straw in each.

Decorate with a sprig of fresh mint.

Variations

Yoghurt Smoothie: Add ½ carton (50ml) of natural bio yoghurt to any basic recipe to increase the probiotic and protein content. Choose natural bio yoghurt with live enzymes as they are very important for a healthy gut or intestine, which is essential for whole-body health.

Kale Smoothie: Add a fistful of raw kale to any smoothie. Kale is high in fibre and nutrients, see page 66. This is a great way of including it in your diet.

Honey Smoothie: Only add 1 teaspoon of honey to a smoothie. Honey is a sugar which, when raw and local, can contain very healthy live enzymes and trace elements, but too much sugar can lead to increased risk of disease and weight gain.

Frozen Yoghurt Smoothie: Add 1 or 2 scoops of low-sugar frozen yoghurt to any recipe.

Watch Out!
Smoothies can become unhealthy if sweetened juices, milks or yoghurts are added. Always read the label.

USING A PROCESSOR, LIQUIDISER, HAND OR BULLET BLENDER

Liquidisers

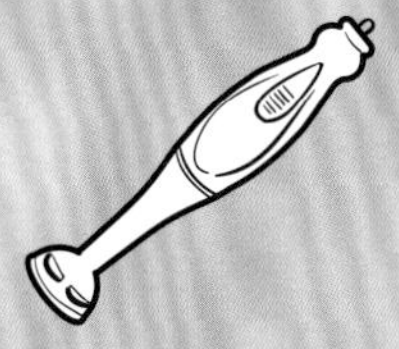

Hand or Stick Blender

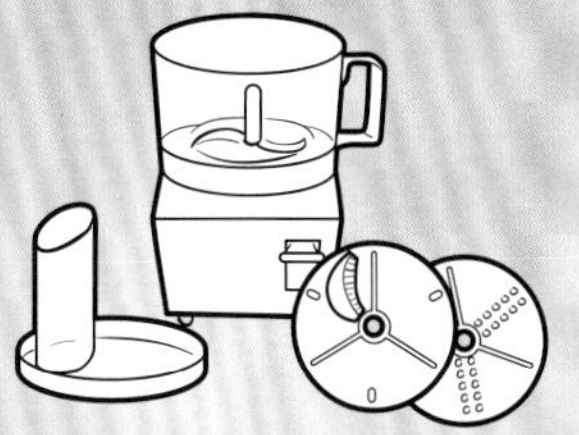

Food Processor showing blades

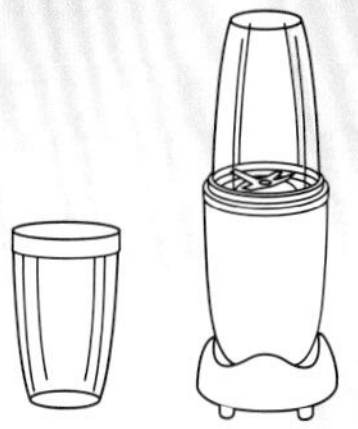

Bullet Blender

1 Make sure you know and understand how to use a food processor or liquidiser or blender before you start. Ask someone to show you if you are not sure.
2 Follow the instructions carefully. Ask for help again if you forget.
3 Bring all the ingredients you need to the machine before you begin.
4 Make sure your hands are dry when plugging in or out the machine.
5 Clean and wash according to the manufacturer's instructions after use.

Food Processor: The food is usually put into the goblet, the cover is clicked into position and the machine is turned on. Food can be added through the small hole in the lid. Processors usually have many other attachments for slicing, grating, whipping, etc.

Liquidiser: Dry food is more often dropped onto the running blades of a liquidiser through the small cap in the lid. Liquids are placed in the goblet, the lid is clicked into position and the machine turned on. Always hold the lid in position with your hand.

Hand or Stick Blender: The blender is put into the saucepan, jug or goblet where the food is to be puréed or processed.

Bullet Blender: The food is placed in the cup and the blade lid is screwed on. The cup is turned upside down and slotted onto the motor unit and turned clockwise. Push down to start.

Food Facts!

Linseeds/flax seed are from the flax or linen plant. They are low in carbohydrates, gluten-free, high in fibre and omega-3 fatty acids. Flax seeds support the digestive system and make skin and hair healthy.

Chia seeds are an energy booster. Buy whole chia as they will be fresher. Chia seeds are gluten-free and contain healthy omega-3 fatty acids, carbohydrates, protein, fibre, antioxidants and calcium.

Cocoa nibs are a raw, pure, gluten-free form of chocolate, which contain antioxidants that help absorb free radicals in the body.

Nut butters are made by grinding nuts into a crunchy or smooth paste. They can be made from any nuts. Nut butters contain healthy fats and are high in protein. Gluten-free.

Turmeric contains a natural anti-inflammatory compound, see page 129. Add 1 teaspoon ground turmeric, a dash of olive oil and a pinch of black pepper to any smoothie for general good health and healing.

Watch Out!
The blades on all machines are sharp and very dangerous. BE VERY CAREFUL. ASK FOR ADVICE.

FRESH MELON

A small melon serves 2, a medium serves 4-6, a large serves 8.

Ingredients

1 melon

Caster sugar and ground ginger

Decoration: glacé cherry, mint leaves and/or kiwi

Equipment

sharp knife, board, dessertspoon, small serving plates.

Chef's Tip!
Choose melons that are in season. They will be sweet and good value.

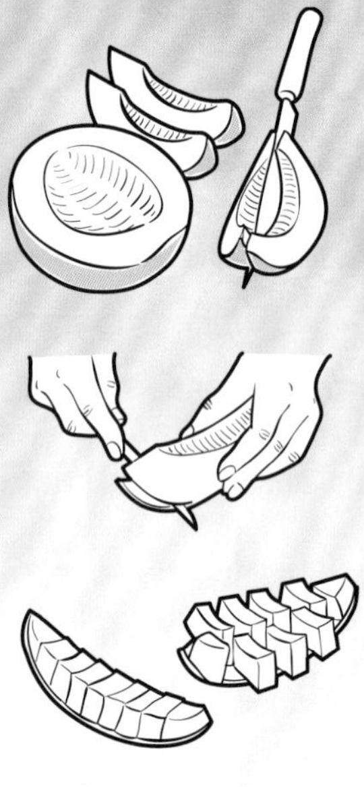

Cutting a melon

Ogen, Watermelon, Honeydew, Charentais and Piel de Sapo

Steps — Method

Gather equipment, collect/weigh ingredients, set worktop.

1 Wash and dry melon.

2 For **large and medium melons** cut in half from top to bottom. Scoop out seeds using a spoon. Cut each half into 3 or 4 wedges and slice between the flesh and skin to loosen flesh. Cut across the flesh in each wedge to make small bite-sized pieces.

3 For **small melons**, cut in half around the 'equator'. Scoop out the seeds using a spoon. Serve ½ to each person.

Serve with caster sugar, if necessary, and ground ginger to sprinkle.

Decorate each with half a glacé cherry, mint leaves and/or kiwi.

Melons

There are many varieties of melon: small, medium and large.

Small melons

Cantaloupe or Charentais and Galia have rough green/beige skin and fragrant orange flesh.

Ogen is small with green and yellow striped skin and pale green flesh.

Medium melons

Honeydew has yellow skin, pale flesh and is often shaped like a rugby ball.

Piel de Sapo has dark green skin, pale greenish flesh and is shaped like a rugby ball.

Large melons

Watermelon is very large with dark green skin and bright pink flesh.

Chef's Tip!
Choosing a melon: The end opposite the stalk will smell fragrant. This part should 'give' a little when pressed.

Fresh Fruit with Melon

VARIATION

Serves: 2

Ingredients

1 small melon
Fresh berries/fruits
Caster sugar

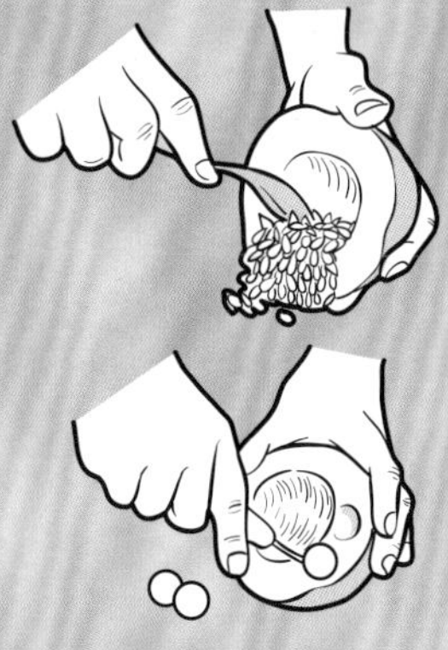

Balling a melon

Steps **Method**

Gather equipment, collect/weigh ingredients, set worktop.

1 Prepare melon as on page 16 for small melons.
2 Fill with washed, fresh strawberries or raspberries or other chopped fruit.
3 Sprinkle with caster sugar.

Serve chilled for breakfast or as a starter.

Melon Cocktail

VARIATION

Serves: 4

Ingredients

2 different melons, e.g. 1 cantaloupe and 1 honeydew
4 mint leaves

Melon lily

Step **Method**

Gather equipment, collect/weigh ingredients, set worktop.

1 Scoop the flesh from two different kinds of melon using a melon baller.

Serve the mixed balls in a wine glass with a doyley on a saucer or serve in half a small melon as in the picture. **Decorate** with mint leaves.

Healthy Hint!
Breastfeeding women should never eat melon, garlic or cabbage as these foods can upset the baby's stomach.

Food Fact!
Live enzymes are abundant in raw fruits and vegetables and live probiotics are found in live bio yoghurt. These are essential for a healthy gut, which promotes a healthy brain and body.

Resource Management: Take care when cutting melons and use all the flesh to avoid waste. Store any unused melon in a clean, covered container and refrigerate. Use within 24 hours, never waste good food.

Avocado Vinaigrette

Serves: 2

Ingredients

1 ripe avocado

Garlic Vinaigrette

1 tablespoon cider vinegar or lemon juice

¼ teaspoon salt

Grind of black pepper

½ level teaspoon Dijon mustard

1 level teaspoon sugar

6 tablespoons oil

½ clove garlic, crushed

Garnish: chopped parsley

Equipment

board, stainless steel knife, brush, garlic press, 2 serving dishes.

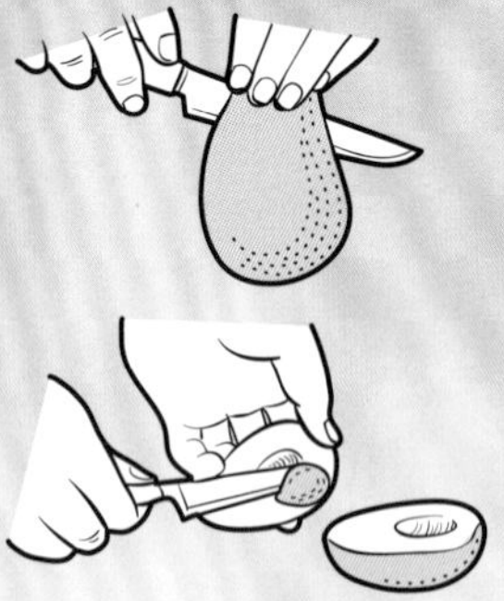

Cutting an avocado

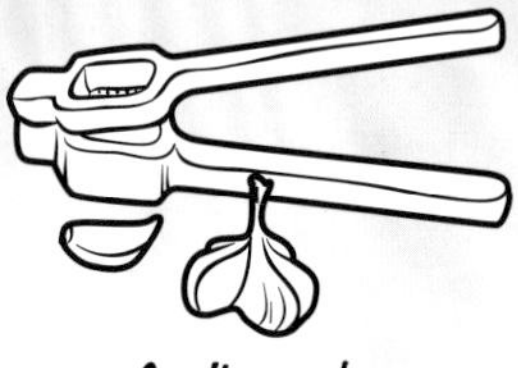

Garlic crusher

Chef's Tip!
To soften an avocado, pierce it in several places. Microwave on HIGH for 1 minute; allow to cool before peeling.

Choosing an Avocado

The skins of avocadoes can be green and smooth or rough and purplish brown. Test for ripeness by gently pressing the narrow end. It should 'give' slightly. Avoid bruised or blemished fruit.

Steps **Method**

Gather equipment, collect/weigh ingredients, set worktop.

1. Whisk or shake all vinaigrette ingredients together (see pages 36/37).
2. Wash the avocado, dry, cut lengthways all round until the stone is reached.
3. Holding each half in your hands, gently rotate avocado in opposite directions until the halves separate.
4. Plunge the blade of the knife into the stone, then rotate it to remove the stone. If the avocado is soft, use a teaspoon.
5. Put each half on a serving dish and brush flesh with vinaigrette to prevent discolouring. Fill each hole with dressing.

Garnish with chopped parsley. **Serve** as a starter/first course.

Chef's Tip!
Avocados discolour easily so prepare just before serving and brush the flesh with lemon juice or vinaigrette to prevent enzymic browning.

Food Fact!
Enzymic browning occurs when foods such as avocados, apples and bananas are cut and their flesh exposed to oxygen in the air. Brushing or tossing the foods with lemon juice will prevent this happening.

Healthy Hint!
Avocadoes have a low sugar content and contain healthy monounsaturated fatty acid, which is a healthy fat. They contain a number of essential vitamins and minerals. Avocadoes are good for healthy skin and the absorption of fat-soluble vitamins, minerals and other nutrients that help boost the immune system. Avocadoes are easily digested by infants and the elderly.

Stuffed Fresh Avocado

Serves: 4

Ingredients

2 avocadoes
1 tablespoon mayonnaise
½ small onion or chives
1 small eating apple (red)
50g cooked chicken **or** ham **or** tuna
Lemon juice
Garnish: parsley or chives

Equipment

small bowl, spoon, sharp knife, scissors.

Chef's Tip!
Use cold leftover chicken, ham, fish or grilled crispy rasher.

Avocadoes can be filled with a variety of ingredients to create a tasty dish

Steps	Method
	Gather equipment, collect/weigh ingredients, set worktop.
1	Peel and dice onion very finely or snip chives.
2	Wash apple, quarter and core, dice 3 quarters very finely. Slice the other quarter for garnish, brush with lemon juice.
3	Dice meat or fish finely. Mix with apple, onion and mayonnaise.
4	Prepare avocado as on page 18 and brush flesh with lemon juice. Pile stuffing neatly on top. Put an apple wedge on each.

Serve in individual dishes as a starter.

Garnish with parsley or chives.

Smashed Avocado on Toast

VARIATION

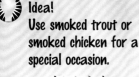

Idea!
Use smoked trout or smoked chicken for a special occasion.

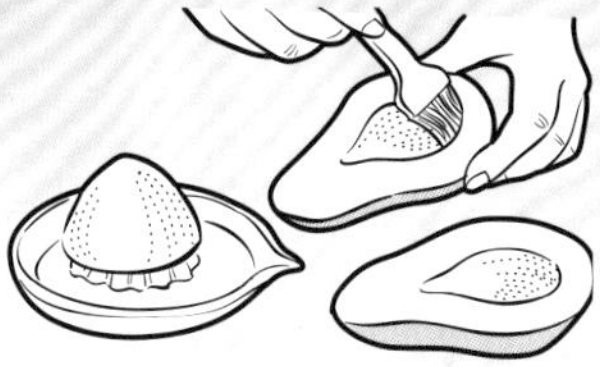

Brushing avocadoes with lemon juice

Dicing onion

Steps	Method
	Follow Steps 1 to 4 from Avocado Vinaigrette recipe on previous page.
5	Using a dessertspoon, scoop out the flesh from each avocado half onto a plate.
6	Add 1 tablespoon of vinaigrette and mash together with a fork. Keep the mixture slightly chunky.
7	Toast 2 slices of bread, spread mixture onto toast, garnish with sliced tomato and drizzle with a little vinaigrette.

Serve warm.

Variation

Serve with toasted pumpkin, sesame or sunflower seeds, a poached egg or smoked trout on top and drizzle with balsamic glaze.

Crudités

BITE-SIZED PIECES OF FRESH VEGETABLES THAT ARE USUALLY SERVED WITH DIPS

Ingredients

Choose colourful vegetables from the following list:
1 carrot, 2 sticks celery
1 red or yellow pepper
½ cucumber, ½ cauliflower
small head broccoli
6 scallions, 12 radishes
6 baby sweetcorn

Dips: Choose one or two.

Cream cheese dip, page 22

Avocado dip, page 22

Cheese and chilli dip, page 23

American sour cream dip, page 23

Hummus, page 21

Curry-flavoured mayonnaise, page 39

Garlic-flavoured mayonnaise, page 39

Equipment

sharp knife, board, serving platter.

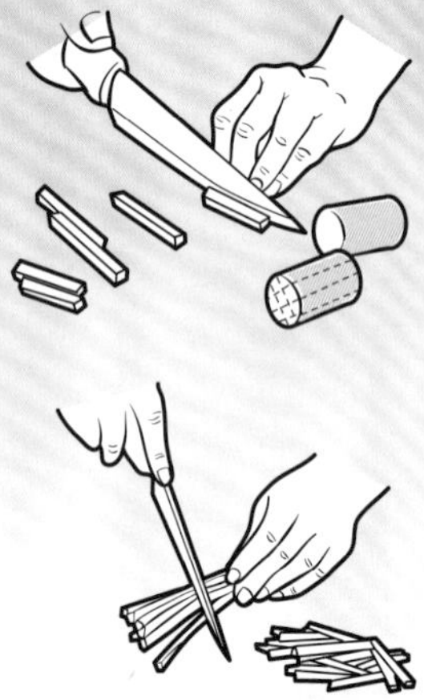

Julienne strips

Buy Local, Buy Irish!
Buy locally grown vegetables at farmers' markets.

Steps Method

Gather equipment, collect/weigh ingredients, set worktop.

1 First make the dips and chill.

2 Wash each vegetable carefully. Peel carrot.

3 Cut carrot, celery, cucumber, peppers and scallions evenly into very narrow 8cm long strips (Julienne strips). See diagram.

4 Cut cauliflower and broccoli into small, bite-sized florets. Trim the stalks as necessary.

5 Trim radishes. If very large, cut in half. Trim baby sweetcorn only if necessary.

6 Arrange in neat piles around a bowl of 'dip' on the serving platter.

7 Cover with cling film until ready to serve.

Serve with one or two dips (see pages 22/23) or with flavoured mayonnaise as 'nibbles' before a party or in portions as a starter.

Healthy Hint!
Vegetables add variety, colour and flavour to the diet. They are cheap, nutritious and filling. Many vegetables can be eaten raw.

Smoked Seafood Pâté

BLENDER/PROCESSOR/LIQUIDISER

Serves: 4

Ingredients

- 250g smoked mackerel, trout or salmon
- 100g Philadelphia cheese
- 1 teaspoon lemon juice
- Black pepper
- **Garnish:** parsley, lemon

Equipment

sharp knife, board, food processor, tablespoon, spatula, serving bowl.

Chef's Tip!
Soften this with a spoon of mayonnaise or water if it is too thick.

Smoked Seafood Pâté and Hummus Dip

Steps — Method

Gather equipment, collect/weigh ingredients, set worktop.

1 Skin the fish if necessary. Blend the flesh with all other ingredients in a processor. Use spatula to scrape down the sides of goblet.

2 Place in serving dish and chill.

Serve with fingers of toast, brown bread or crackers.

Garnish with lemon twist and chopped parsley.

Hummus

MIDDLE-EASTERN

Ingredients

- 100g chickpeas, drained
- 50ml reserved juice
- 1 tablespoon lemon juice
- 1 tablespoon tahini
- 1 tablespoon virgin olive oil
- 1 small clove garlic
- Salt and black pepper
- **Garnish:** pinch of paprika or poppy seeds, olive oil or lemon wedges.

Equipment

processor, sharp knife, board, sieve, measuring jug, cutlery, spatula, shallow serving dish.

Steps — Method

Gather equipment, collect/weigh ingredients, set worktop.

1 Drain chickpeas into a sieve and reserve the juice.

2 Smash garlic, peel and place in a blender or food processor with all ingredients. Add chickpeas and half the reserved juice. Blend to make a thick paste, adding more juice to make a creamy consistency.

3 Taste, add more salt, lemon or oil according to taste.

Garnish with a pinch of paprika, poppy seeds or lemon wedges.

Serve in a shallow dish drizzled with olive oil.

Store in a screw-topped jar in a fridge for 3-4 days.

Use as a dip for crudités, a spread, starter or sauce with pita bread, vegetable sticks, roasted vegetables, kebabs or burgers.

Variation

Add in 1 beetroot or 1 sweet potato, cooked and puréed or a big bunch of coriander at Step 2.

Food Fact!
Hummus is high in protein and a good complement for vegan dishes.
Tahini is puréed sesame seed paste. It is rich in calcium.
See Tahini Sauce/Dressing, page 141.

DIPS

Dips are made on a 'base' with flavourings added. Bases can be mayonnaise, cream cheese, crème fraîche, soured cream, cottage cheese, natural yoghurt. The most calories are found in mayonnaise, and the least in natural yoghurt. For other dips, see Mayonnaise, pages 38/39, Tahini Sauce/Dressing, page 141 and Hummus, page 21.

Cream Cheese Dip

Ingredients

225g cream cheese

Dash of lemon juice

Salt and pepper

100g tuna, sardine or crisp bacon or smoked salmon or cooked ham

¼ clove garlic

8-10 chives, chopped

Garnish: chives

Equipment

wooden spoon, bowl, scissors, serving bowl, garlic crusher.

Cream Cheese Dip and Avocado Dip

Steps **Method**

Gather equipment, collect/weigh ingredients, set worktop.

1 Wash chives and snip with scissors.

2 Blend all ingredients together with wooden spoon or in a blender.

3 Soften with a little more lemon juice or milk if necessary.

Serve piled into a bowl.

Garnish with chives.

Use with crudités, baked potatoes or as a spread to fill rolls or pinwheel sandwiches (see page 31).

Avocado Dip

Ingredients

1 avocado

25g cream cheese

2 rashers

½ clove garlic (optional)

2 tablespoons lemon juice

1 tablespoon parsley

Salt and pepper

Garnish: chopped parsley

Equipment

sharp knife, board, tablespoon, scissors, garlic crusher, bowl, serving bowl.

Steps **Method**

Gather equipment, collect/weigh ingredients, set worktop.

1 Grill rashers, cool, cut into small pieces.

2 Peel garlic then crush. Wash, dry and chop parsley (pages 53 and 73).

3 Wash avocado, dry, cut lengthways all around until the stone is reache

4 Holding each half in your hands, gently twist the avocado in opposite directions until the halves separate.

5 If the avocado is soft, remove stone using a teaspoon. If hard, plunge the knife into the stone, then twist it to remove.

6 Mash avocado with a fork, beat in the cream cheese, garlic, rashers, lemon juice and parsley.

Serve in a small decorative dish. **Garnish** with chopped parsley.

Use as a low-calorie dip, as a filling for baked potatoes or in rolls and sandwiches.

Cheese and Chilli Dip

Ingredients

- 100g sour cream or Greek yoghurt
- 50g grated cheese
- ¼ clove garlic, crushed
- ½ teaspoon chilli powder
- 2 teaspoons tomato ketchup
- 1 teaspoon Worcestershire sauce
- 1-2 tablespoons milk

Equipment

sharp knife, board, tablespoon, teaspoon, garlic crusher, bowl, serving bowl.

Chef's Tip!
Store leftover cheese in foil or greaseproof paper in the fridge.

Look Up!
Kimchi, kefir and sauerkraut.

Cheese and Chilli Dip, American Sour Cream Dip

Steps **Method**

Gather equipment, collect/weigh ingredients, set worktop.

1 Mix all ingredients together. Taste and adjust seasoning.

Serve with crudités or salads.

Healthy Hint!
Greek yoghurt is high in protein and calcium. Probiotics are live, good bacteria present in live yoghurt, kimchi, sauerkraut, fermented vegetables and kefir. By increasing your intake of probiotic rich foods, a proper balance of good bacteria in the gut is maintained which helps with bowel immunity and good health.

American Sour Cream Dip

Ingredients

- 100g sour cream or crème fraîche
- I tablespoon mayonnaise
- 1 teaspoon tomato purée
- 1 teaspoon chives
- 1 teaspoon fresh basil or parsley
- 1 small clove garlic, crushed
- Salt and pepper
- **Garnish:** snipped chives

Equipment

sharp knife, board, tablespoon, teaspoon, garlic crusher, bowl, serving bowl.

Steps **Method**

Gather equipment, collect/weigh ingredients, set worktop.

1 Wash, dry and chop herbs very finely. Put some aside for garnish.

2 Blend all the ingredients together with a wooden spoon.

Serve piled into a serving bowl.

Garnish with snipped chives.

Use with crackers, baked potatoes, potato wedges, kebabs, baked fish or chicken dishes.

Food Fact!
Sour cream is produced when lactic acid bacteria are added to acidify and thicken pasteurised cream. It has a nice sharp taste, and can be used in cakes, desserts and stroganoffs.
It is high in fat, Vitamin D, calcium and phosphorous.

STOCKS

Stock is a well-flavoured liquid that is used to give a good flavour to soups, sauces and stews. It is made by simmering bones and vegetables in water to draw out the flavours.

Stock cubes are made from concentrated dried stock. They are best kept for emergencies as they are highly seasoned and can contain **artificial additives.** If using a stock cube, use an **organic** one and use ½ or even ¼ cube at a time. They can contain a lot of salt, so look for salt-free cubes when buying ingredients.

VEGETABLE STOCK

Cooking Time: 45 minutes

Makes 1 litre of stock

Ingredients

2 onions
2 carrots
2 sticks celery
1 leek
½ parsnip
Bouquet garni*

Equipment

sharp knife, board, saucepan, pot stand, colander, measuring jug.

Herbs wrapped in a piece of celery make a good bouquet garni.

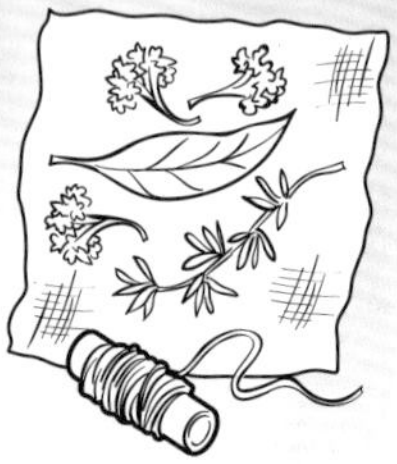

Herbs wrapped in muslin

Making your own stock is the best option.

Steps — Method

Gather equipment, collect/weigh ingredients, set worktop.

1 Prepare vegetables, as on page 25 – wash, peel and chop.

2 Put into saucepan with **bouquet garni*,** 1 litre of water and seasoning. Cover tightly.

3 Bring to the boil and simmer for a minimum of 45 minutes, but at least two hours is recommended.

4 Strain, use as required or cool and store in fridge or freeze for later use in soups and sauces.

Chef's Tip!
TO FREEZE: Fill freezer containers or plastic bags supported in plastic basins. Label, date and freeze when cold.

Watch Out!
Stock should be stored CLEAN, COLD AND COVERED in a fridge and used within three days of making.

***BOUQUET GARNI** — TECHNIQUE

A bunch of herbs, e.g. a bay leaf, 2 cloves, parsley, peppercorns and a blade of mace which are tied together in a piece of muslin and used to give flavour. Remove before serving. This can be bought in a sachet like a tea bag and popped into stocks or soups.

Chicken Stock or Bone Broth

Cooking Time: 1 hour

Makes 1 litre of stock

Ingredients

1 raw carcass or the bones from a cooked chicken

Bouquet garni (page 24)

1 onion

1 carrot

1 stick celery

1 leek (optional)

½ parsnip (optional)

Chef's Tip!
Add a teaspoon of dried sea kelp or kombu to stock to add flavour, iodine and trace elements.

Steps — Method

Gather equipment, collect/weigh ingredients, set worktop.

1 Prepare vegetables – wash, peel and chop.

2 Put into saucepan with chicken bones, bouquet garni, 1 litre of water and seasoning.

3 Bring to the boil, cover and simmer for at least 1 hour.

4 Strain, use as required or cool and store in fridge.

USE In soups, sauces and stews or as a hot health drink seasoned with pepper and a little salt.

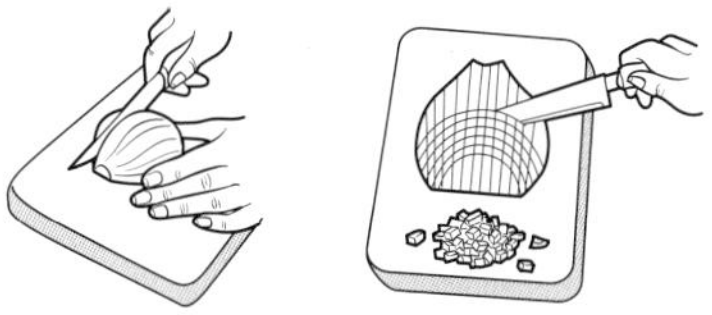

To dice onion, first cut lengthways

Cutting carrots into chunks, rings or batons

Preparing celery

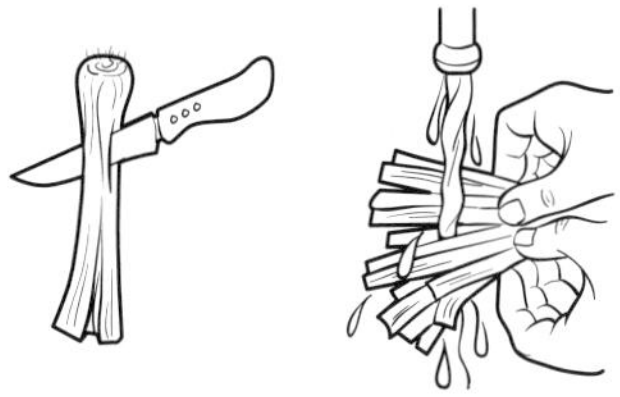

Preparing and washing a leek

Beef Bone Stock or Broth

VARIATION

Ingredients

500g beef bones
1 tablespoon oil
1 tablespoon cider vinegar or ½ glass white wine

Use the vegetables for the stock above

Food Fact!
Bone broth is full of minerals and benefits the gut, brain, muscles and ligaments. The long simmering causes the bones and ligaments to release collagen, which help to keep the gut and body healthy.

Steps — Method

Preheat oven to 200°C/Fan 180°C/Gas Mark 5.

Gather equipment, collect/weigh ingredients, set worktop.

1 Put 500g beef bones into a roasting tin, drizzle with 1 tablespoon oil and brown in a hot oven for 30-40 minutes.

2 Place in a large saucepan, cover with cold water, the vinegar or white wine, and allow to soak while preparing the vegetables as above.

3 Add all ingredients, bring to the boil with the lid on and allow to simmer gently for 2 hours. Skim off any froth/foam that collects with a tablespoon and throw it away.

4 When cooked, turn off heat, cool and strain using a sieve. Store in glass jars or covered bowls in the fridge or freezer.

***SIMMER** — COOKING METHOD

Water simmers when bubbles break gently on the surface at 95°C. It extracts flavour and tenderises most foods. Most foods are simmered with the lid on the pot.

FRESH VEGETABLE SOUP

Cooking Time: 40 minutes

Serves: 4

Ingredients

Basic Soup

1 small potato

1 small onion

25g butter

1 tablespoon cooking oil

800ml organic/fresh chicken stock (made with ½ cube)

Bouquet garni (see page 24)

Salt and pepper

25g flour (optional/to thicken)

Mixed Vegetable Soup

500g mixed vegetables, e.g.

1 leek, 1 carrot, 2 sticks celery, 1 tablespoon frozen peas

Garnish: 2 tablespoons cream, chopped chives or parsley

Equipment

sharp knife, board, measuring jug, liquidiser, large saucepan, wooden spoon, pot stand, serving bowls or tureen.

Fresh Vegetable Soup, Mushroom Soup, Carrot and Sweet Potato

Steps — Method

Gather equipment, collect/weigh ingredients, set worktop.

1 Prepare vegetables – wash, peel and dice.

2 Heat butter and oil, add vegetables and **sweat*** (see Technique, page 27) for about 5 minutes. Do not brown.

3 Add stock, seasoning and bouquet garni.

4 Bring to the boil, cover and simmer gently for 30 minutes until vegetables are soft.

5 Liquidise or blend with an electric hand blender (see page 15).

If consistency is too thin, blend flour until smooth with a little water anc whisk into soup, bring to a boil and simmer for 5 minutes to cook the flour and thicken.

Serve in a warmed soup tureen or dish with melba toast or croûtons (page 34) or garlic bread (page 32).

Garnish with a swirl of cream sprinkled with chopped chives or parsley

MUSHROOM SOUP

VARIATIOI

Ingredients

1 x Basic Soup ingredients

400g mushrooms

Use the Basic Soup Ingredients from the recipe above. Wash and chop mushrooms. Follow the same method, adding mushrooms at **Step 2**.

CARROT AND SWEET POTATO SOUP

VARIATIO

Ingredients

1 x Basic Soup ingredients

1 carrot

1 sweet potato

Use the Basic Soup Ingredients from the recipe above. Wash and dice carrot. Wash, peel and dice sweet potato and add at **Step 2**.

Resource Management: Buy local and organic produce where possible. Peel vegetables thinly to avoid waste. Cover any unused vegetables in a clean container and store in a fridge. Use within 2 days.

Potato and Leek Soup

Cooking Time: 40 minutes

Serves: 4

Ingredients

- 250g potatoes
- 250g leeks
- 1 onion
- 2 sticks celery (optional)
- 25g butter
- 1 tablespoon cooking oil
- 25g flour (optional)
- 800ml organic chicken stock (made with 1 stock cube)
- Bouquet garni (page 24)
- Salt and pepper
- **Garnish:** chopped chives or parsley

Equipment

sharp knife, board, measuring jug, saucepan, wooden spoon, liquidiser, serving bowls/tureen.

Idea!
Swirl a teaspoon of pesto into each bowl before serving or top with grated cheese.

Chef's Tip!
Wrap the herbs in a piece of celery instead of making a bouquet garni.

Dicing an onion

Steps **Method**

Gather equipment, collect/weigh ingredients, set worktop.

1 Prepare vegetables – wash, peel and dice. (See page 25 for washing and dicing).
2 Heat butter and oil, add vegetables, **sweat*** for 5 minutes. Do not brown.
3 Add stock, bouquet garni and seasoning. Bring to the boil, cover and simmer gently for 30 minutes until vegetables are soft.
4 Liquidise or blend with an electric hand blender (see page 15). If consistency is too thin, blend flour with 5 tablespoons water until smooth and whisk into soup. Bring to boil, simmer for 5 minutes to thicken.

Serve in warmed bowls with croûtons, melba toast (see page 34) or homemade brown scones or rolls.

Garnish with chopped chives or parsley (see Chef's Tip).

In a hurry!
Homemade stock is tasty and nutritious, see page 24, but organic, low-salt stock cubes can be used. There are a variety of stock flavours available, e.g. beef, chicken, fish, vegetable, but always read packets to avoid any artificial ingredients. Stock cubes can be very concentrated so only use half at any one time. Always taste and check the seasoning before adding further salt to a dish.

Watch Out!
The blades of a processor, liquidiser or hand blender are sharp and very dangerous.

***SWEAT** TECHNIQUE

This refers to the initial cooking of vegetables in butter or oil, in a covered saucepan, over a very low heat in order to extract the juices and flavour without colouring. A paper cover is pressed down onto the vegetables to trap the steam and intensify the flavours.

TOMATO SOUP

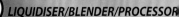

LIQUIDISER/BLENDER/PROCESSOR

Cooking Time: 25 minutes

Serves: 4

Ingredients

- 25g butter
- 1 tablespoon cooking oil
- 1 onion
- 1 clove of garlic
- 2 sticks celery
- 1 carrot
- 1 medium potato
- Bunch of fresh herbs, chopped
- Pinch of thyme or oregano
- 1 tin chopped tomatoes
- 1 teaspoon tomato purée
- 1 teaspoon sugar
- 1 level teaspoon salt
- Pinch of pepper
- 400ml organic vegetable stock (made with ½ cube)
- **Garnish:** 1 tablespoon cream, chopped chives or parsley

Equipment

sharp knife, board, liquidiser, measuring jug, saucepan, wooden spoon, pot stand, serving bowls or tureen.

Chef's Tip!
Adding a little salt when sweating prevents onions from burning.

Idea!
Serve with melba toast or croûtons, page 34.

Chef's Tip!
Add a pinch of sugar when cooking tomatoes as it will bring out the flavour.

Steps — Method

Gather equipment, collect/weigh ingredients, set worktop.

1 Prepare vegetables – wash, peel and dice. See page 25.

2 Heat butter and oil, **sauté*** onion, garlic and celery for 3 minutes. Stir, do not brown.

3 Add potato and carrot, sweat for 1 minute. See page 27.

4 **Add stock** (page 24), tin of tomatoes, purée, sugar, herbs and seasoning.

5 Bring to the boil, cover and simmer gently for about 15 minutes until vegetables are soft. Liquidise or blend with an electric hand blender (see page 15).

If consistency of soup is too thin, blend 25g flour (or cornflour for coeliacs) with a little water until smooth and whisk into soup. Bring to the boil and simmer for 5 minutes. Check seasoning.

Serve in hot soup bowls.

Garnish with a blob of cream and chopped chives or parsley.

Food Fact!
The quality of tinned or packaged tomatoes can vary. Canned cherry tomatoes are sweet and tasty. Use 'chopped tomatoes' for soups and sauces. Buy organic tomatoes free from artificial flavours and additives when possible. Passata is sieved or puréed tomato and is used for making soups and sauces.

***SAUTÉ** — TECHNIQUE

Sauté means to fry food rapidly in hot fat. The food is sometimes browned and sometimes not. This method is used to intensify the flavours and so develop a better taste in the finished dish.

Seafood Chowder (Fresh or Smoked)

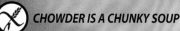

CHOWDER IS A CHUNKY SOUP

Cooking Time: 35 minutes

Serves: 4

Ingredients

- 400g fish – smoked or fresh or a mixture of each
- 25g butter
- 1 tablespoon oil
- 1 onion
- 1 stick celery (optional)
- 1 medium potato
- 500ml water
- Salt and pepper
- Pinch of powdered mace or nutmeg
- 1 bay leaf
- 75g sweetcorn – fresh, frozen or tinned
- 2 tablespoons cream
- 1 dessertspoon parsley
- **Garnish:** 1 tablespoon cream and parsley or snipped chives

Equipment

sharp knife, board, measuring jug, tablespoon, large saucepan, pot stand, metal/wooden spoon, scissors, whisk, soup tureen or bowls.

To skin a fish:
Hold skin in one hand and use salt to help you grip. Hold the knife at a 45° angle. Use a sawing action to cut flesh from the skin while pushing away from you.

Seafood Chowder served with Melba Toast and Brown Bread

Steps — Method

Gather equipment, collect/weigh ingredients, set worktop.

1. Wash, peel and dice the potato, onion and celery neatly.
2. Heat butter and oil, sweat (see page 27) onion, potato and celery for 3 minutes. Stir, do not brown.
3. Add water, bay leaf, mace or nutmeg, salt and pepper. Bring to the boil, cover and **simmer*** gently for 15 minutes until vegetables are soft.
4. Meanwhile wash fish, remove skin and bones. Cut into 2cm dice.
5. Remove bay leaf from chowder.
6. Add fish, sweetcorn and parsley and **simmer*** for 15 minutes. Check consistency (see Chef's Tip below) and seasoning. Stir in the cream.

Serve in a warm tureen or bowls with croûtons, melba toast (page 34) or fresh wholemeal bread or scones.

Garnish with a swirl of cream and parsley or snipped chives.

Chef's Tip!
If consistency of soup is too thin, blend 1 heaped teaspoon cornflour with a little water and whisk into soup, bring to boil and simmer for 5 minutes.

Idea!
Add 100g frozen, diced vegetables for more nutrients and colour.

***SIMMER** — COOKING METHOD

Water simmers when bubbles break gently on the surface at 95°C. It extracts flavour and tenderises most foods. Most foods are simmered with the lid on the pot.

Super Sandwiches, Filled Rolls and Wraps

Look for interesting fresh Irish breads and rolls, brown and white, with added seeds and nuts, etc. If the bread is really fresh, there is no need to remove the crusts, unless dainty sandwiches are needed. A variety of sandwiches can be made by varying the bread, the spread or the filling.

Breads

Baps, bagels, batons, Vienna rolls, pitta, country grains, cheese scones, corn breads, walnut bread, rye, crispbread, beetroot or spinach, gluten-free wraps or multiseed tortilla wraps.

Spreads

A spread makes a waterproof layer that prevents the bread becoming soggy. Use butter, hummus, low-fat spreads, mayonnaise or flavoured cream cheese.

Fillings

Choose lots of interesting fresh ingredients. Vary colour, texture and flavour.

Combine soft foods with crispy fresh foods. Put the filling right to the edges.

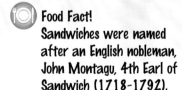

Food Fact!
Sandwiches were named after an English nobleman, John Montagu, 4th Earl of Sandwich (1718-1792).

Idea!
Try making the following: An Open Sandwich and a Double Decker.

Brown Bread Sandwich, Filled Roll and Wrap

Try the following delicious fillings!

- BLT: Crispy grilled bacon, lettuce and tomato.
- Tuna, scallions and sweetcorn.
- Mozzarella, vine-ripened tomato, avocado and scallions.
- Roast pepper, pesto and crisp lettuce.
- Egg, spring onion and fresh cucumber.
- Grilled chicken with Cajun spice and cream cheese.
- Smoked salmon, cream cheese, lemon juice and beansprouts.

Toasting

If toasting, lightly butter the bread on the outside only. Toast it in a heated sandwich maker or under a hot grill. Avoid fillings such as lettuce.

Cutting

Always use a sharp knife and a chopping board. Press the sandwich well together. Cut into triangles or fingers. Cut rolls across at an angle.

Garnish

Fresh herbs always add freshness to a sandwich. Chives, flat-leaf parsley or fresh coriander are all wonderful additions. Tomato wedges give a good colour.

Presentation

Serve sandwiches on a plate/basket with a folded serviette or doyley.

Wrapping

Wrap sandwiches in cling film or tinfoil to keep them fresh and clean. If they have to be carried, put them into a small polythene box. Chill the sandwiches well in a fridge if they are to be kept for a time. Sandwiches may be wrapped and kept fresh in a fridge overnight.

Croque Monsieur

A TRADITIONAL HOT FRENCH SANDWICH MADE OF TOASTED CHEESE AND HAM

Cooking Time: 6-8 minutes

Serves: 1

Croque Monsieur and Party Pinwheel Sandwiches

Ingredients

2 slices of sliced pan bread

A little butter to spread

25g Gruyère cheese or mild Irish Cheddar

1-2 slices cooked ham

Salt and pepper

Garnish: fresh parsley

Equipment

grater with large holes, board, buttering knife, sharp knife, grill, plate to serve.

Steps — Method

Preheat the grill. Gather equipment, collect/weigh ingredients, set worktop.

1 Grate cheese. Do not butter the bread at this stage.

2 Make a sandwich with bread and ⅓ of the cheese, then the ham, then ⅓ cheese again.

3 Butter the top slice of bread and place the buttered side facing up. Grill until brown.

4 Turn the sandwich over, sprinkle with remaining cheese and grill until just brown. Cut into triangles.

Serve hot on a clean plate.

Garnish with fresh parsley.

Party Pinwheel Sandwiches

Serves: 2-3

Ingredients

6 slices brown sliced pan

2 sticks celery

Filling

½ quantity of the Cream Cheese Dip on page 22

Fresh herbs, e.g. parsley, dill

Equipment

sharp knife, board, rolling pin, cling film, serving plate with doyley, cocktail sticks.

Steps — Method

1 Make dip for filling.

2 Wash and cut celery lengthways into 6 sticks.

3 Wash, dry and chop the herbs very finely.

4 Remove crusts from bread, roll out lightly with rolling pin. Spread thickly with the filling. Place a celery stick across one side of each slice then roll up tightly.

5 Chill until required, wrapped in cling film. Before serving, cut into 2cm slices with a sharp knife. Sprinkle with herbs.

Serve on a plate with a doyley and cocktail sticks.

Chef's Tip!
Serve some toasted for a change of texture.

Resource Management: Use a processor or bullet blender to make breadcrumbs from crusts or leftover bread. Store in the freezer in freezer bags for later use in stuffing, or mix with cheese and herbs and use as a savoury topping on pies or fish bakes. See page 56.

Garlic Bread

Cooking Time: 20 minutes

Serves: 4

Ingredients

1 small French stick or baton

2 cloves garlic

¼ level teaspoon salt

50g butter or spread

2 tablespoons chopped herbs (optional)

Garnish: chopped parsley

Equipment

sharp knife, board, garlic crusher, pot stand, pyrex bowl, tinfoil, wooden spoon, baking tin, serving plate/basket.

Cutting bread

Garlic Bread and Bruschetta

Steps **Method**

Preheat oven to 190°C/Fan 180°C/Gas Mark 5.

Gather equipment, collect/weigh ingredients, set worktop.

1. Soften butter in a pyrex bowl in the oven or in the microwave.
2. Smash garlic, peel and crush. Wash and chop herbs. Beat butter, garlic, salt and chopped herbs together.
3. Slice bread diagonally, leaving a little hinge.
4. Butter each slice and reassemble the loaf. Spread any remaining butter on top of loaf.
5. Wrap in foil. Place on tin, bake for 15 minutes. Open foil for final 5 minutes to crisp the top.

Garnish with chopped parsley. Add fresh herbs for Herby Garlic Bread.

Serve hot as an accompaniment to a meal.

Bruschetta

PRONOUNCED 'BRUSKETTA' IN ITALY

Cooking Time: 10-15 minutes

Serves: 3

Ingredients

1 small ciabatta loaf or 1 large lunch roll or baton

1 clove garlic

Rock salt or table salt

4 tablespoons virgin olive oil

Topping

3 very ripe tomatoes

Salt and black pepper

Garnish: fresh herbs

Equipment

sharp knife, board, fork, bowl, tablespoon, grill or toaster, serving plate.

Steps **Method**

Gather equipment, collect/weigh ingredients, set worktop.

1. Peel tomatoes for topping and chop very finely.
2. Peel garlic, cut in two.
3. Preheat the grill or use pop-up toaster. Cut bread into thin slices on the diagonal. Toast.
4. Rub a little garlic over one side of each slice. Drizzle with olive oil and sprinkle with a little rock salt.
5. Top with tomatoes, and season with salt and pepper.

Serve as a hot snack or starter.

Garnish with fresh herbs and serve straight away.

To serve the Catalan way – a regional speciality and a fun way to begin a dinner party. Provide each guest with ½ a tomato, ½ a clove of garlic and some hot toast. Have olive oil and salt to pass around. Tell your guests to rub the toast first with garlic then with the cut tomato, then sprinkle with oil and salt. With sweet, vine-ripened tomatoes this is bliss!

Italian Crostini

LIKE LARGE FRENCH CROÛTONS

Cooking Time: 10 minutes

Serves: 1

Ingredients

1 x 20cm lunch roll or ½ French stick or 2 slices thickly cut bread

1-2 cloves garlic

3 tablespoons olive oil

Salt and black pepper

Topping

Choose from the list below.

Equipment

sharp knife, board, garlic crusher, tablespoon, small Swiss roll tin, pot stand, wire tray, serving plate.

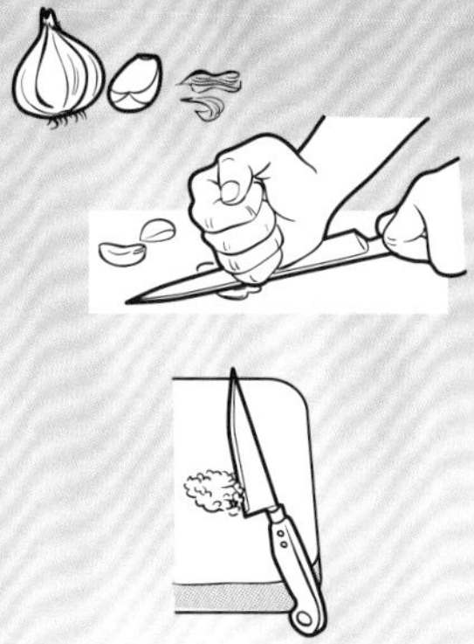

Smashing and crushing garlic

Idea!

Crostini for soups: Make small crostini, spread with green pesto and pop into hot soup – delicious!

Steps **Method**

Preheat oven to 180°C/Fan 170°C/Gas Mark 4.

Gather equipment, collect/weigh ingredients, set worktop.

1. Cut bread roll or French stick at an angle into thick slices or cut loaf into even-sized pieces.
2. Peel and crush garlic, place on baking tin. Add the oil, salt and pepper. Mix all about. Dip each slice into the oil, on both sides, to coat lightly.
3. Bake for 5-7 minutes until crisp.

To serve hot: Top each slice with the chosen toppings and bake for 5 minutes.

Garnish and **serve** hot as a snack or starter.

To serve cold: Cool the crostini and top just before serving.

Crostini Toppings

Hot Toppings

- **Cheese, tomato and basil:** Top each crostini with sliced tomato and a piece of cheese. Irish Cheddar or mozzarella cheese is nice, but for a Mediterranean effect, try goats cheese or feta. Bake for 5 minutes. **Garnish** with a black olive and a basil leaf.
- **Chopped salami, tomato and cheese.**

Cold Toppings

- **Cream Cheese:** Use the cream cheese dip recipe on page 22 with bacon, sardine or tuna.
- **Avocado:** Pile with mashed avocado and vinaigrette. Garnish with a slice of tomato. (See page 18 for preparation and use of avocado).

Resource Management: Leftover cheese can be grated or finely diced and frozen for later use or sprinkled over pies and bakes.

FRENCH CROÛTONS

Cooking Time: 15 minutes

Ingredients

- 2 slices thickly cut bread
- Salt
- 2 tablespoons olive oil
- 1 clove garlic, crushed (optional)

Equipment

plastic bag for tossing, baking tin.

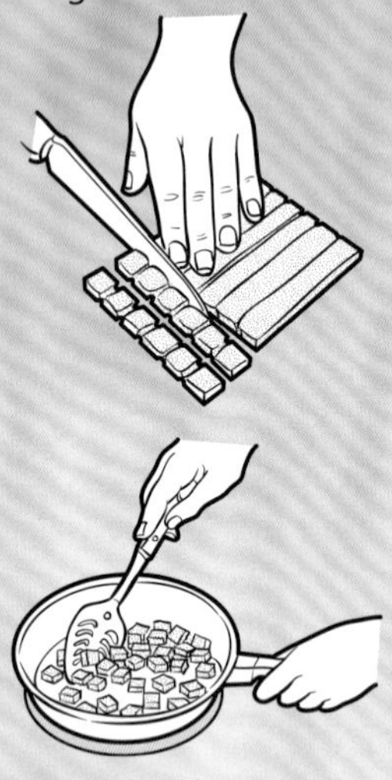

Cutting and frying croûtons

Croûtons and Melba Toast

Steps **Method**

Preheat oven to 180°C/Fan 170°C/Gas Mark 4.

Gather equipment, collect/weigh ingredients, set worktop.

1. Cut bread into 1cm cubes. Put into a freezer bag with the oil, salt and crushed garlic, toss to coat.
2. Spread on a baking tin. Bake for 15 minutes until crisp (or fry until crisp).

Serve hot or cold with soups, chowders or salads.

Keep fresh in a sealed plastic bag or jar in the fridge.

Chef's Tip!
These can be fried instead of baked but can burn easily.

MELBA TOAST

Ingredients

1 slice thick sliced pan bread

Equipment

sharp knife, board, serving basket and napkin.

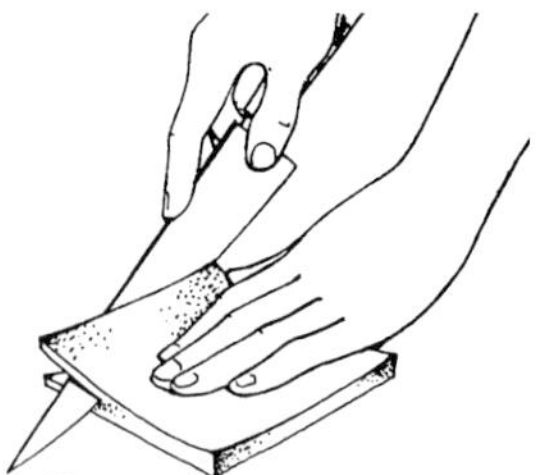

Slicing the toasted bread for melba toast

Steps **Method**

Gather equipment, collect/weigh ingredients, set worktop.

1. Preheat the grill to high or use pop-up toaster.
2. Toast each side of the bread until golden.
3. Cut off the crusts from each side, using a sharp knife.
4. Holding the toast flat, slice horizontally through the centre of the slice, between the toasted sides, to make 2 thin slices. Cut each piece into 4 triangles or 3 fingers.
5. Toast the uncooked sides under the grill for a few moments to just brown or bake in a moderate oven until crisp and golden.

Serve with soup or use for dips.

Resource Management: Croûtons, melba toast, bruschetta and crostini are great ways to upcycle unused bread. See bread and butter pudding page 154 and breadcrumbs page 31.

Chapter 2

Dressings, Mayonnaise, Salsa and Sauces

Extra Virgin Cold Pressed Olive Oil

Olive Oil

Irish Cold Pressed Rapeseed Oil

Virgin Coconut Oil

Irish Butter

Always choose a good-quality First Cold Pressed Olive Oil when making dressings. Oils that contain Omega-3 fats are known to be anti-inflammatory and reduce the risk of coronary heart disease and stroke. Choose fats and oils that are rich in Omega-3 and low in Omega-6, such as olive oil and butter.

Eggs are used to emulsify oil and vinegar when making mayonnaise. Butter gives the best flavour when making a sauce.

Key Words and Skills

- ❖ emulsion
- ❖ blend
- ❖ roux
- ❖ boil
- ❖ grate
- ❖ infuse
- ❖ consistency
- ❖ crush
- ❖ mix
- ❖ melt
- ❖ sauté
- ❖ grill
- ❖ scald
- ❖ zest

Other suitable recipes:

Raita (page 129), Tahini Sauce/Dressing (page 141), Vegetarian Nut Cream (page 142), Coconut Cream (page 152), and Apple Sauce (page 156).

Evaluation! See pages 223 and 224.

- ❖ Did you meet the brief and did you refer to the specific requirements of the task or dish/dishes?
- ❖ Discuss the results of your finished dish/dishes including the presentation, colour, taste and texture.
- ❖ What aspects were done well and what aspects could be improved?
- ❖ Did you correctly cost and budget for all ingredients?

DRESSINGS

Ingredients for dressings

Oil: Good-quality oils give the best flavour. Use any of the following: (a) extra virgin cold pressed olive oil, (b) sunflower oil, (c) avocado oil, (d) cold pressed rapeseed oil.
Olive oil on its own can be heavy so mix it with sunflower or avocado oil.

Vinegar: Choose a good-quality vinegar to give flavour to your dressing. If you find the taste too sharp, reduce the amount used. Use any of the following: (a) cider vinegar, (b) wine vinegar, (c) tarragon vinegar, (d) balsamic vinegar. Coeliacs are to avoid plain malt vinegar.

Mustard: English, Dijon or grainy mustards can be used. Avoid pre-made mustards as they contain gluten.

Sugar: This gives sweetness to dressings. Try honey for a change.

FRENCH DRESSING

BASIC VINAIGRETTE
TEMPORARY EMULSION

Ingredients

1 tablespoon cider vinegar
¼ teaspoon salt
Generous grind of black pepper
½ level teaspoon Dijon mustard
1 level teaspoon sugar
6 tablespoons oil

Equipment

tablespoon, teaspoon, bowl, whisk or screw-top jar.

Chef's Tip!
Do not toss green salads until ready to serve. Put the dressing in the bottom of the salad bowl. Put the greens gently on top and toss at table just before serving.

Making French dressing

Dressing Ingredients

Steps	Method

Gather equipment, collect/weigh ingredients, set worktop.

1 Whisk all the ingredients in a bowl until the mixture **emulsifies*** (see page 38) or shake vigorously in a screw-top jar.
2 Taste and adjust flavour. Add more vinegar, salt or sugar to taste. Use as required.
3 Store in a screw-top jar in a fridge.

Garlic Vinaigrette

🔑 VARIATION

Ingredients

1 x French Dressing ingredients (see page 36)

½ clove garlic, crushed

Healthy Hint!
Always use cold pressed extra virgin olive oil for making salad dressings.

Look Up!
Modified Atmosphere Packaging (MAP).

Use fresh mixed salad leaves and fresh herbs mixed together with the vinaigrette of your choice. Toss just before serving.

Steps **Method**

Whisk or shake the ½ clove crushed garlic with the French Dressing ingredients.

Herb Vinaigrette

🔑 VARIATION

Ingredients

1 x French Dressing ingredients

1 tablespoon chopped herbs

Steps **Method**

Whisk or shake 1 tablespoon finely-chopped herbs (try basil, coriander, parsley or mint) with the French Dressing ingredients.

Roquefort Dressing

🔑 VARIATION

Ingredients

1 x French Dressing ingredients

50g Roquefort cheese

Steps **Method**

Mash 50g Roquefort cheese with a fork and whisk with the French Dressing ingredients. Try using Cashel Blue, Crozier Blue or Stilton for a change.

Orange Dressing

🔑 VARIATION

Ingredients

1 x French Dressing ingredients

1 orange juice and zest

Steps **Method**

Whisk or shake the orange juice and zest with the French Dressing ingredients.

Resource Management: Wash and spin salad leaves and place between 2 sheets of kitchen paper. Place in a sealed container and store in fridge.

Whole Egg Blender Mayonnaise

Each ingredient affects the taste of mayonnaise; choose cider or wine vinegar if possible. Use a mixture of sunflower oil and 'first cold pressed extra virgin olive oil' for a great flavour. Free-range eggs give the best result.

Ingredients

- 1 fresh egg, free-range if possible
- ½ teaspoon salt
- 1 level teaspoon sugar
- 1 teaspoon Dijon mustard
- 1 small clove garlic
- 1 tablespoon wine vinegar
- 250ml olive oil or mixture of oils

Equipment

liquidiser or processor, teaspoon, tablespoon, measuring jug, spatula, clean screw-top jar to store.

Watch Out!
Uncooked eggs should not be given to the very young, the elderly or pregnant women.

Chef's Tip!
A mayonnaise will absorb a little more oil and become even thicker. Be careful! It can suddenly go thin again! If this happens, put the mixture into the measuring jug and begin again with all the ingredients except the oil. Pour the curdled mixture onto the egg in a slow, steady stream and then add just 100ml more oil. Do not make the same mistake twice!

Steps — Method

Gather equipment, collect/weigh ingredients, set worktop.

1. Put egg, sugar, salt, mustard, garlic and vinegar into the liquidiser/processor and blend for 20 seconds.
2. Remove the small lid from the middle hole and dribble the oil slowly onto the running blades. Continue until all the oil has been absorbed and the mayonnaise has thickened (**emulsified***). Scrape down the sides of goblet with the spatula and buzz once again.
3. Use as it is or flavour as required.
4. Store in a clean, screw-top jar in a fridge for 1 week.

Chef's Tip!
See use of liquidiser/processor/blender (page 15).

Idea!
Use wholegrain mustard in place of Dijon mustard. Coeliacs should use gluten-free powder mustard.

*EMULSION — TECHNIQUE

When oil and vinegar are shaken vigorously as in French dressing, they form a **temporary** emulsion. Temporary means that it doesn't stay together for too long. A **permanent** emulsion is made by adding an emulsifier, e.g. egg yolk. Mayonnaise is a permanent emulsion.

Curry-Flavoured Mayonnaise

VARIATION

Ingredients

3 tablespoons mayonnaise (see page 38)

For Curry Dip use:

1-2 teaspoons curry paste or powder

1-2 teaspoons sweet chutney

Equipment

teaspoon, tablespoon, bowl, serving bowl.

Steps **Method**

Blend all the ingredients together in a bowl. Taste and adjust the seasoning if necessary.

Use as a dip with baked potatoes, with egg mayonnaise, with a salad or at a barbecue.

Serve in a polished bowl or store in a screw-top jar in a fridge. (Use within 10 days.)

Garlic-Flavoured Mayonnaise

VARIATION

Ingredients

3 tablespoons mayonnaise

For Garlic Dip use:

1 clove garlic

Dash of lemon juice

Finely-chopped parsley

Equipment

tablespoon, sharp knife, board, garlic crusher, serving dish.

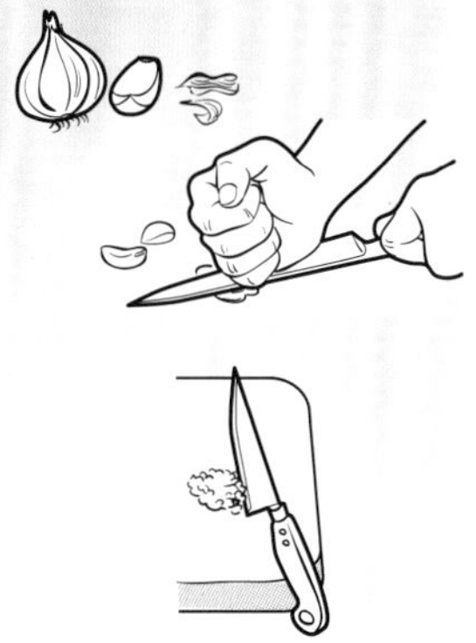

Smashing and crushing garlic

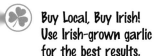

Flavoured mayonnaise goes very well with baked potatoes.

Steps **Method**

1 Peel and crush garlic.

2 Wash, dry and chop 1 tablespoon parsley very finely.

3 Blend all together with mayonnaise and a dash of lemon juice.

Use as a dip with baked potatoes, with fish or chicken kebabs, with spring rolls or as a barbecue accompaniment.

Serve in a polished bowl or store in a screw-top jar in a fridge. (Use within 10 days.)

Buy Local, Buy Irish! Use Irish-grown garlic for the best results.

Resource Management: Never put egg shells into a compost heap as they can attract vermin.

SAUCES

Chef's Tip!
Keep some cooked roux in a screw-topped jar in the fridge and whisk a little at a time into hot soup or sauce that you want to thicken. Boil for a minute to cook the flour.

A **roux** means equal quantities of fat and flour cooked together.
It is used to thicken sauces, stews and soups. Varying the fat, liquid and flavourings makes sauces different.

Fat*: For white sauces, choose butter as it has the best flavour.
For dark sauces, choose butter, oil or the sediment from roasts or sautés.

Liquid:** For white sauces, use milk or milk and cream. For other sauces, use stock, water or half stock and another liquid such as milk, cream, wine, cider, fruit or tomato juice.

BASIC PROPORTIONS FOR ROUX SAUCES (including quick method)

The consistency or **thickness** of a sauce depends on the amount of liquid used.

Types of sauce (consistency)	Flour plain white	Fat* butter/oil	Liquid** milk/stock/water	Examples
Pouring sauce (thinnest)	25g	25g	**500ml**	Parsley sauce
Stewing sauce	25g	25g	**375ml**	Sauce for brown stew
Coating sauce	25g	25g	**250ml**	To coat cauliflower/fish
Binding sauce/ Panard (very thick)	25g	25g	**125ml**	To bind fish cakes/ vegetable burgers

WHITE SAUCE ('ALL-IN-ONE' QUICK METHOD)

Ingredients
- 25g butter
- 25g flour
- 500ml milk = pouring sauce
- White pepper and salt

Equipment
small non-stick saucepan, wooden spoon, plastic/nylon whisk, measuring jug, pot stand.

Buy Local, Buy Irish!
Buy Irish butter, cheese and full-fat milk.

Steps **Method**

Gather equipment, collect/weigh ingredients, set worktop.

1 Put the flour, fat* and liquid** into a saucepan and whisk until it boils and thickens.
2 Use a wooden spoon to stir the mixture out from the corners.
3 Reduce the heat, simmer for 3 minutes to cook the flour properly, stirring all the time.
4 Add flavourings as required – see variations on page 42.

Roux Sauce (Traditional Method)

Ingredients

25g butter
25g flour
500ml milk = pouring sauce
White pepper and salt

Equipment

small non-stick saucepan, wooden spoon, plastic/nylon whisk, measuring jug, pot stand.

Chef's Tip!
Use a whisk to rescue a lumpy sauce – use a nylon one in a non-stick saucepan.

Look Up!
Whole milk, low-fat milk, lactose-free milk, dairy-free milk and goats milk.

Idea!
To keep a sauce warm for a time before serving, lay a piece of cling film directly over the surface of the sauce to prevent a skin from forming.

1. Melt fat add flour
2. Remove from heat, add liquid and stir
3. Boil and simmer for five minutes to thicken
4. Season to taste

Steps **Method**

1 Melt the fat in a saucepan.
2 Add the flour and cook **gently** while stirring for 1 minute.
3 Remove from heat and cool slightly on a pot stand.
4 Gradually beat in ½ the liquid little by little. Use the wooden spoon to get into the corners of the pot, but a whisk is best for removing all the lumps. It is also the quickest!
5 Beat out all lumps before adding the remaining liquid.
6 Return to heat. **Continue to stir** and boil for 3-5 minutes.
7 Add the flavourings now. Correct the consistency and check the taste.

Resource Management: Use a spatula to clean out the saucepan. Always steep the saucepan in cold water to make the wash-up easier.

***ROUX** COOKERY TERM

A roux is equal quantities of fat and flour cooked together. It is used to thicken sauces, soups and stews or casseroles.

Béchamel Sauce

VARIATION

Ingredients

25g butter

25g flour

375g milk = stewing sauce

White pepper and salt

Additional ingredients

2 cloves
1 bay leaf
1 small onion
Pinch powdered mace

Steps — Method

Heat the milk with the additional ingredients slowly to draw out the flavours gently (**infuse***). Leave aside for 15 minutes, strain and then make the sauce as in the Quick Method (see page 40).

Serve with, or use for, savoury pancakes or vol-au-vent fillings.

***INFUSE** — TECHNIQUE

Infuse means to flavour a liquid by heating it slowly with vegetables, herbs and/or spices to slowly draw out the flavours.

Cheese Sauce

VARIATION

Ingredients

1 x Roux Sauce ingredients (page 40), see Chef's Tip

Additional ingredients

50g strong Cheddar cheese, grated

1 teaspoon readymade mustard

Steps — Method

Add the grated cheese and ½ teaspoon mustard to hot Roux sauce. Do not boil; just let the cheese melt gently.

Serve with or use for fish, cauliflower, lasagne or macaroni cheese.

Chef's Tip!
The consistency or thickness of a sauce depends on the amount of liquid used. See types of sauces on page 40 and vary the quantity of liquid as required, e.g. Stewing Sauce for lasagna and Coating Sauce for cauliflower cheese.

Parsley Sauce

VARIATIO

Ingredients

1 x Roux Stewing Sauce ingredients (page 40)

Additional ingredients

1-2 tablespoons finely-chopped parsley

Steps — Method

Add the finely-chopped fresh parsley to hot sauce just before serving.

Serve with bacon, ham or fish.

Chef's Tip!
If chopping parsley, put into a cup and use a scissors for chopping, see diagrams on pages 53 and 73.

Mushroom Sauce

VARIATIO

Ingredients

1 x Roux Coating Sauce ingredients (page 40)

Additional ingredients

200g mushrooms

1 tablespoon oil

25g butter

Steps — Method

Wash mushrooms, dry well on kitchen paper. Chop into small pieces. Heat oil and butter in frying pan, cook mushrooms gently allowing the juices to evaporate, but do not let brown. Stir into white sauce and check the seasoning.

Serve with fish, meat or as a savoury pancake filling, see page 79.

Grilled Pepper Salsa

SPANISH/MEXICAN

Ingredients

- 2 red peppers
- 8 cherry tomatoes
- 2 sprigs fresh coriander
- ½ small onion
- 1 clove garlic
- 3 tablespoons oil
- 2 teaspoons vinegar
- Salt and black pepper

Equipment

sharp knife, board, garlic crusher, grater, small bowl, cling film, tablespoon.

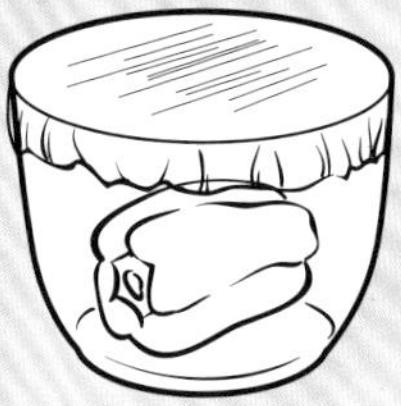

Seal the bowl with cling film

Steps — Method

Gather equipment, collect/weigh ingredients, set worktop.

1. Preheat the grill. Wash the peppers, cut lengthways into quarters. Grill until the skins blacken. Put into bowl and cover with cling film. When cool, the skins will slip off.
2. Peel and grate the onion, peel and crush the garlic, chop the coriander finely, dice tomatoes.
3. Skin, deseed and dice the peppers. Combine with all other ingredients, taste and add a pinch of sugar if desired.

Serve in a bowl. Use with grilled or baked meat or fish.

Variation

Add a chopped avocado or ½ a deseeded, very finely diced chilli.

Tomato and Avocado Salsa

MEXICAN

Ingredients

- 1 clove garlic
- 2 tomatoes
- Bunch coriander or parsley
- ½ lime or lemon
- 1 teaspoon tomato purée
- 1 teaspoon wine vinegar
- 1 red chilli or dash of Tabasco
- 1 teaspoon sugar
- 1 ripe avocado

Equipment

teaspoon, sharp knife, board, squeezer, garlic crusher, bowl.

Chef's Tip!
Salsa is best eaten on the day it is made.

Steps — Method

Gather equipment, collect/weigh ingredients, set worktop.

1. Peel and crush garlic. Chop herbs very finely.
2. Wash, dry and dice the tomatoes. Juice the lemon or lime.
3. Cut avocado in two (page 18), remove stone and skin, dice flesh very finely. Mix all ingredients together.

Serve in a clean bowl. Use with meat dishes, baked potatoes and barbecued, grilled or baked fish dishes.

Fresh Tomato Sauce

Cooking Time: 30 minutes

Ingredients

- 1 onion
- 1 clove garlic
- 1 carrot (optional)
- 1 tablespoon olive oil
- 300g fresh tomatoes or 1 can chopped tomatoes
- 1 rounded teaspoon flour
- 150ml water
- 1 tablespoon tomato purée
- 1 teaspoon dried oregano
- ½ teaspoon sugar
- Salt and black pepper

Equipment

grater, sharp knife, board, garlic crusher, tablespoon, saucepan with lid, teaspoon, wooden spoon, pot stand, liquidiser or processor (optional).

Fresh Tomato Sauce, Barbecue Sauce, Sweet and Sour Sauce

Steps **Method**

Gather equipment, collect/weigh ingredients, set worktop.

1 If using a liquidiser/processor, chop vegetables roughly. When cooking is finished, liquidise (see safety note on page 15). If not using a liquidiser/processor, wash and chop tomatoes very finely.

2 Smash garlic, peel and crush. Peel onion and carrot, grate on large holes of grater.

3 Heat oil, **sauté*** onion, carrot and garlic until soft (about 5 minutes).

4 Add flour and stir for 1 minute. Remove from heat.

5 Slowly stir in the liquid and tomatoes and all other ingredients. If using fresh tomatoes, make a cross into the skin with a sharp knife and follow the instructions below for skinning

6 Cover and simmer gently for 20 minutes. Liquidise until smooth.

7 Taste the sauce, correct the seasoning and serve.

Serve with hot pasta and top with basil leaves. Stir 50g diced mozzarella into the sauce to melt just before serving.

Grating a carrot

How to skin a tomato

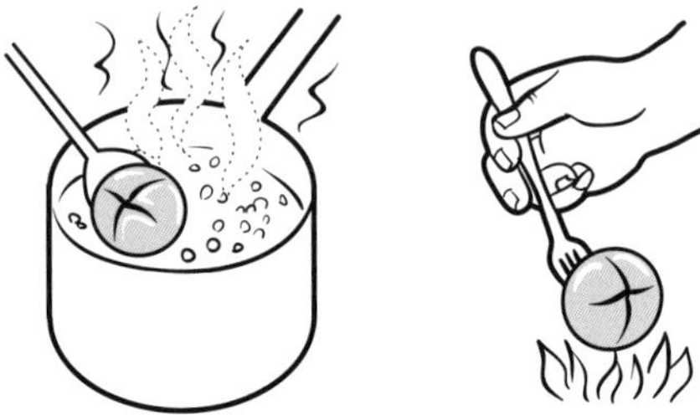

Scald in boiling water for 1 minute or hold it on a fork over a low flame.

Carefully pull away the loosened, blistered skin with a sharp knife.

Chef's Tip!
Stirring 2 tablespoons mayonnaise into the sauce before serving makes it very creamy and it sticks to the pasta beautifully. It is a non-dairy alternative to cheese or cream.

***SAUTÉ** TECHNIQUE

Sauté means to fry food rapidly in hot fat. The food is sometimes browned and sometimes not. This method is used to intensify the flavours and so develop a better taste in the finished dish.

Barbecue Sauce

VARIATION

Ingredients

1 x Fresh Tomato Sauce ingredients but omit carrot
2 teaspoons mustard powder
2 teaspoons brown sauce
1-2 teaspoons honey
1 teaspoon brown vinegar

Steps / Method

1 Make as for Fresh Tomato Sauce (omitting carrot).
2 Add all extra ingredients at Step 5.

Serve hot or cold with barbecued or grilled meats, fish or vegetables.

Idea!
Use brown sugar if you have no honey.

Sweet and Sour Sauce

VARIATION

Ingredients

1 x Fresh Tomato Sauce ingredients but omit carrot
1 dessertspoon soy sauce
1 teaspoon sugar
1 dessertspoon cider vinegar
100g crushed pineapple

Spring Rolls with Sweet and Sour Sauce

Steps / Method

1 Make as for Fresh Tomato Sauce (omitting carrot).
2 Add all extra ingredients at Step 5.

Serve hot or cold with barbecued or grilled meats, fish or vegetables.

Sweet Chilli Sauce

VARIATION

Ingredients

1 small onion
1 clove garlic
2 tablespoons oil
3cm piece fresh ginger
½ red pepper
¼ teaspoon chilli powder
100ml stock or water
2 tablespoons dark soy sauce
1 tablespoon lemon juice
1 tablespoon brown sugar

Steps / Method

1 Heat oil in frying pan, sauté the onion, garlic, ginger and pepper for 5 minutes but do not brown.
2 Add the stock or water, chilli, soy sauce, sugar and lemon juice. Simmer for 10 minutes.

Serve with meatballs or burgers.

Healthy Hint!
Too much salt can lead to high blood pressure, increased strain on your heart, kidneys and brain. Look for natural salt substitutes, e.g. ginger, herbs and spices. Look for low sodium soy sauce or miso.

Chef's Tip!
If you have no chili powder, use ½ a fresh finely diced chilli.

Curry Sauce (Vindaloo style)

Cooking Time: 30-40 minutes

Ingredients

1 onion
1 clove garlic
1 small carrot (optional)
1 tablespoon olive oil
2 tablespoons curry paste or powder
2 teaspoons flour
400ml stock or water
1 eating apple
2 teaspoons chutney
1 teaspoon tomato purée
Black pepper and salt
Garnish: fresh coriander

Equipment

saucepan with lid, pot stand, sharp knife, board, tablespoon, garlic crusher, teaspoon, wooden spoon, sauce boat/bowl.

Chef's Tip!
These curry sauces are useful for cooking or reheating small pieces of meat or fish or even cooked vegetables. They are quick to make, and using a liquidiser makes preparation even quicker.

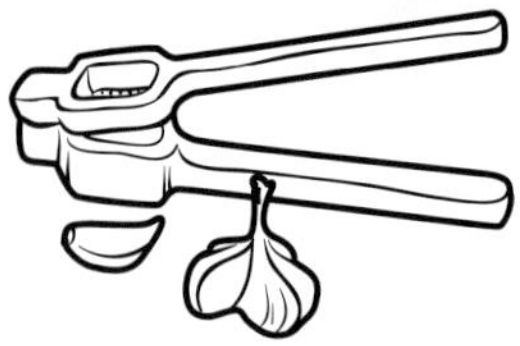

Garlic crusher

Vindaloo Sauce with rice

Steps **Method**

Gather equipment, collect/weigh ingredients, set worktop.

1 Peel onion and carrot, dice or grate. Wash, peel, core and dice or grate apple. Smash garlic, peel and crush.

2 Heat oil, **sauté*** onion and carrot for 5 minutes until soft. Stir in garlic and curry paste or powder, cook for 1 minute.

3 Add flour, stirring for 1 minute. Remove from heat.

4 Gradually beat in ½ the stock, apple, chutney, tomato purée, salt and pepper. When well mixed, add the remaining stock.

5 Bring to the boil, stirring all the time. Reduce the heat and simmer for 5 minutes.

6 Now add vegetables or see vegan serving idea, below. If you are an omnivore, add fish or small pieces of meat that you might wish to cook or reheat. Cover and simmer gently until meat is thoroughly cooked or reheated.

7 Taste the sauce and correct the seasoning.

Serve with Basmati rice (see page 100).

Garnish with chopped fresh coriander, see pages 53 and 73.

Serving Idea: Reheat cooked chicken or meatballs in the sauce.

See also **Chicken Curry** and **Vegetarian Curry** on page 129.

Vegan Serving Idea: Add ½ tin of drained chickpeas, ½ tin drained lentils and 400g frozen sweetcorn/peas to the sauce. Simmer gently until cooked through.

***SAUTÉ** **TECHNIQUE**

Sauté means to fry food rapidly in hot fat. The food is sometimes browned and sometimes not. This method is used to intensify the flavours and so develop a better taste in the finished dish.

Thai Green Curry Sauce

THAILAND

Cooking Time: 35-40 minutes

Ingredients

1 small onion

1 clove garlic

1 teaspoon grated ginger

½ lemon, juice and zest

1 tablespoon oil

2 teaspoons Thai green curry paste

1 teaspoon sugar

200ml can coconut milk

1 sprig fresh coriander

Salt to taste

Equipment

saucepan with lid, pot stand, sharp knife, board, garlic crusher, wooden spoon, juice squeezer, teaspoon, grater, tablespoon.

Green Thai Curry Sauce, Basmati Rice

Steps — Method

Gather equipment, collect/weigh ingredients, set worktop.

1 Peel onion, dice finely. Peel garlic and dice or crush.

2 Peel ginger, grate using medium holes of grater.

3 Wash lemon, cut in two, zest (see page 150) and juice one half.

4 Wash and dry the coriander. Keep some for garnish and chop remaining leaves and stalks.

5 Heat oil, add the onion, sauté for 5 minutes. Add the ginger, garlic and curry paste, stir once.

6 Add the coconut milk, lemon zest, juice, sugar and chopped coriander.

7 Simmer for 1 minute. If you are an omnivore, now add fish, small pieces of chicken or vegetables that you might wish to cook or reheat. Simmer gently until meat is thoroughly cooked or reheated.

Serve with Basmati rice, see page 100.

Garnish with fresh coriander.

Serving Idea: Reheat cooked chicken or meatballs in the sauce for a really quick and tasty meal or prepare **vegan option** on page 46.

Zesting a lemon

Watch Out!
When buying cans of coconut milk or cream, buy organic where possible. Avoid the 'low-fat' or 'lite' variety as these contain mostly water.

Chef's Tip!
Use Red Thai Curry Paste for Thai beef and lamb dishes – it is much hotter! Use red peppers in these sauces and some tomato purée to improve the colour.

Food Fact!
Ginger is a natural anti-inflammatory and aids digestion. The Ancient Greeks grated it into many dishes, including sauces and breads. Add grated or chopped fresh ginger to curries and savory dishes, or crystallised or ground dried ginger to desserts.

Chapter 3

Salads, Vegetables and Potatoes

Parsnips

Carrots

Sweet Potato

Celeriac

Beetroot

Always choose vegetables in season and if possible visit farmers' markets to buy locally grown, Irish, organic produce. Food in season is fresher, the enzymes are still alive and the vitamins are intact. Look for quality, freshn and class when selecting vegetables. Compare quantities and weights and take advantage of special offers.

Other suitable recipes:

Vegetarian Bolognese Sauce (page 91), Vegetarian Chilli (page 122), Red Lentil Dal and Comforting Kitchari (page 137), Buddha Bowl (page 141), Chickpea Patties (page 138), Vegetable Accompaniments (page 140).

Evaluation! See pages 223 and 224.

- Did you meet the brief and did you refer to the specific requirements of the task or dish/dishes?
- Discuss the results of your finished dish/dishes including the presentation, colour, taste and texture.
- What aspects were done well and what aspects could be improved?
- Did you correctly cost and budget for all ingredients?

Key Words and Skills

- peel
- parboil
- shred
- marinade
- reduce
- bake

Coleslaw

IT IS IMPORTANT THAT WE EAT SOME FRESH, RAW FOOD EVERY DAY FOR GOOD HEALTH

Serves: 4

Ingredients

¼ hard white cabbage
1 carrot
1 small red pepper
1 dessert apple
50g seedless raisins
Salt and ground pepper
2 teaspoons parsley

Dressing

3 tablespoons mayonnaise
2 teaspoons cider vinegar
1 teaspoon caster sugar

Garnish: parsley

Equipment

sharp knife, board, large bowl, tablespoon, teaspoon, serving bowl.

Shredding cabbage

Healthy Hint!
As vegetables contain no fat, they are important for those on a low-kilocalorie or low-cholesterol diet.

Steps **Method**

Gather equipment, collect/weigh ingredients, set worktop.

1 **Dressing:** Put all the dressing ingredients into a bowl and whisk until smooth (or shake in a screw-topped jar).
2 **Vegetables:** Remove outer leaves of cabbage, trim hard stalks, wash, dry and shred finely with a sharp knife or food processor.
3 Peel and grate carrot, wash and dice pepper and apple.
4 Wash, dry and chop parsley, see diagrams on pages 53 and 73.
5 Combine the cabbage, carrot, pepper, apple, raisins, parsley, dressing and seasoning and mix well. Spoon into a salad bowl.

Garnish with chopped parsley.

Serve with grilled, baked or barbecued foods or in lunch rolls.

Chef's Tip!
To make coleslaw more interesting, add any of the following: 2 sticks finely-chopped celery, shredded red cabbage, 100g sweetcorn, 25g cashew nuts. Sprinkle the coleslaw with 25g sesame or sunflower seeds.

Fruity Coleslaw

VARIATION

Add an extra diced apple, grapes or diced mango to the coleslaw.

Coleslaw with Croûtons

VARIATION

See recipe for French Croûtons on page 34. Scatter them over the coleslaw before serving.

Green Salad

Serves: 4

Ingredients

1 head of lettuce or mixed lettuce leaves

3 scallions

½ small cucumber

½ small green pepper

Parsley or other fresh herbs

Equipment

sharp knife, board, scissors, salad spinner or tea towel, colander, salad bowl.

Food Fact!
Modified Atmospheric Packaging (MAP).
Avoid packets of pre-washed leaves as the chlorine used to wash the leaves and the nitrogen in the packets destroy most of the vitamins. Buy or grow fresh lettuce and salad leaves.

Chef's Tip!
A little cheese served with lettuce is delicious and provides calcium.

Healthy Hint!
Lettuce contains live enzymes and is high in fibre. Eating some lettuce leaves every day keeps the bowel clean and functioning.

Steps	Method

Gather equipment, collect/weigh ingredients, set worktop.

1. Wash lettuce and dry in a salad spinner if possible. Otherwise use a clean tea towel. Arrange in a salad bowl.
2. Wash and chop scallions, deseed and wash green pepper and slice into fine strips. Wash and slice cucumber.
3. Arrange nicely in bowl, sprinkle with chopped parsley.

Serve tossed in French Dressing (pages 36/37).

Store lettuce and salad washed and dried, but not dressed, in a polythene bag or salad spinner in the fridge.

Butterhead Lettuce

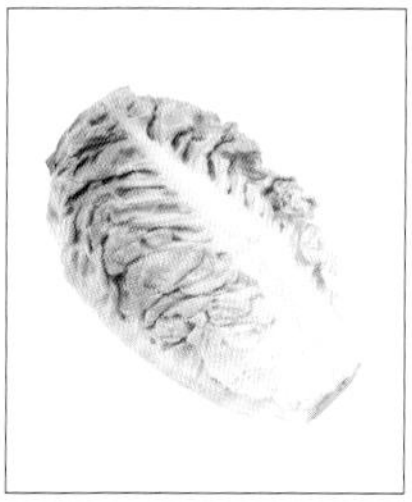

Baby Gem Lettuce

Rocket Leaves

Baby Spinach Leaves

Red Leaf/Lollo Rossa Lettuce

Waldorf Salad

USA

Serves: 4

Ingredients

3 sticks celery
1 small red eating apple
Lemon juice
50g chopped walnuts

Dressing

1 tablespoon lemon juice or wine vinegar
½ teaspoon sugar
Salt and pepper
½ teaspoon mustard
3 tablespoons sunflower oil

Garnish: lettuce, tomatoes, cucumber

Equipment

sharp knife, board, lemon squeezer, tablespoon, whisk, 2 bowls, serving bowl.

Chef's Tip!
To soften avocado, see page 18.

In a hurry!
Use 2 tablespoons mayonnaise instead of making the dressing.

Waldorf Salad and Avocado, Apple and Walnut Salad

Steps **Method**

Gather equipment, collect/weigh ingredients, set worktop.

1 **Dressing:** Mix the lemon juice or vinegar with seasonings in a small bowl with a whisk. Add the oil gradually while whisking until the dressing thickens or place ingredients in a screw-topped jar and shake vigorously.

2 Wash, quarter, core and dice the apple. Place in a bowl and sprinkle with lemon juice to prevent enzymic browning, see Food Fact on page 18.

3 Wash and dice celery, chop walnuts into small pieces. Add to apple in bowl.

4 Add the dressing, mix gently and check the seasoning. Turn into the serving bowl.

Garnish with lettuce leaves, sliced tomato and cucumber.

Serve with grilled, baked or roasted meats.

Avocado, Apple and Walnut Salad

VARIATION

Serves: 4

Ingredients

1 x Waldorf Salad ingredients but omit celery
2 avocadoes

Steps **Method**

1 Make dressing.

2 Cut avocadoes in two, remove the stones (see page 18). Using a tablespoon, remove flesh from each avocado in one piece. Dice flesh, put into bowl and sprinkle with lemon juice.

3 Add diced apple and chopped walnuts as above. Stir in the dressing.

Serve in a bowl or fill into the avocado shells and arrange on a plate.

Garnish as above.

Potato Salad

Serves: 4

Ingredients

400g potatoes (3-4 potatoes)

1 scallion or 1 small onion

1 teaspoon fresh parsley, chopped (see pages 53/73)

Salt and pepper

4-5 teaspoons mayonnaise

Vinaigrette Dressing

2 tablespoons cider vinegar

½ teaspoon sugar

½ teaspoon French or English mustard

Salt and pepper

2 tablespoons sunflower oil

Garnish: chopped parsley or chives

Equipment

tablespoon, saucepan, pot stand, sharp knife, board, screw-top jar, salad bowl.

Steps **Method**

Gather equipment, collect/weigh ingredients, set worktop.

1 Wash and peel potatoes, cut into quarters, cook in salted water until tender. Drain.

2 Peel and chop scallion very finely or grate onion.

3 **Dressing:** Place all the ingredients for the dressing in a jar and shake vigorously until mixture emulsifies. Dressing should have a fairly sharp taste with a good mustard flavour.

4 Dice potatoes evenly. Place in a bowl, sprinkle with the dressing while still hot. Add the scallion/onion, parsley and plenty of seasoning. Allow to cool.

5 Mix the mayonnaise gently through the potatoes and pile into a serving dish.

Garnish with chopped parsley or chives.

Serve with barbecued or roasted meat or fish dishes.

Healthy Hint!
Cooked potato starch is very easy to digest, making it suitable for invalids and anyone with digestive problems. It is also suitable for weaning babies.

Food Fact!
Floury potatoes are best for mashing as they break up easily. A good idea is to steam or microwave them in their skins then peel and mash, e.g. Oilean, Kerr's Pinks, King Edwards, Queens, Golden Wonders.

Waxy potatoes, e.g. Pentland Dells, have a creamy, waxy texture that does not break up when cooked. They are perfect for salads, for boiling and for use in gratins.

All-purpose potatoes, e.g. Records and Roosters, are neither waxy nor floury and are good for roasting and general use.

Idea!
Visit your local farmers' markets.

Buy Local, Buy Irish!
Support Irish growers. Irish potatoes have great flavour.

Warm Potato Salad (German potato salad)

Serves: 4

Ingredients

400g small potatoes
4 rashers
Dressing
1 small red onion
1 tablespoon cooking oil
1 tablespoon honey
3 tablespoons cider vinegar
2 teaspoons cornflour
3 tablespoons water
2 tablespoons fresh dill
Garnish: fresh dill, chopped

Equipment

sharp knife, board, saucepan, tablespoon, scissors, small frying pan, wooden spoon, teaspoon, small bowl, salad server.

Dicing an onion

Quick method for chopping herbs

Steps — Method

Gather equipment, collect/weigh ingredients, set worktop.

1 Scrub and wash potatoes well, cut into quarters, cook in boiling salted water until soft. Drain well (there is no need to peel potatoes unless the skins are very thick and old).
2 Grill rashers, cut into small pieces with scissors.
3 **Dressing:** Peel, chop and dice onion and then sauté in oil until soft.
4 Mix cornflour, vinegar and water and add to the onion mixture. Bring to the boil and cook until thickened.
5 Add the honey and chopped dill (keep some dill aside for garnish).
6 Mix dressing with warm potatoes and rashers and pile into serving bowl.

Garnish with fresh dill.

Serve warm (or cold) with grilled, baked or barbecued foods.

Chef's Tip!
Use frankfurter or German sausage sliced and arranged on top instead of rasher. Serve with large, sweet gherkins.

Idea!
Use fresh herbs, e.g. mint, coriander or thyme instead of dill.

In a hurry!
Make potato salad using leftover mashed potato. Add some finely chopped scallions or diced red onion. Mix some grainy mustard with mayonnaise and chopped parsley. Gently mix together and season to taste. Serve with hard-boiled eggs cut into wedges and cherry tomatoes.

Hawaiian Salad

Serves: 4

Ingredients

- 1 small head of lettuce
- 2 pineapple rings
- 1 eating apple
- 100g Cheddar cheese

Dressing

- 150ml soured cream
- 1 teaspoon lemon juice
- 1 teaspoon icing or caster sugar
- Salt and pepper
- **Garnish:** 1 orange, 6-8 black olives (optional)

Equipment

sharp knife, board, fork, plate, screw-top jar, small bowl, salad bowl, grater.

In a hurry!
Break a satsuma into segments instead of using an orange.

Hawaiian Salad, Carrot, Apple and Orange Salad

Steps **Method**

Gather equipment, collect/weigh ingredients, set worktop.

1 Wash and dry lettuce, tear leaves into bite-size pieces, use to cover the base of a serving dish.

2 Wash and dice apple, grate or dice cheese. Drain pineapple and chop.

3 **Dressing:** In a screw-topped jar, combine the soured cream with the lemon juice, sugar, salt and pepper and shake vigorously.

4 Add the soured cream mixture to the apples, cheese and pineapple and toss lightly together. Arrange attractively on top of the lettuce.

Garnish with orange slices or segments and olives.

Serve with grilled or baked dishes. This salad can be used as a main course salad with fresh bread rolls.

Carrot, Apple and Orange Salad

Serves: 3

Ingredients

- 2-3 large carrots
- 1 red apple
- 1 orange
- 25g raisins
- Small bunch chives or 2 scallions
- 1 tablespoon mayonnaise
- Salt and pepper
- **Garnish:** 4 orange slices and chives

Equipment

sharp knife, board, plate, bowl, grater, scissors, tablespoon, salad bowl.

Steps **Method**

Gather equipment, collect/weigh ingredients, set worktop.

1 Wash orange, cut into two around 'equator' (put aside half for garnish). Zest (see page 150) one half only, then cut away the rind and chop flesh into small pieces, removing the pips and pith and saving the juice.

2 Wash and finely dice apple and chop chives or scallions.

3 Wash, peel and grate carrot using large holes on grater, see page 63. Mix with orange flesh, zest, mayonnaise and raisins. Season with pepper and salt to taste.

Garnish with the orange slices and chopped chives.

Serve with grilled or baked dishes.

Idea!
This is lovely sprinkled with toasted sesame seeds and great in a Buddha Bowl or Bento Box, see page 141.

Pasta or Rice Salad

Serves: 4

Ingredients

150g pasta shapes or 160g rice (long-grained)

50g grated cheese

100g mushrooms

2 tablespoons frozen peas

2 scallions

1 red or green pepper

Dressing

125ml olive or salad oil

2-3 tablespoons vinegar

1 tablespoon tomato purée

1 teaspoon poppy seeds

Salt and pepper

Fresh basil for pasta salad or fresh coriander for rice salad

Garnish: fresh basil or coriander or parsley

Equipment

sharp knife, board, saucepan, pot stand, scissors, colander, 2 tablespoons, measuring jug, large screw-top jar, serving plate.

Pasta Salad, Rice Salad, Curried Rice Salad

Steps **Method**

Gather equipment, collect/weigh ingredients, set worktop.

1 Cook pasta or rice in boiling salted water for about 10 minutes (see pages 84 and 100). Drain and allow to cool completely.

2 Wash and slice mushrooms thinly. Deseed, wash and dice peppers.

3 Wash, trim and chop scallions. Wash and chop the basil or coriander for dressing.

4 Add all vegetables and grated cheese to the pasta or rice.

5 **Dressing:** Place oil, vinegar, tomato purée, poppy seeds, basil or coriander and seasoning into a large screw-top jar and shake vigorously until thoroughly combined.

6 Pour over the salad mixture, stirring well until all the ingredients are coated with the dressing. Chill before serving.

Garnish with coarsely-chopped fresh basil or coriander.

Serve with grilled, baked or barbecued foods.

Variation

Sprinkle the salad with 2-3 tablespoons sunflower seeds, toasted flaked almonds or cashew nuts.

Curried Rice Salad

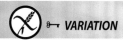

VARIATION

Serves: 4

Ingredients

1 x Rice Salad ingredients

1-2 dessertspoons curry paste or powder

1 dessertspoon chutney

Steps **Method**

1 Add 1-2 dessertspoons curry paste or powder to the rice immediately after draining and then stir in 1 dessertspoon chutney.

2 Continue as above, omitting the tomato purée if wished.

Garnish with freshly-chopped coriander and toasted almonds.

Resource Management: Cook extra rice and pasta when making dinner and use the remainder for salads, evening meals, next-day lunches, Bento Boxes and Buddha Bowls, see page 141.

Stuffed Tomatoes

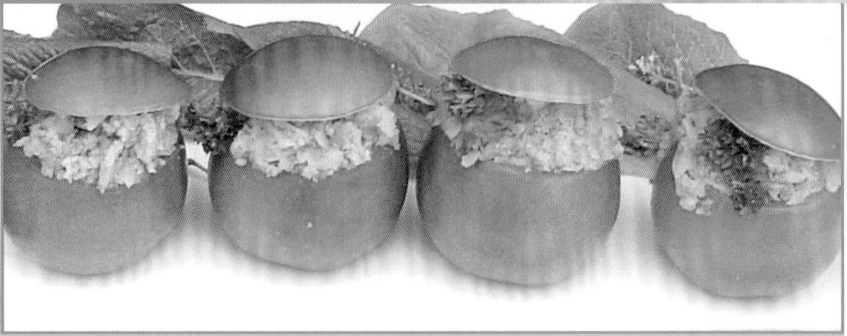

Cooking Time: 20 minutes

Serves: 4

Ingredients

4 large tomatoes

Stuffing

25g butter

Salt and pepper

50g breadcrumbs (2 slices)

¼ onion, finely chopped

2 slices ham or rashers, diced

25g grated cheese

Garnish: chopped parsley

Equipment

sharp knife, board, small bowl, teaspoon, scissors, saucepan (small), pot stand, circle of greaseproof paper to cover, casserole dish.

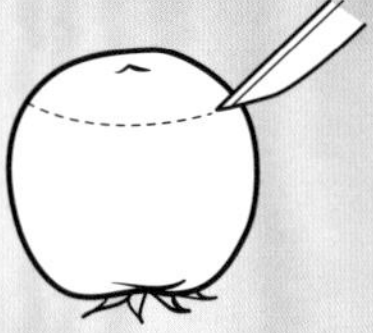

Cutting a tomato

Filling a tomato

In a hurry!
Use 100g of steeped couscous in place of breadcrumbs.

Steps — Method

Preheat oven to 160°C/Fan 150°C/Gas Mark 4.

Gather equipment, collect/weigh ingredients, set worktop.

1. Wash tomatoes, cut slice from smooth end (not the tops) of each for a lid (see diagram). Scoop out the pulp with a teaspoon.
2. **Stuffing:** Melt butter, add onion (and rasher if using) and cook for 2 minutes. Remove from heat, add pulp, breadcrumbs, ham, cheese and seasoning. Mix well.
3. Pile the hot mixture into the tomato shells and replace lids.
4. Put into casserole dish. Cover with greased greaseproof paper and bake for 15-20 minutes.

Garnish with parsley.

Serve for lunch with a side salad or as a starter or vegetable dish.

Variation

Gluten-free: Use 100g cooked rice or quinoa (see page 98) in place of breadcrumbs.

Vegan: Replace rasher/ham with 25g chopped cashew nuts. Fry in 1 tablespoon of coconut oil until just toasted. Use vegan cheese.

Dairy-free: Replace butter with coconut oil and serve with vegan cheese.

To make breadcrumbs

Cut stale bread into small pieces. Using a **processor** or **liquidiser**, drop bread onto the running blades through the hole in the cover.

Bullet Blender: Place some cut bread in the cup. Screw on the blade lid. Turn it upside down and slot it into the motor unit. Use a pulse action.

Grater: Rub large chunks of stale bread on a sharp metal grater.

You can also buy **readymade breadcrumbs**, but check the 'sell-by' date.

Freeze unused breadcrumbs in a sealed bag for use later.

Resource Management: Use a processor or bullet blender to make breadcrumbs from crusts or leftover bread. Store in the freezer in freezer bags for later use in stuffing, or mix with cheese and herbs and use as a savoury topping on pies or fish bakes. See page 56.

Roasted Root Vegetables

Cooking Time: 40 minutes

Serves: 2-3

Ingredients

1 parsnip
2 carrots
200g swede or turnip
1 small onion
Marinade
1 clove garlic
1-2 tablespoons olive oil
1 teaspoon honey or sugar
1 tablespoon lemon juice
Sea salt and pepper
Garnish: chopped parsley

Equipment

garlic crusher, sharp knife, board, pot stand, baking sheet, teaspoon, freezer bag, vegetable peeler, tablespoon, serving dish.

Root Vegetables

Steps — Method

Preheat oven to 200°C/Fan 190°C/Gas Mark 6.

Gather equipment, collect/weigh ingredients, set worktop.

1 Wash, peel and cut vegetables into large chunks, approximately 4cm.
2 **Marinade*:** Smash garlic, peel and crush. Put into freezer bag with lemon juice, honey, oil, salt and pepper. See technique below.
3 Add the vegetable chunks to the bag and mix well to coat.
4 Spread on a baking sheet and roast for 35-40 minutes until just tender. Stir once during cooking. Test with a fork or skewer.

Garnish with parsley.

Serve with roast meats or fish.

Variation

Add red pepper chunks, courgette, aubergine or sweet potato.

Healthy Hint!
Sweet potato and carrot are excellent sources of Vitamin A (beta carotene), Vitamin B, Vitamin C, minerals and fibre. Cooked together and mashed, they purée easily for invalids, the elderly and weaning babies.

Resource Management: Always wash vegetables before use. Peel thinly and compost the peelings. Use waste water for watering plants. Wrap and refrigerate any leftovers.

*MARINADE — TECHNIQUE

This is a good way to flavour and tenderise uncooked food. The marinade is made by mixing oil, acid (vinegar, lemon juice or wine), herbs and/or spices together. The food is then tossed or steeped in this mixture.

Creamy Vegetable Pie

Cooking Time: 45 minutes

Serves: 4

Creamy Vegetable Pie, Vegetable Stuffed Pancakes, Pastry Topped Pie

Ingredients

Vegetables

400g mixed fresh vegetables or 1 x 450g pack frozen vegetables

White Sauce

25g butter

25g flour

300ml milk

½ teaspoon made mustard

Potato Topping

4 medium potatoes

25g butter

½ teaspoon salt

Pinch pepper

Garnish: chopped parsley

Equipment

sharp knife, board, potato peeler, tablespoon, colander, wooden spoon, whisk, 3 saucepans, potato masher, teaspoon, ovenproof dish.

Steps **Method**

Preheat oven to 180°C/Fan 170°C/Gas Mark 4.

Gather equipment, collect/weigh ingredients, set worktop.

1 **Potato Topping:** Wash, peel and quarter potatoes, boil in salted water until soft. Drain, keeping some cooking water aside to soften the mash. Mash with salt and pepper, soften with potato water.

2 **Vegetables:** If using fresh vegetables, wash, peel and dice them. Cook vegetables in boiling salted water until tender. Strain. Grease dish.

3 **White Sauce (see Quick Method on page 40):** Whisk butter, flour, salt, pepper, mustard and milk in a saucepan while bringing to the boil. Boil for 2 minutes, stirring, add vegetables and pour into dish. Spread potato on top, score with fork and dot with butter.

4 Bake in preheated oven for 25-30 minutes until golden.

Garnish with parsley.

Serve with baked or grilled fish or meats.

Vegetable Stuffed Pancakes

VARIATION

Ingredients

1 x vegetables and sauce from Creamy Vegetable Pie

1 x Pancake recipe (page 78)

75g grated Cheddar cheese

Butter to grease

Steps **Method**

1 Make pancakes following recipe and method (page 78).

2 Make vegetable and sauce mixture (see above recipe). Grease ovenproof dish. Use the creamy vegetable mixture to fill pancakes.

3 Roll up, place in dish, sprinkle with grated cheese and bake for 15 minutes until cheese melts.

Pastry Topped Vegetable Pie

VARIATION

Ingredients

1 x vegetables and sauce from Creamy Vegetable Pie

100g shortcrust or rough puff pastry

Beaten egg to glaze

Steps **Method**

1 Put the vegetable and sauce mixture into a greased ovenproof dish.

2 Roll out pastry to fit dish. Damp the top edge of dish. Place pastry on top, press onto dish, trim edges and fork to decorate.

3 Use trimmings to make pastry leaves (see page 121).

4 Glaze with a pastry brush and bake at 190°C/Fan 180°C/Gas Mark 5 for 30 minutes until golden brown.

Roast Mediterranean Vegetables

Cooking Time: 20 minutes

Serves: 4

Ingredients

1 red pepper
1 aubergine
1 courgette
1 red onion
2 cloves garlic
2 tomatoes
Marinade (see page 57)
2 tablespoons olive oil
Salt and pepper
1 tablespoon fresh herbs
1 teaspoon honey
Garnish: fresh herbs

Equipment

sharp knife and board, large freezer bag, teaspoon, tablespoon, roasting tin, pot stand, serving dish.

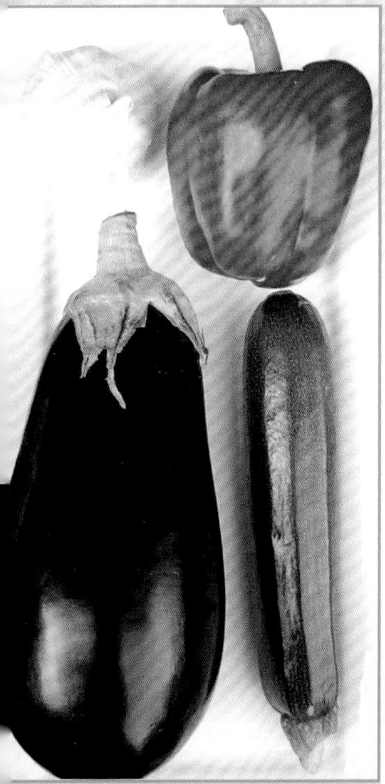

Mediterranean Vegetables

Steps — Method

Preheat oven to 220°C/Fan 210°C/Gas Mark 7.

Gather equipment, collect ingredients, set worktop.

1 Wash and dry the pepper, aubergine, courgette and tomatoes. Peel and chop onion and garlic into quarters.

2 Halve the pepper lengthways, remove the stalk and seeds and cut each half in 4 pieces.

3 Take the stalk from aubergine, divide in 4 lengthways, slice each piece into thick chunks.

4 Slice the courgette thickly. Cut the tomatoes into quarters.

5 **Marinade:** Put the oil, herbs, honey, salt and pepper into the freezer bag, add all the prepared vegetables, shake well to coat. If time permits, leave aside to marinate for 15 minutes.

6 Spread vegetables on the roasting tin, roast for 20 minutes until the vegetables are just soft and starting to brown. Turn onto the serving dish.

Garnish with chopped, fresh herbs or balsamic glaze.

Serve hot with roast meat or fish and baked potato or cold with French dressing (page 36) or Tahini Sauce/Dressing (page 141) and garlic bread (page 32).

*ROASTING — COOKING METHOD

Roasting means cooking food in hot air in an oven. Vegetables and meats are often brushed or tossed in oil and seasoned before roasting to prevent the food from drying out and to add flavour.

Quick Ratatouille

FRANCE/ITALY

Cooking Time: 20 minutes

Serves: 3-4

Ingredients

1 red pepper
1 aubergine
1 courgette
1 tin chopped tomatoes
1 large onion
1 clove garlic
1 level teaspoon salt
Black pepper
1 tablespoon parsley
Pinch mixed herbs
Pinch sugar
1 tablespoon oil
Garnish: fresh herbs, parsley

Equipment

saucepan, sharp knife, board, pot stand, tablespoon, wooden spoon, serving dish.

Chef's Tip!
Add 1 tablespoon pesto for a change of flavour.

Aubergine

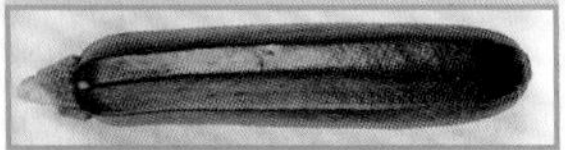

Courgette

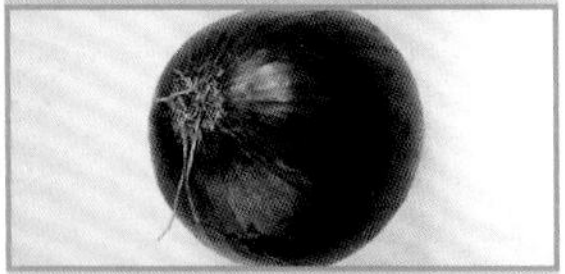

Red Onion

Red Pepper

Steps — Method

Gather equipment, collect/weigh ingredients, set worktop.

1 Wash, deseed and slice pepper. Wash and slice courgette and aubergine.

2 Peel and dice onion and garlic.

3 Heat oil, **sauté*** onion gently for 5 minutes.

4 Add all vegetables, tinned tomatoes, garlic, herbs, sugar, salt and pepper. Cover and simmer for 15 minutes.

5 Wash and chop parsley for garnish.

Garnish with chopped fresh herbs and parsley.

Serve with grilled meat/fish.

Healthy Hint!
Tomatoes are a good source of Vitamin C and the antioxidant lycopene. People who eat tomatoes and tomato products have a lower risk of certain cancers and heart disease than those who rarely eat them.

Food Fact!
Throughout history, garlic has been used to treat everything from athlete's foot to colds and flus. Scientific evidence now supports that allicin, the compound that gives sliced, diced or crushed garlic its smell and taste, is a powerful antibiotic that has anti-viral and anti-fungal properties. See Chef's Tip and diagrams on page 72.

Buy Local, Buy Irish!
Support local industry and growers when possible.

*SAUTÉ — TECHNIQUE

Sauté means to fry food rapidly in hot fat. The food is sometimes browned and sometimes not. This method is used to intensify the flavours and so develop a better taste in the finished dish.

Ratatouille Lasagne

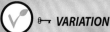

VARIATION

Cooking Time: 40 minutes

Serves: 3-4

Ingredients

1 x basic Ratatouille recipe (page 60)

6 sheets lasagne

Basic white sauce recipe

50g flour

50g butter

500ml milk

50g strong Cheddar cheese

Garnish: parsley

Equipment

lasagne dish and equipment from page 60.

Chef's Tip! To increase protein, stir in pre-cooked Puy lentils, butter beans or kidney beans.

Steps **Method**

Preheat oven to 180°C/Fan 170°C/Gas Mark 4.

1 Make quick method white 'coating' sauce (page 40).

2 Grease a lasagne dish/casserole. Put in ½ the ratatouille followed by a layer of lasagne followed by ⅓ of the sauce. Repeat. Soften remaining sauce with 2 tablespoons milk or water. Spread over top. Sprinkle with cheese.

3 Bake for 35-40 minutes.

Garnish with chopped parsley.

Serve with green salad and garlic bread or rolls.

Ratatouille Pastry Pie

VARIATION

Cooking Time: 30 minutes

Serves: 3-4

Ingredients

1 x basic Ratatouille recipe

½ packet frozen shortcrust pastry, thawed or home-made (page 167)

1 tin butter beans or chick peas

Equipment

shallow ovenproof dish, rolling pin, flour dredger, knife.

Steps **Method**

Preheat oven to190°C/Fan 180°C/Gas Mark 4-5.

1 Grease overproof dish, pour in the ratatouille and drained peas or beans.

2 Roll out pastry, fit onto the top of casserole dish. Trim and decorate with pastry leaves made from the trimmings (see page 121).

3 Brush with beaten egg. Slash a hole to allow steam to escape.

4 Bake for 30-40 minutes until just golden.

Serve hot with grilled or roast meat, fish or root vegetables (page 57).

Vegetarian Shepherd's Pie

Cooking Time: 50 minutes

Serves: 4

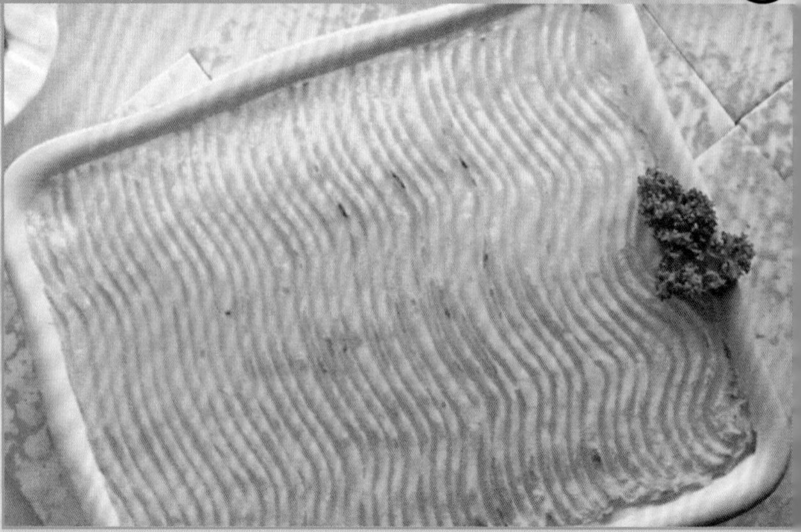

Ingredients

1 small onion
1 small red pepper
1 small carrot
1 small head of broccoli
1 tin tomatoes
1 tin kidney or baked beans
25g butter
1 tablespoon oil
25g wholemeal flour
250ml vegetable stock cube
1 tablespoon tomato purée
1 teaspoon chopped parsley
Pinch of herbs
Salt and pepper

Topping

4 medium potatoes
Knob of butter
Salt and pepper
Little milk
50g grated cheese

Garnish: chopped parsley

Equipment

sharp knife, board, 2 large saucepans, colander, 2 pot stands, masher, spatula, measuring jug, tablespoon, teaspoon, casserole dish.

Idea!
Vegans can modify recipes by substituting butter for olive or coconut oil. Use non-dairy milk and vegan cheese.

Steps — Method

Preheat oven to 180°C/Fan 170°C/Gas Mark 5.

Gather equipment, collect/weigh ingredients, set worktop.

1 **Topping:** Wash, peel and quarter potatoes, boil in boiling salted water until soft.
2 Make stock. Dissolve ½ stock cube in 250ml boiling water.
3 Peel and chop onion. Wash, peel and dice carrot and pepper. Wash broccoli, cut into florets. Drain and rinse the kidney beans in cold water using a colander.
4 Heat butter and oil, **sauté** (see page 60) onion, carrot and pepper for 3 minutes. Add wholemeal flour, cook for 2 minutes. Add broccoli, parsley, herbs, salt and pepper. Mix well.
5 Stir in kidney beans, tomatoes, purée and stock. Bring to the boil, cover and simmer for 15 minutes. Stir.
6 Drain potatoes and mash with butter, milk, salt and pepper until soft.
7 Turn the vegetable mixture into a greased casserole dish and cover with the potato mash.
8 Sprinkle with the grated cheese. Bake for 30 minutes.

Garnish with chopped parsley.

Serve with a crisp salad.

Healthy Hint!
Use a low-salt stock cube as too much salt is bad for your health. Try incorporating natural alternatives to salt when cooking, e.g. herbs and spices.

Resource Management: Buy local and organic produce. Always wash vegetables before use. Peel finely and compost the peelings. Cover and refrigerate any leftovers. Use waste water for watering any plants.

Vegetable Burger

Cooking Time: 18 minutes

Serves: 4

Ingredients

1 medium potato
1 small carrot
2 scallions
1 stick celery
½ pepper (optional)
1 clove garlic, crushed
50g butter
30g porridge oats or breadcrumbs (page 56)
1 teaspoon Worcestershire sauce
50ml water
½ teaspoon curry paste or powder
½ teaspoon salt
Black pepper
1 tablespoon oil to fry
Garnish: lettuce, tomato

Equipment

peeler, sharp knife, board, grater, wooden spoon, teaspoon, measuring jug, egg lifter, saucepan, pot stand, plate, garlic crusher, flour dredger, frying pan, serving dish.

Grating a carrot

Look Up!
Smoke point.

Steps — Method

Gather equipment, collect/weigh ingredients, set worktop.

1. Cut the celery, scallions and pepper into ½cm dice – very small.
2. Peel garlic and dice finely. Wash, peel and grate the carrot and potato.
3. Melt butter, **sauté** (page 60) all vegetables very gently over a low heat for 3 minutes.
4. Stir in oats or breadcrumbs, water, Worcestershire sauce, salt, pepper and curry paste or powder. Cook, stirring for 3 minutes.
5. Spread mixture on a plate, put aside to cool and set.
6. Divide into 4 pieces, form into burgers using a little flour.
7. Fry burgers in 1 tablespoon oil (see Chef's Tip) over medium heat for 6 minutes on each side or until brown. Drain on kitchen paper.

Serve in a soft bun with lettuce, tomato and onion or with a baked potato and a side salad.

Variation

Add red pepper chunks, courgette, aubergine or sweet potato.

Gluten-free: Use gluten-free oats or breadcrumbs, gluten-free flour or cornflour to thicken when necessary. Omit the Worcestershire sauce.

Dairy-free: Use coconut oil or olive oil in place of butter.

Chef's Tip!
Always heat the oil first before adding food to a frying pan. This prevents the juices running out of the food. Never allow a pan to smoke.

Idea!
Use 1 small, raw beetroot instead of carrot and add 1 tablespoon of hummus.

Mashed Potato

Cooking Time: 20 minutes

Serves: 3

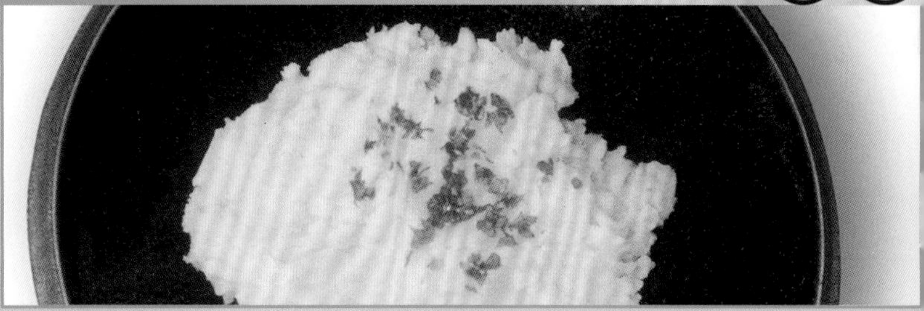

Ingredients

500g potatoes (about 4 medium-sized)

Level teaspoon salt

Pinch of pepper

Knob of butter

2 tablespoons milk

Equipment

sharp knife, board, peeler, saucepan, pot stand, tablespoon, potato masher.

Steps **Method**

Gather equipment, collect/weigh ingredients, set worktop.

1 Wash, peel and quarter potatoes. Boil water in kettle.

2 Cook potatoes in boiling salted water for 20 minutes or until soft.

3 Drain, reserving some of the liquid to soften the mash.

4 Mash, adding salt, pepper, knob of butter, a little milk and 2 tablespoons of the reserved liquid (or extra milk).

5 Reheat and serve immediately.

Pea Mash

VARIATION

Ingredients

1 x Mashed Potato recipe

200g frozen peas

Salt and pepper

Steps **Method**

1 Add the peas to the potatoes for the last 10 minutes of cooking.

2 Add salt and pepper. Mash very well.

Serve with fish, chicken or pork.

Garlic Mash

VARIATION

Ingredients

1 x Mashed Potato recipe

1-2 cloves of garlic

Equipment

garlic crusher.

Steps **Method**

1 Smash, peel and crush the garlic and add to the potatoes for the last 5 minutes of cooking.

2 Drain. Add salt and pepper to taste. Mash well.

Serve with roast lamb, lamb chops or steak.

Carrot or Sweet Potato Mash

VARIATION

Ingredients

1 x Mashed Potato recipe

1 carrot or sweet potato

Equipment

grater with large holes.

Steps **Method**

1 Grate carrot or sweet potato on a grater with large holes. Add carrot or sweet potato to potatoes for the last 10 minutes of cooking.

2 Drain, reserving some of the water to soften the mash. Add salt and pepper and mash well. Correct the seasoning.

Serve with chicken, fish or any meat dish.

Healthy Hint!
Use extra virgin olive oil in place of butter.

CHAMP (CEAILE OR POUNDIES)

VARIATION – TRADITIONAL IRISH

Ingredients

1 x Mashed Potato recipe
2 scallions, chopped
75ml milk
Salt and pepper
25g butter
Garnish: parsley

Salmon and Champ

Mashed potato equipment

Steps	Method
1	Put the milk, scallions, salt and pepper into a saucepan and simmer gently for 5 minutes.
2	When potatoes are soft, drain and mash with the milk and scallions to form a soft but not sloppy mixture. Correct the seasoning.

Serve piled on a dish. Make a hollow on top, place butter in hollow and allow to melt.

Garnish with parsley.

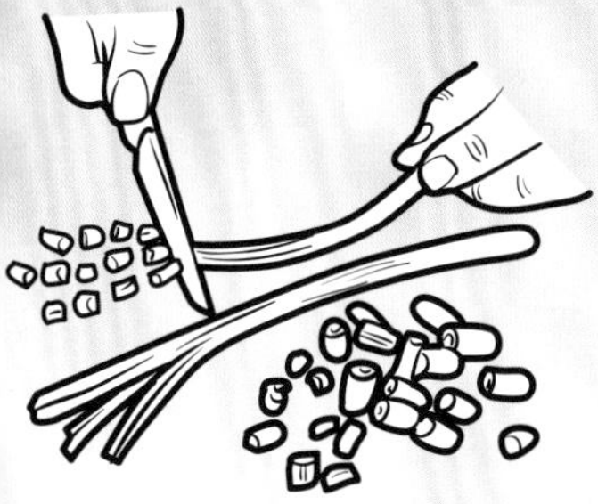

Chopping scallions

WHICH POTATO TO USE? IF YOU ARE ...

BOILING – Queens, Home Guard, Record, Rooster, Kerr's Pink, Golden Wonder.
BAKING – Queens, Record, Kerr's Pink, Golden Wonder, Rooster, Orla.
ROASTING – Queens, Record, Rooster, Golden Wonder, Kerr's Pink.
MASHING – Kerr's Pink, Golden Wonder, Rooster, Orla.
CHIPPING – Maris Piper is the usual suggestion, but this is one area where Roosters really shine.
MAKING A SALAD – Waxy is best. Try Orla, Nicola, Cara or Charlotte.
EATING NEW POTATOES – They're best simply boiled or steamed and lightly tossed with a knob of butter and some chopped mint.

Resource Management: Buy local and organic produce where possible. Peel vegetables thinly to avoid waste. Cover any unused vegetables in a clean container and store in a fridge. Use within 2 days.

Healthy Hint!
Try to cut back on salt when cooking as too much salt is bad for your health.

*BOILING — COOKING METHOD

Boiling means cooking the food covered in boiling liquid (100°C). However, most foods are best simmered just below boiling point (95°C). It is best to cover the pot with a lid so that the liquid does not evaporate.

Colcannon

TRADITIONAL IRISH

Cooking Time: 35 minutes

Serves: 3-4

Ingredients

- 500g potatoes
- 4 small green cabbage leaves or 2 stalks of kale
- 4 scallions or 1 small onion
- 150ml milk or cream
- 75g butter
- Salt and pepper

Equipment

peeler, sharp knife, board, scissors, measuring jug, saucepan, pot stand, masher, wooden spoon, serving dish.

Chopping kale

Shredding cabbage

Kale

Steps	Method
	Gather equipment, collect/weigh ingredients, set worktop.
1	Wash, peel and quarter potatoes. Boil in salted water for 15 minutes.
2	Wash and shred the cabbage or kale very finely. Add to potatoes, continue cooking for 15 minutes.
3	Chop scallions, simmer in milk or cream for 5 minutes.
4	Drain the potatoes and cabbage. Then mash really well with milk, half the butter, pepper and salt. Pile onto a dish.
5	Make a well in the centre and drop in the remaining butter to melt.

Serve with meat, fish or egg dishes.

Food Fact!

Traditionally Colcannon was served at Hallowe'en and eaten with a glass of fresh buttermilk.

Healthy Hint!

- Cabbage is rich in antioxidants, fibre and full of Vitamin K, manganese and potassium. Research has found that eating cruciferous vegetables such as cabbage, can help reduce the risk o Alzheimer's disease and help prevent cancer.
- Kale is rich in fibre, calcium, magnesium and Vitamins A, C and K. It can help lower cholesterol and keep the body healthy. It can be cooked or eaten raw in salads or added to smoothies, see page 14.
- Dark green, leafy vegetables should be included in the diet to provide iron and prevent anaemia.
- Vegetables provide the body with roughage and fibre, especially if the skins are eaten. They help move fibre through the digestive system (peristalsis).

Traditional Potato Cakes (Fadge)

IRISH

Cooking Time: 10 minutes

Serves: 4

Ingredients

250g cooked boiled potatoes

50g self-raising flour

Salt and pepper

50g butter, melted

Oil or butter to fry

Garnish: chopped parsley

Equipment

peeler, sharp knife, board, bowl, saucepan, wooden spoon, flour dredger, rolling pin, masher, palette knife, frying pan, pot stand, serving plate.

Keep potatoes covered in cold water to prevent them from discolouring.

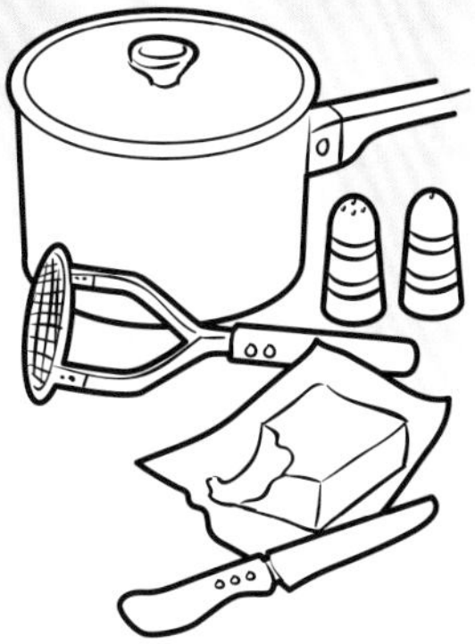

Mashed potato equipment

Resource Management:
This is a great recipe for using up leftover potatoes.

Steps — Method

Gather equipment, collect/weigh ingredients, set worktop.

1 Use leftover potatoes or peel and boil potatoes until soft. Drain well.

2 Mash potatoes in bowl, add flour, pepper and salt, mix.

3 Add melted butter, mix well.

4 Turn onto floured board. Knead lightly, cut into two.

5 Roll out each piece into a little circle about 2cm thick. Cut each into 4 triangles.

6 Heat oil on pan. **Fry*** each cake until golden on both sides.

Garnish with chopped parsley.

Serve hot as a snack with butter and salt. It is suitable as a lunch or supper dish with a salad and coleslaw (page 49).

Healthy Hint!
Eat lots of vegetables because:

- Vegetables are a good source of vitamins.
- Protein is low in most vegetables except in pulses.
- Low in fat, any fat present is polyunsaturated.
- Starch, sugar and fibre are present, depending on the type.
- Dark green, leafy vegetables are an excellent source of iron. Calcium, potassium and iodine are also present.
- Vegetables contain a high percentage of water.

*FRYING — COOKING METHOD

Frying is a quick method of cooking in hot fat between 150ºC and 195ºC. The food is in direct contact with the fat or oil, which sears the food, and it cooks quickly. Frying does not tenderise so foods must be already tender. Foods should be dry before frying. There are three methods of frying: (a) shallow frying, (b) deep frying and (c) stir-frying.

BAKED POTATOES OR SWEET POTATOES

PLAIN OR FILLED

Cooking Time: 1 hour

Serves: 4

Ingredients

4 medium-sized potatoes or sweet potatoes

Vegetable oil

Filling of your choice – see page 69.

Topping (optional)

25g Gruyère cheese or mild Cheddar cheese

Equipment

sharp knife, board, baking tin, fork, kitchen paper, pastry brush, skewer, pot stand, tablespoon, serving plate, piece of foil.

Different methods of cutting potato skins for baking

Steps **Method**

Preheat oven to 200°C/Fan 190°C/Gas Mark 6.

Gather equipment, collect/weigh ingredients, set worktop.

1. Wash and scrub potatoes or sweet potatoes well and dry with kitchen paper.
2. Pierce the skin in 2 places with a fork or with a skewer. Cut a cross on the top of each one. Brush with oil and sprinkle with salt if wished.
3. Place on the tin (line tin with foil if baking sweet potatoes) and **bake*** uncovered for 50-60 minutes until soft (test with skewer). Sweet potatoes will take a little less time. Cut a cross on top, turn back skin.
4. Add optional cheese topping.

***BAKING** — COOKING METHOD

This means cooking food in an oven. Food can be cooked in the dry air or covered to partially cook in its own steam, e.g. foil-wrapped baked potatoes.

MICROWAVE POTATOES OR SWEET POTATOES

VARIATION

Cooking Time:
Potatoes
7-10 minutes
Sweet potatoes
6-8 minutes

Equipment

microwave (800 watts), skewer, kitchen paper, oven mitt, fork.

Chef's Tip!
Standing time means giving food time to complete the cooking process.

Steps **Method**

Gather equipment, collect/weigh ingredients, set worktop.

1. Prepare potatoes or sweet potatoes using Steps 1 and 2 above. Arrange potatoes in a circle, on kitchen paper in the microwave and cover with a plate or microwave cover.
2. Microwave on HIGH for 4 minutes. Using an oven mitt, turn the potatoes.
3. Check for doneness. Repeat again for 3 minutes. Leave to stand (see Chef's Tip) for 5 minutes. Small potatoes will take less time and large potatoes will take longer.
4. Open back the skin, place a knob of butter into each or remove the middle and fill with a filling as in stuffed baked potatoes on page 69.

Food Fact!
Sweet potatoes are rich in orange-coloured Vitamin A (beta carotene), which is a powerful antioxidant and great for eye health. The skin of the sweet potato is high in fibre and potassium.

Stuffed Baked Potatoes or Sweet Potatoes

VARIATION

Cooking Time:
Potatoes 50 minutes
Sweet potatoes 40 minutes

Ingredients

4 medium-sized potatoes or sweet potatoes

Extra virgin olive oil or butter

Salt and pepper

Filling of your choice

Grated cheese (optional)

Equipment

skewer, kitchen paper, oven mitts, baking sheet, foil.

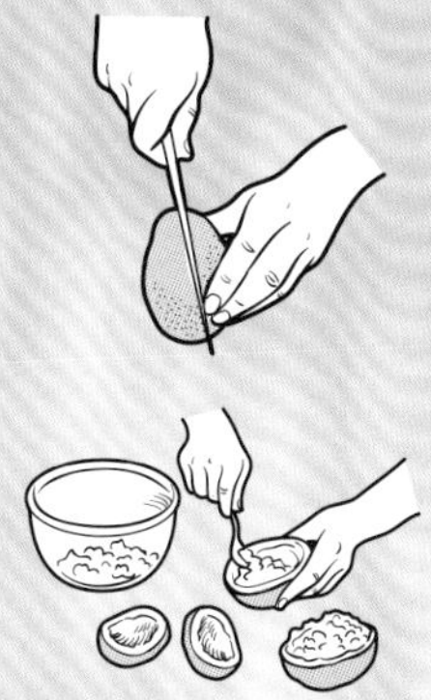

Cutting and filling potatoes

Sweet potato is a tuber with orange or yellow flesh. *See Food Fact on page 68.*

Steps — Method

Preheat oven to 200°C/Fan 190°C/Gas Mark 6.

Gather equipment, collect/weigh ingredients, set worktop.

1 Scrub potatoes, dry well, pierce with a fork or skewer. Place sweet potatoes on foil on a baking sheet, place potatoes directly onto oven rack and bake until the insides are soft. Bake medium potatoes for 50-60 minutes and sweet potatoes for 40-50 minutes.

2 Cut baked potatoes in half lengthways and scoop out flesh into a bowl. Add butter, salt and pepper and mash well.

3 Fold the filling of choice gently through the mash.

4 Spoon into the potato shells. Top with grated cheese if you like. Brown under a grill.

Garnish with chives or chopped parsley.

Serve hot.

Filling Variations

- Grilled, chopped rashers and finely-chopped scallions.
- Baked beans with grated Cheddar cheese topping.
- Finely diced celery, cream cheese and tuna.
- Ricotta and sundried tomatoes topped with Gruyère cheese.

Variation

Vegan: Chop ½ onion, 1 stick of celery, 3 finely diced sundried tomatoes. Mix in 2 tablespoons of cooked Puy lentils and 2 teaspoons of olive oil. Dust with chilli flakes to serve.

Resource Management: To conserve fuel, make full use of oven space by baking two or three dishes at the one time, e.g. Top shelf: baked potatoes. Middle shelf: apple pie. Bottom shelf: baked casserole. Always turn off oven after use.

Potato and Bacon Rosti

SWISS

Cooking Time: 15-20 minutes

Serves: 4

Ingredients

- 2 large potatoes
- 3 tablespoons oil
- 1 rasher
- ¼ onion
- 1 clove garlic
- 1 tablespoon chopped fresh parsley
- ½ teaspoon salt
- Grind pepper
- **Garnish:** 1 tomato

Equipment

sharp knife, board, scissors, wooden spoon, saucepan, pot stand, frying pan (non-stick), palette knife, bowl, grater with large holes, serving plate.

Chopping parsley

Snipping rashers

Steps — Method

Gather equipment, collect/weigh ingredients, set worktop.

1. Scrub potatoes, **parboil*** in boiling water for 5 minutes only.
2. Peel and dice onion and garlic very finely. Snip the rasher into very small pieces using a scissors.
3. Heat 1 tablespoon oil, **sauté*** bacon and onion until soft.
4. Drain, cool, peel and grate potato into a bowl. See grating image, page 63.
5. Mix potato with garlic, parsley, salt, pepper, onion and bacon.
6. Heat the remaining oil on pan. Put spoonfuls of the mixture onto hot pan and flatten a little.
7. Reduce heat and cook gently for 5-7 minutes until golden. Turn, then brown other side. Wash and chop parsley. Wash and slice tomato for garnish.
8. Drain rosti on kitchen paper. Place on serving dish.

Garnish with sliced tomato or tomato wedges.

Serve immediately. These are best served with a salad.

*PARBOIL — TECHNIQUE

To partially or half cook in boiling water (or microwave) before some other form of cooking.

*SAUTÉ — TECHNIQUE

Sauté means to fry food rapidly in hot fat. The food is sometimes browned. This method is used to intensify the flavours and so develop a better taste in the finished dish.

Potato Wedges

Cooking Time: 40 minutes

Serves: 4

Ingredients

4 medium potatoes
1 tablespoon olive oil
Salt and pepper

Equipment

sharp knife, board, plastic bag, kitchen paper, tablespoon, non-stick baking sheet, pot stand, serving plate.

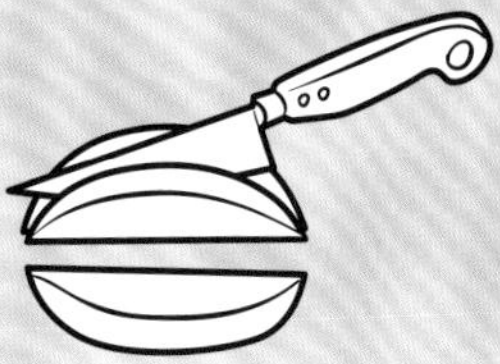

Cutting potato wedges

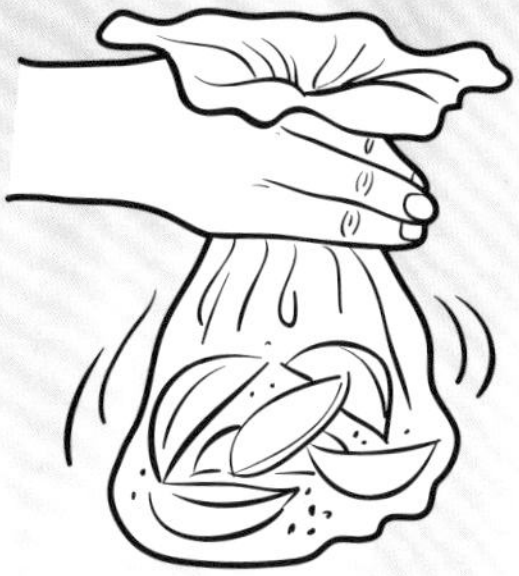

Seasoning potato wedges in a bag

In a hurry!
Put wedges into a microwaveable bowl with olive oil and seasoning, cover with a plate. Microwave for 2 minutes and stir. Place back into the microwave for 2 minutes then roast for 20-25 minutes until soft.

Steps — Method

Preheat oven to 220°C/Fan 210°C/Gas Mark 8.

Gather equipment, collect/weigh ingredients and set worktop.

1 Wash and scrub the potatoes well, dry on kitchen paper. Cut in half lengthways, then cut each half lengthways into 4-5 wedges.

2 Put the oil and seasoning into the bag and shake well. Add wedges and shake to coat well.

3 Oil the baking sheet lightly and spread the wedges on top. **Roast***/bake uncovered for 40 minutes until lightly browned.

Serve with flavoured mayonnaise (pages 38/39), dips (pages 22/23) or salsa (page 43).

Chef's Tip!
When preparing and cooking vegetables:

- Always use a sharp knife.
- Prepare vegetables just before cooking.
- Use the cooking water for soups and sauces.
- Avoid overcooking vegetables.
- Avoid steeping in liquid before cooking.
- Steam vegetables when possible.
- Use a tight-fitting lid on the saucepan.

Idea!
Make sweet potato wedges and place them on a tin covered with non-stick baking paper. They should cook in 30 minutes.

***ROASTING** — COOKING METHOD

Roasting is a dry method of cooking in dry air in an oven. The food should be dry but brushed or tossed in a little fat or oil to brown and crisp the outside.

Potato Dauphinoise

FRENCH

Cooking Time: 45 minutes

Serves: 4

Ingredients

- Knob butter
- 500g potatoes
- Salt and pepper
- 100ml milk
- 150ml water
- 100ml cream
- 1 small clove garlic
- Pinch nutmeg
- 50g grated white cheese
- **Garnish:** parsley

Equipment

sharp knife, board, potato peeler, wooden spoon, measuring jug, large non-stick saucepan with lid, pot stand, casserole dish.

Food Fact!
See Food Fact GARLIC on page 60.

Bulb of garlic

Crushing garlic

Slicing a clove ofgarlic

Steps — Method

Preheat oven to 200°C/Fan 190°C/Gas Mark 6.

Gather equipment, collect/weigh ingredients, set worktop.

1 Grease saucepan bottom with a knob of butter.

2 Wash and peel potatoes, cut in half and slice **very** thinly.

3 Put into saucepan with salt and pepper and stir. Add the milk and water and bring to the boil.

4 Cover and simmer for 8 minutes. Smash, peel and crush garlic.

5 Add the cream, garlic and nutmeg and simmer for 8 minutes, stirring occasionally so that the potatoes do not stick to saucepan. (A non-stick saucepan is best.)

6 When potatoes are just soft, turn into a greased casserole dish along with any liquid remaining from saucepan and sprinkle with grated cheese.

7 Cook in the oven for 20-25 minutes until golden on top.

Garnish with chopped parsley.

Serve hot with grilled meats or fish.

Chef's Tip!
To peel garlic: Place a clove of garlic on a board and put the widest part of a knife flat over the clove to cover. Holding the knife steady with one hand, smash down with the heel of the other hand. Remove the skin.

Potato and Leek Dauphinoise

VARIATION

Ingredients

- 1 leek

Steps — Method

Wash and prepare 1 leek as on page 25. Slice thinly and add at Step 5.

Dublin Coddle

IRISH

Cooking Time: 50 minutes

Serves: 4

Ingredients

1 large onion

4 large pork sausages

2 tablespoons parsley, finely chopped

4 rashers

400g potatoes

200ml stock or water

Salt and pepper

Garnish: parsley

Equipment

sharp knife, board, scissors, tablespoon, measuring jug, pot stand, saucepan, greaseproof paper, serving dish.

Chopping parsley

Snipping rashers

Steps — Method

Gather equipment, collect/weigh ingredients, set worktop.

1 Chop rashers and sausages into bite-sized pieces. Wash, peel and slice potatoes thinly. Peel and slice the onion.

2 Layer onion, rashers, sausages, potatoes and parsley in a saucepan, seasoning with pepper and salt between layers.

3 Pour on the stock, bring to the boil and then press a sheet of greaseproof paper on top of the coddle.

4 Cover, reduce to a simmer and cook for 50 minutes until the liquid is reduced and the potatoes are broken-down and thickening the liquid. Look into the coddle during cooking and add a little water if necessary. Turn onto a serving dish.

Garnish with the remaining parsley.

Serve with soda bread.

Healthy Hint!
If using stock cubes, choose an organic low-salt one and only use ½ or ¼ at a time, see page 24.

Wicklow Coddle

VARIATION

Ingredients

1 x Dublin Coddle ingredients

1 tin tomatoes

100g yellow split peas, soaked

100g red lentils, soaked

Steps — Method

1 Steep peas and lentils for 30 minutes in cold water.

2 Follow steps and method for Dublin Coddle but brown the sausages in a dry frying pan until nicely golden brown on all sides.

3 Drain the peas and lentils. Layer with the other ingredients as in Step 2 above.

4 Add the tomatoes with the stock and continue cooking as above.

Chapter 4

Egg Dishes and Batters

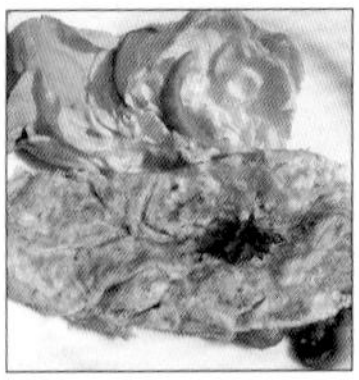

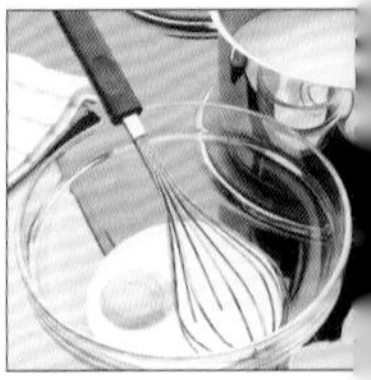

Eggs

Buy Irish eggs, check the date and store in the fridge with the pointed end downwards.

Organic eggs: These eggs are laid by hens that are free to roam over fresh, green paddocks. They are fed special organic feed made from grains and pulses.

Barn Fresh Eggs: The hens are fed a premium vegetarian grain diet and have complete freedom to roam and perch in large barns.

Free-Range Eggs: These hens are fed a premium vegetarian grain diet and are free to nest, forage, perch and roam over fresh, green pastures.

Corn Fed Eggs: These eggs are from free-range hens that have been fed a meal rich in maize instead of wheat. This gives the yolk a rich, yellow colour.

Omega-3 Eggs: The free-range hens have been fed a diet rich in Omega-3 fatty acid. Levels of Omega-3 in these eggs are double those found in normal eggs. Omega-3 oils promote healthy cells, are known to be anti-inflammatory and decrease the risk of heart disease and stroke.

Other suitable recipes

Quiche Lorraine (page 176), Salmon and Broccoli Quiche (page 112), Dingle Quiche (page 112).

Key Words and Skills

- ❖ palette knife
- ❖ fried
- ❖ separate
- ❖ peel
- ❖ coagulation
- ❖ whisk
- ❖ dice
- ❖ shallow fry
- ❖ fish slice/egg lifter
- ❖ glaze
- ❖ beat
- ❖ sauté
- ❖ deep fry
- ❖ poach

Evaluation! See pages 223 and 224.

- ❖ Did you meet the brief and did you refer to the specific requirements of the task or dish/dishes?
- ❖ Discuss the results of your finished dish/dishes including the presentation, colour, taste and texture.
- ❖ What aspects were done well and what aspects could be improved?
- ❖ Did you correctly cost and budget for all ingredients?

Scrambled Eggs

Cooking Time: 5 minutes

Serves: 1

Ingredients

2 large eggs
2 tablespoons milk
15g butter
Salt and pepper
Garnish: parsley

To serve:
Toast – 2 slices bread
Butter for spreading

Equipment

small bowl, knife, whisk/fork, pot stand, tablespoon, small saucepan (non-stick is best), wooden spoon, serving plate.

Chef's Tip!
When heating milk, use a non-stick saucepan or rinse the saucepan with cold water beforehand as it makes it easier to clean.

Steps **Method**

Gather equipment, collect/weigh ingredients, set worktop.

1. Make toast and butter it. Put onto serving plate and keep warm.
2. Whisk eggs, add salt and pepper.
3. Rinse saucepan with water. Put milk and butter into saucepan and heat gently until fat melts.
4. Add the eggs, stir with a wooden spoon over a gentle heat until it just thickens. It should look glossy, not dry.
5. Pile the scrambled egg onto the buttered toast.

Garnish with parsley.

Serve immediately with more triangles of hot toast.

Variations

To add to the eggs just before serving:

1 cooked rasher, chopped **or**
25g grated cheese **or**
1 tomato, chopped **or**
1-2 tablespoons smoked salmon, chopped.

Poached Egg

Cooking Time: 10 minutes

Serves: 1

Ingredients

1 egg
Pinch of salt
1 teaspoon white vinegar (optional)

Equipment

1 small saucepan, teaspoon, slotted spoon, 1 cup.

Steps **Method**

Gather equipment, collect/weigh ingredients, set worktop.

1. Boil water in a kettle. Half fill the saucepan with boiling water. Add vinegar.
2. Break the egg into the cup, swirl the water and gently slip the egg into the centre. **Poach*** gently for 4 minutes, until the yolk is set but soft.
3. Using a slotted spoon, lift the egg and drain very well.
4. **Serve** on toast. **Garnish** with parsley.

Serving suggestion: with smashed avocado (page 19), fish, tomato or on top of a warm salad.

***POACHING** — COOKING METHOD

Poaching is a quick, moist method of cooking in a liquid at a temperature between 75°C and 93°C. The liquid should just 'shiver' or barely move but not boil (100°C). Poached food is ideal for invalids as it is very easily digested.

French Savoury Omelette

FRANCE

Cooking Time: 5-6 minutes

Serves: 1

Ingredients

2 large eggs
1 tablespoon water
Salt and pepper
Pinch of mixed herbs
15g butter, melted
1 tablespoon of oil to fry
Filling of your choice (see Step 2)
Garnish: parsley

Equipment

small bowl, whisk, tablespoon, pot stand, small frying pan (non-stick), plastic palette knife, serving plate.

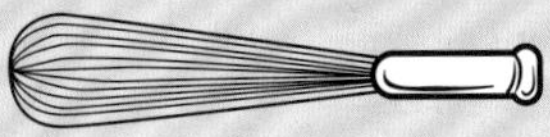

Balloon whisk: for whisking egg whites, stirring sauces, whipping cream

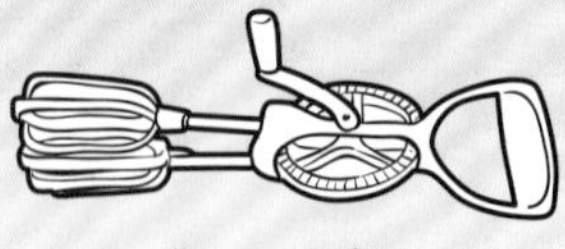

Rotary whisk: for whipping cream, beating eggs and other light mixtures

Palette knife

Fish slice or egg lifter

Steps — Method

Gather equipment, collect/weigh ingredients, set worktop.

1 Gently whisk all the ingredients together except the oil and the filling.

2 **Filling:** Prepare one filling from the following choices:
- 2 tablespoons cheese, grated.
- 50g mushrooms, sautéed in a little butter.
- 2 tablespoons ham/cooked rashers, chopped.
- ½ onion and ½ a red pepper, sautéed.
- 50g finely chopped, raw spinach.

3 Heat oil, pour in the egg mixture. When the egg starts to set, quickly tilt the pan and using a palette knife, push the cooked edges of omelette towards the centre. Now run any remaining liquid egg onto the hot pan to cook. Continue cooking until the egg mixture is nearly set. The top will look glossy and creamy. Sprinkle on the filling.

4 Fold omelette across in three and slip onto warm plate.

Garnish with parsley.

Serve immediately with a fresh salad and brown bread.

Healthy Hint!

Avoid serving an omelette or other fried foods with chips as the high quantity of fat is unhealthy. Choose a salad and brown bread.

Spanish Tortilla or Potato Omelette

SPAIN

Cooking Time: 25 minutes

Serves: 4

Ingredients

- 1 medium potato
- 1 small onion
- 1 clove garlic
- 1 tablespoon peas
- 3 large eggs
- 1 large sprig parsley
- Salt and black pepper
- 3 tablespoons olive oil
- **Garnish:** parsley

Equipment

sharp knife, board, medium bowl, whisk, medium-sized frying pan, pot stand, palette knife, large plate, serving plate.

Chef's Tip!
A non-stick pan is best for this recipe.

Food Fact!
In Spain, tortilla is eaten hot or cold at all times of the day - for breakfast, lunch or as a snack. The Spanish cut cold tortilla into 2cm cubes and serve it topped with an olive, cherry tomato or anchovy on a cocktail stick.

Dicing an onion

Steps — Method

Gather equipment, collect/weigh ingredients, set worktop.

1. Wash, peel and slice potato very thinly.
2. Peel and dice onion very finely. Peel and crush garlic.
3. Wash and chop parsley. Keep some for garnish.
4. Heat oil, add potato, fry on medium heat for 10 minutes. Add onion, fry until golden and potato is soft.
5. Beat eggs, garlic, parsley, salt and pepper in a medium-sized bowl. Add peas.
6. Add potatoes to the eggs, mix. Heat 1 teaspoon oil in pan, and return mix to the pan. Cook over a low heat for 10 minutes until the top has just set.
7. Place a large plate over the pan, turn out the tortilla, then slide it back onto pan to cook the other side for 5 minutes.
8. Slide onto a warm serving plate. Cut into wedges.

Garnish with parsley.

Serve with a tomato or pepper salad.

Variation

Add a finely-diced red pepper with the peas at Step 5.

Chef's Tip!
Buy free-range or organic eggs as they contain good Omega-3 fatty acids.

Resource Management: Wash fruit or vegetables in cold water, but never under a running tap. Compost vegetable peelings. Turn off the hob or oven immediately after use.

Batters

A batter is a smooth mixture of flour, egg and liquid that is well beaten. It can be thin or thick.
Thin batter is used for making pancakes or crêpes and Yorkshire pudding.
Thick batter is used for coating fish and making chicken or fish goujons or fruit fritters.

Thin Pancake Batter

Cooking Time: 25 minutes

Serves: 3

Ingredients

100g plain flour
1 egg
Pinch of salt
250ml milk
Oil for frying
Caster sugar to sprinkle

Equipment

bowl, sieve, balloon whisk, spatula, measuring jug, non-stick frying pan.

Chef's Tip!
For a lighter pancake or crêpe, make with cold water instead of milk and stand the batter for one hour before cooking.

In a hurry!
Buzz all ingredients together in a liquidiser/processor or use an electric hand/stick blender, see page 15.

Hand or stick blender

Steps	Method

Gather equipment, collect/weigh ingredients, set worktop.

1 **Batter:** Sieve flour and salt into bowl, make a well in the centre.

2 Drop in egg and half the measured milk. Beat with a whisk, allowing the flour to fall in gradually from the sides. Beat until the batter is completely smooth – no lumps.

3 Add remaining liquid, beat well for 5 minutes to entrap air. Pour into jug and store in fridge if not using straight away.

4 **Cooking Pancakes:** Heat 1 teaspoon oil on pan. Pour on a small amount of batter, just enough to coat the base of pan. Tilt pan to spread the batter.

5 Cook until the edges begin to brown and lift from pan. Shake the pan to loosen the pancake.

6 Turn using the spatula or toss and cook the other side. Put onto plate Cover and keep hot on plate over simmering water.

7 Repeat Steps 5-8 with the remaining batter.

8 Sprinkle or spread each with filling of choice. Roll up.

Sweet pancake finishes

❖ Lemon juice and caster sugar.
❖ Nutella or chocolate spread.
❖ Golden syrup or honey.

Serve on a plate with a doyley.

Sweet Stuffed Pancakes

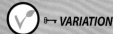

VARIATION

Cooking Time: 30 minutes

Serves: 3

Ingredients

1 x Thin Pancake Batter (see page 78)

Icing sugar to sprinkle

Filling of choice

- sweetened stewed apples flavoured with cloves or cinnamon
- raisins or bananas fried in butter with a little rum poured over
- raspberries or strawberries and whipped cream or mascarpone cheese

Sweet Stuffed Pancakes

Steps **Method**

1 Make pancake batter (see page 78, Steps 1-3) and keep warm.

2 Prepare filling.

3 Cook pancakes (see page 78, Steps 4-7).

4 Put 1 tablespoon of filling into the centre of each and roll up. Sprinkle with sieved icing sugar.

Serve with cream, ice cream or fresh berry coulis (page 156).

Savoury Stuffed Pancakes

VARIATION

Cooking Time: 30 minutes

Serves: 3

Ingredients

1 x Thin Pancake Batter but omit icing sugar

25g Parmesan to sprinkle

Oil for frying

10g butter to melt

Filling of choice

- 150g grated cheese and 125g chopped ham
- chopped grilled bacon with pineapple chunks and cottage cheese
- mixed seafood in white coating sauce (page 40)
- diced cooked chicken, mushrooms and leeks in white coating sauce (page 40)

Steps **Method**

Preheat oven to 170°C/Fan 160°C/Gas Mark 4.

1 Make pancakes, keep warm. Prepare filling and put 1 tablespoon of filling into the centre of each, roll up.

2 Put pancakes on a greased serving dish, coat with 10g melted butter and sprinkle with a little Parmesan cheese.

3 Bake for 10-15 minutes until heated through.

Garnish and **serve** hot as a starter, for a snack or for lunch.

Chef's Tip!

If batter becomes lumpy use a hand or stick blender to make it smooth, see page 15.

Watch Out!

If oil catches fire, cover the pot or frying pan as fast as you can. A plate or saucepan lid is good for this or throw a fire blanket or a damp tea towel over it, if you have one. Don't forget to turn off the heat at source. If this fails, shut the door, get everyone out of the house and call the fire brigade.

Thick Batter – Fish, Chicken, Onion Rings or Fruit Fritters

Cooking Time: 5 minutes

Ingredients

100g plain flour

1 egg

Pinch of salt

125ml milk

4-5 tablespoons of rapeseed oil for shallow frying

25g flour for dusting

Fish in Batter

300g boneless fish fillet, cut into thick fingers.

Chicken Goujons

2 chicken fillets cut into thick fingers.

Onion Rings

1 big onion sliced thickly into rings, separated.

Fruit Fritters

1 apple peeled, cored and sliced thickly into rings.

1 banana peeled and cut in half, lengthways.

Pineapple Rings

Drained pineapple rings.

Equipment

bowl, sieve, balloon whisk, spatula, measuring jug, frying pan (non-stick, if possible), fish slice/egg slice, plate, teaspoon, skewer, kitchen paper.

Healthy Hint!
Fried foods have a high-fat content. Avoid eating them every day as too much fat causes obesity.

Fish in Thick Batter

Steps — Method

1. **Batter:** Sieve flour and salt into bowl, make well in centre.
2. Drop in egg and half the measured milk. Beat with a whisk, allowing the flour to fall in gradually from the sides. Beat until the batter is completely smooth – no lumps.
3. Add remaining liquid, beat well for 5 minutes to entrap air.
4. Prepare fish, chicken, onion or fruit pieces. Dust with flour.
5. Drop the food pieces one by one gently into the batter. Heat oil and check it sizzles nicely by testing with a drop of batter.
6. Using a skewer, lift out the food pieces one at a time. Allow excess batter to drain off.
7. Place pieces carefully into oil. **Fry*** a few pieces at a time, turning once and cook until just golden on both sides. The chicken will take a bit longer to cook through.
8. Drain on kitchen paper and place in oven to keep warm. Repeat with remaining food. Turn off the heat immediately when finished.

Serve fish with lemon wedges and chips or baked potatoes, tartare sauce or mayonnaise.

Serve chicken or onion rings with a flavoured mayonnaise, dip or salsa.

Serve onion rings with steak, fish or potato wedges and a green salad.

Serve fruit sprinkled with caster sugar, cream or ice cream.

*FRYING — COOKING METHOD

Frying is a quick method of cooking in hot fat between 150°C and 195°C. The food is in direct contact with the fat or oil, which sears the food, and it cooks quickly. Frying does not tenderise so foods must be already tender. Foods should be dry before frying.

Deep-fat frying: Always use a thermostatically-controlled, deep-fat fryer placed on a heat-resistant surface. Use clean oil. Set the temperature according to instruction on cooker. Add the foods. Never overfill the basket. Drain food well on kitchen paper. Foods are often sealed and protected from the hot fat by coating in batter or flour or egg and breadcrumbs before deep frying.

Crumpets or Dropped Scones

USA

Cooking Time: 20-30 minutes

Serves: 8-10

Ingredients

200g plain flour
1 rounded teaspoon baking powder
25g caster sugar
Pinch of salt
1 tablespoon golden syrup
25g butter
1 egg
200ml milk
Butter for frying

Equipment

bowl, sieve, teaspoon, measuring jug, tablespoon, wooden spoon, pot stand, saucepan, frying pan, balloon whisk, palette knife, spatula, plate and doyley.

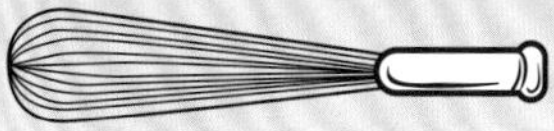

Balloon whisk: for whisking egg whites, stirring sauces, whipping cream

Palette knife

Idea!
Act quickly to treat a burn. Immerse the burnt area of skin in cold water for 5 minutes. Apply burn gel, aloe vera or Vitamin E cream.

Steps — Method

Gather equipment, collect/weigh ingredients, set worktop.

1 Melt butter, add golden syrup, remove from heat. **Do not boil.**
2 Sieve flour, salt and baking powder into a bowl and add sugar.
3 Drop in egg, melted butter and half the milk. Beat well with a balloon whisk. Add remaining milk and pour back into jug.
4 Heat the pan to a medium heat and grease with butter. Use a tablespoon to pour on the mixture, forming round shapes.
5 When the scones set and holes appear on top, turn over with a palette knife. Cook the other side. Repeat the process until all the batter has been used up.
6 Keep warm over a pan of hot water and serve immediately.

Serve with butter and golden syrup or caster sugar.

If your clothes catch fire, you must **STOP, DROP** and **ROLL**. That means drop to the ground and roll over to quench the flames.

Watch Out!
If oil or fat catches fire DO NOT try to quench it with water. Instead use a fire blanket, an extinguisher or smother it with a large plate or saucepan lid. Turn off the gas or electricity at source if you can and close any windows and doors. If the fire becomes out of control, leave the premises and phone the fire brigade on 112.

Spaghetti –
smooth, long strands

Fresh and Dried Tagliatelle –
smooth, long, flat strands

Lasagne –
smooth, flat sheets

Farfalle –
smooth 'bows'

Penne –
smooth or
ridged quills

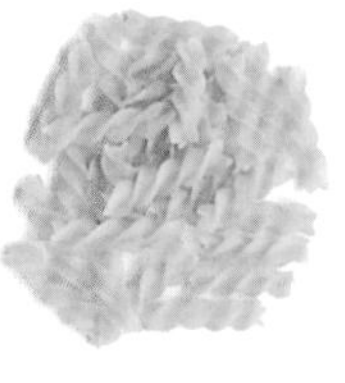

Fusilli –
smooth spirals

Macaroni –
smooth, short tubes

Fresh Tortellini –
smooth, stuffed
crescents

Fresh Ravioli –
smooth, stuffed
'pillows'

White Short-Grain –
sushi and paella

White Long-Grain–
Chinese cooking

Basmati –
Indian cooking

Arborio –
risotto

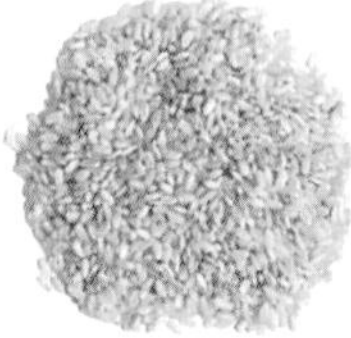

Brown Short-Grain –
soups and patties

Brown Long-Grain –
salads, vegetarian
and accompaniment

Wild Rice –
salads and
accompaniment

White Glutinous –
Asian sweet dishes
and sticky rice

Couscous –
African cooking,
salads and tagines

Corn Polenta –
Italian cooking

Chapter 5

Pasta, Pizza, Couscous and Rice

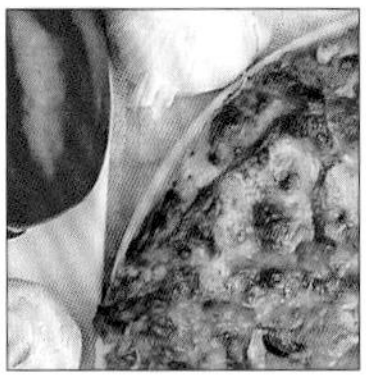

Fresh pasta is made in Ireland but most is imported from Italy. Traditionally, pasta is made from durum wheat, but pasta made from rice, quinoa or corn is available for coeliacs. Soba rice noodles are a good substitute for pasta, but always read the labels. Quinoa contains High Biological Value (HBV) protein and is very nutritious. Rice is a staple food in many diets in countries around the world.

Key Words and Skills

- strain
- drain
- roux
- sear
- freeze
- dice
- al dente
- roll
- grate
- reheat
- modify
- shred

Other suitable recipes:

Pasta or Rice Salad (page 55), Curried Rice Salad (page 55), Ratatouille Lasagne (page 61), Crunchy Seafood Pasta (page 113), Crunchy Chicken Pasta (page 113).

Evaluation! See pages 223 and 224.

- Did you meet the brief and did you refer to the specific requirements of the task or dish/dishes?
- Discuss the results of your finished dish/dishes including the presentation, colour, taste and texture.
- What aspects were done well and what aspects could be improved?
- Did you correctly cost and budget for all ingredients?

Cooking Pasta

ITALY

Serves: 2 (75g-100g per person)

Ingredients

150g pasta (dried or fresh)
1½ litres water
3 teaspoons salt

To serve

Black pepper and salt
See suggestions on page 85

Equipment

large saucepan, teaspoon, wooden spoon, colander and bowl, serving dish.

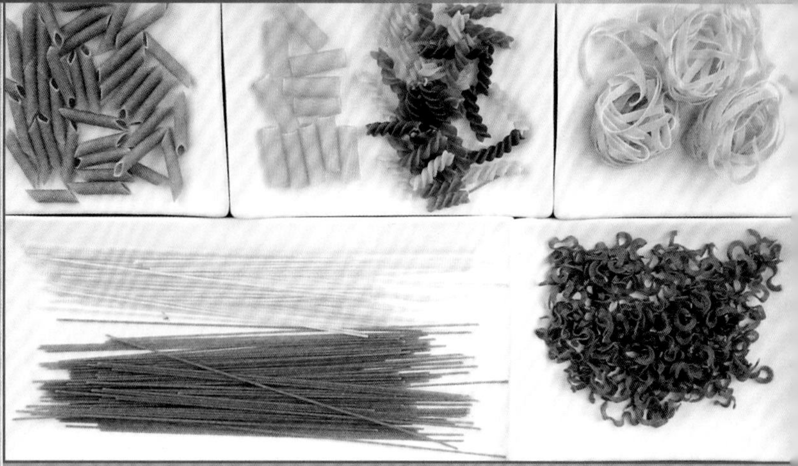

Pasta – Wholewheat, Gluten-Free, Spelt, White and Coloured

Steps — Method

Gather equipment, collect/weigh ingredients, set worktop.

1. Boil lots of water in a kettle. Pour boiling water into saucepan and add salt.
2. Bring water to the boil again. When it bubbles, add pasta, stir and do not cover. Lower heat, simmer until pasta is cooked **al dente***.

   Cooking times: Fresh pasta cooks in 3-4 minutes. Dried pasta takes 10-14 minutes depending on size. Follow the instructions on the packet.
3. **Testing:** Remove a little pasta and run under the cold tap to cool. Eat a piece to test if it is done.
4. **Draining:** Place a colander into a bowl in the sink and turn the cooked pasta into the colander. Be very careful as steam can burn.
5. Turn the pasta back into the saucepan and use as required. See Chef's Tip below.

Serve with variations (page 85) and Bolognese (pages 90/91).

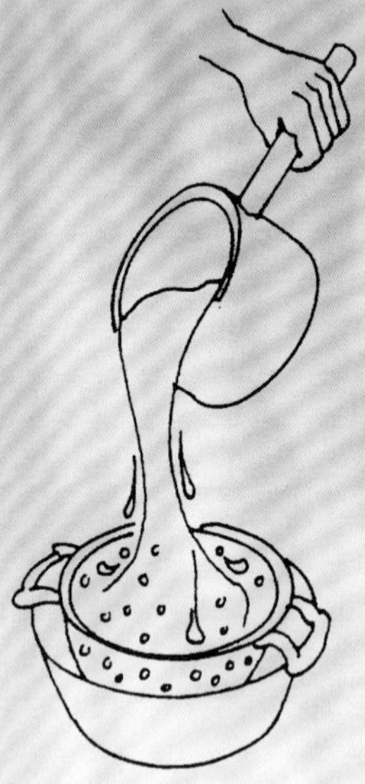

Draining pasta

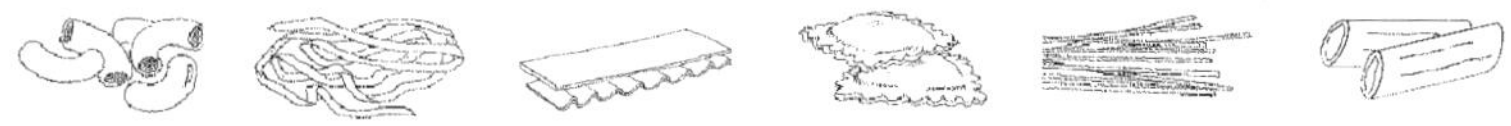

Chef's Tip!
Save some of the pasta's cooking water to pour over the pasta before serving to make it juicier.

Resource Management: Leftover pasta is very tasty tossed in pesto and allowed to cool. Ideal in lunchboxes or Buddha Bowls.

AL DENTE — COOKING TERM

Al dente is an Italian cookery term. It describes food that is cooked so it is still firm or 'has a bite'. Food cooked al dente should not be too soft or soggy. Pasta and rice should be cooked *al dente*.

Buttered Pasta

Ingredients

1 x Pasta ingredients (page 84)
25g butter
Salt and black pepper
Fresh parsley/basil, chopped
25g fresh Parmesan or Cheddar cheese

Pasta with Butter, Pesto, Olive Oil and Herbs, Pasta Verde

Steps **Method**

1 Cook pasta (see page 84).
2 Toss hot pasta with butter, salt and freshly ground black pepper.

Garnish with chopped fresh herbs. Top with grated cheese.

Pasta with Pesto

Ingredients

1 x Pasta ingredients (page 84)
1-2 dessertspoons pesto, green or red
Fresh herbs or parsley

Steps **Method**

1 Cook pasta (see page 84).
2 Toss hot pasta with pesto softened with 1-2 dessertspoons of hot water drained from the pasta.

Garnish with chopped fresh herbs and ground black pepper.

Pasta with Olive Oil and Fresh Herbs

Ingredients

1 x Pasta ingredients (page 84)
1 tablespoon olive oil
2 tablespoons fresh herbs

Steps **Method**

1 Wash, dry and chop herbs finely. Cook pasta (see page 84).
2 Toss hot pasta with the olive oil, herbs, salt and freshly ground black pepper. Taste to check seasoning.

Pasta Verde

Ingredients

1 x Pasta ingredients (page 84)
6 lettuce leaves
3 tablespoons frozen peas
25g butter or pesto

Steps **Method**

1 Cook pasta (see page 84).
2 Shred lettuce. Add peas to cooking pasta for last 5 minutes.
3 Drain and top with shredded lettuce, butter or pesto and seasoning.

Pasta Carbonara

Cooking Time: 20 minutes

Serves: 2-3

Ingredients

175g-200g tagliatelle
1 tablespoon olive oil
2-3 streaky rashers
1 large egg
2 tablespoons cream
Salt and pepper
Garnish: fresh parsley, 1 tomato, 25g fresh Parmesan or Cheddar cheese

Equipment

large saucepan, teaspoon, colander, bowl, frying pan, scissors, whisk, serving dish.

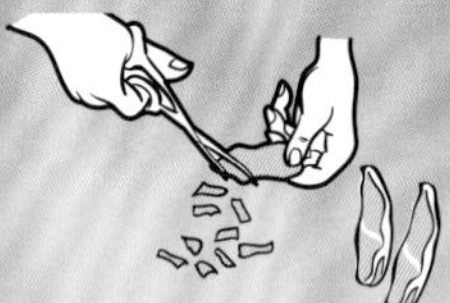

Snipping rashers

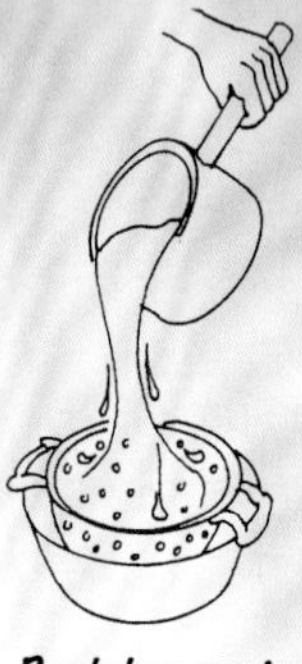

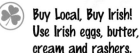

Draining pasta

Steps — Method

Gather equipment, collect/weigh ingredients, set worktop.

1 **Boil** lots of water in a kettle. Pour boiling water into saucepan and add salt and oil if using.

2 **Cooking Pasta:** Bring water to the boil again. When it boils, add pasta, stir, lower heat and **simmer** until pasta is cooked al dente. Do not cover. **Al dente** means that it should have a bite. See **al dente** on page 84.

3 Grate cheese, chop parsley, cut tomato into 6-8 wedges to garnish.

4 Cut rashers into strips. Fry gently in hot oil. Turn off heat.

5 Whisk egg, cream, pepper and salt in a bowl.

6 **Testing:** Remove a little pasta and run under the cold tap to cool. Eat a piece to test if it is done. See al dente, page 84.

7 **Draining:** Place a colander into a bowl in the sink and turn the cooked pasta into the colander. Be very careful as steam can burn.

8 Turn bacon and frying oils into the hot pasta saucepan, add the hot pasta and egg mixture. Mix together.

9 Cover for a few minutes to allow egg to cook in the heat of the pasta only. Turn into heated serving dish.

Garnish with chopped fresh parsley and tomato wedges, fresh Parmesan or Cheddar cheese.

Buy Local, Buy Irish! Use Irish eggs, butter, cream and rashers.

BOILING — COOKING METHOD

This is cooking in rapidly bubbling liquid at 100°C. Fast boiling is used for rice, pasta, green vegetables and jams. It is used to thicken sauces by evaporating the liquid.

SIMMER — COOKING METHOD

Water simmers when bubbles break gently on the surface at 95° C.
It extracts flavour and tenderises most foods. Most foods are simmered with the lid on the pot.

Macaroni Cheese

Cooking Time: 30 minutes

Serves: 2-3

Ingredients

125g macaroni

Cheese Sauce

25g flour

25g butter

1 teaspoon readymade mustard

Salt and pepper

400ml milk

150g cheese

Garnish: parsley, tomato. See Idea below.

Equipment

ovenproof pie dish, grater with large holes, saucepan, wooden spoon, measuring jug, whisk.

Grating cheese

Steps — Method

Preheat oven to 180°C/Fan 170°C/Gas Mark 4.

1 Cook macaroni according to recipe for pasta on page 84.

2 Grate cheese and reserve ¼ for the top. Grease pie dish.

3 **Roux Sauce:** Melt butter, add flour and seasoning, cook for 1 minute. Remove from heat. Stir in milk a little at a time. It will look very thin but will thicken when it boils. Add mustard, see Step 7 on page 41.

4 Return to heat and boil, stirring all the time. Reduce the heat and barely simmer for 5 minutes. **Remove from heat.**

5 Stir in the cheese and the cooked drained macaroni, see Idea below.

6 Put mixture into pie dish, sprinkle with cheese. Brown under a grill or bake until golden for 20-30 minutes in a moderate oven.

Garnish with parsley and tomato.

Serve with a colourful salad of tomato, sweetcorn and peppers.

Cheese and Potato Pie

VARIATION

Ingredients

1 x Cheese Sauce (see above)

5 medium potatoes (cooked or uncooked)

1 clove garlic (optional)

Garnish: chopped parsley

Equipment

ovenproof pie dish, grater with large holes, saucepan, wooden spoon, measuring jug, whisk.

Steps — Method

Preheat oven to 180°C/Fan 170°C/Gas Mark 4.

1 Dice potatoes. If raw, cook in boiling, salted water for 10 minutes. Drain.

2 Make sauce, adding the crushed clove of garlic with the cheese.

3 Stir the diced potato into sauce. Turn into greased pie dish. Cook for 20-30 minutes to brown the top and heat through.

Garnish with parsley.

Serve with baked or grilled fish or meat.

Idea!

Layer sautéd onion and rasher or a sliced hard-boiled egg or tomato or chopped ham or baby spinach between two layers of macaroni or potato. This dish freezes and reheats well.

Luxury Tagliatelle

ITALY

Cooking Time: 20 minutes

Serves: 3

Ingredients

- 25g butter
- 1 tablespoon oil
- 4-5 rashers (hickory or mild)
- 1 onion
- 1 red pepper
- 1 clove garlic
- 100g mushrooms (optional)
- 1 tin chopped tomatoes
- 125ml cream
- 2 bay leaves
- 1 teaspoon oregano or basil
- 100g Cheddar cheese
- 8 balls tagliatelle
- **Garnish:** chopped parsley or basil

Equipment

scissors, sharp knife, board, grater, 2 large saucepans, colander, 2 wooden spoons, garlic crusher, tablespoon, pot stand, serving dish.

Idea!
Do not mix pasta and sauce together. Just serve sauce on top like a bolognese sauce.

Food Fact!
Choose wholewheat pasta instead of refined white pasta. Wholewheat pasta contains more nutrients and fibre and is less processed.

Steps — Method

Gather equipment, collect/weigh ingredients, set worktop.

1. Wash, peel and dice onion and garlic. Wash, deseed and dice pepper. If using mushrooms, wash and slice.
2. Cut rashers into small strips (see Chef's Tip, page 89). Heat oil and butter in saucepan and cook rashers until just golden.
3. Add onions, red pepper, mushrooms and garlic and cook for 5 minutes.
4. Add tomatoes and herbs. Season well, then simmer very gently for 10-15 minutes.
5. Meanwhile cook pasta (page 84).
6. Remove sauce from heat, take out the bay leaves, add cheese and cream. Allow to melt (cooked cheese becomes stringy).
7. When pasta is cooked, add the sauce mixture and mix through using two wooden spoons. Turn into serving dish. Serve immediately.

Garnish with chopped parsley or fresh basil.

Serve with a fresh salad and garlic bread.

Variation

Use 200g mushrooms.

Resource Management: This freezes and reheats well. To Freeze: Place in suitable casserole or container. Cool. Seal, label and freeze. To Reheat: If frozen, allow to thaw and then reheat, covered in a moderate oven for 30 minutes until heated through to the middle.

Buy Local, Buy Irish!
Many ingredients in this recipe are produced or grown in Ireland.

Chicken and Pasta Bake

Cooking Time: 30-40 minutes

Serves: 3-4

Ingredients

120g macaroni
1 tablespoon olive oil
2 chicken fillets
2-3 rashers
1 small carrot
1 medium onion
1 medium courgette
Small carton sour cream
Salt and pepper
50g Cheddar cheese

Sauce

1 x Tomato Sauce (page 44)
or
1 carton of fresh tomato soup

Garnish: chopped parsley

Equipment

sharp knife, board, tablespoon, 2 saucepans, pot stands, grater, wooden spoon, colander, ovenproof dish (medium size).

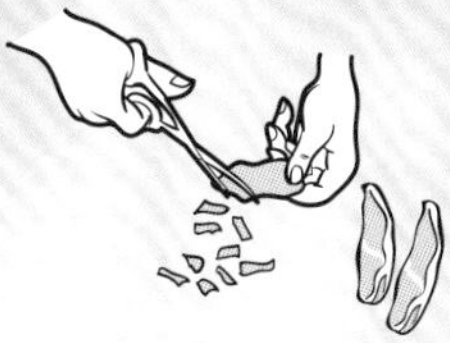

Snipping rashers

Dicing

Steps **Method**

Preheat oven to 180°C/Fan 170°C/Gas Mark 4.

Gather equipment, collect/weigh ingredients, set worktop.

1 Cook macaroni (page 84) and drain in colander.
2 **Make tomato sauce** (page 44) or open a carton of tomato soup.
3 Wash, peel and grate carrot, dice all vegetables and snip rashers (see Chef's Tip). Wash and dry chicken fillets and cut into cubes.
4 Heat oil and fry chicken until just beginning to brown but do not cook through.
5 Add onion, rashers and carrot and stir over medium heat for 10 minutes, add courgette.
6 Combine chicken mixture with pasta, tomato sauce/soup and cream. Season to taste.
7 Turn into dish and top with cheese.
8 Bake for 30 minutes until nicely browned.

Garnish with chopped parsley.

Serve with garlic bread and a green salad.

Chef's Tip!
Cutting rashers or bacon is easier using a scissors.
If you can't find one, sauté the rasher whole, remove from pan, derind, cut into pieces with a sharp knife and fork.

In a hurry!
Use a carton of fresh tomato soup instead of tomato sauce.

Bolognese Sauce

THIS BASIC ITALIAN SAUCE IS USED FOR LASAGNE AND PASTA BAKE

Cooking Time: 35 minutes

Serves: 4

Ingredients

2 tablespoons olive oil
200g lean minced beef
2 streaky rashers (optional)
1 onion
1 fat clove garlic
1 teaspoon dried basil or oregano (or a mixture)
1 tin chopped tomatoes
2 tablespoons tomato purée
Salt and black pepper
100g mushrooms, chopped
1 carrot, diced or grated
1 dessertspoon soy sauce (optional)
1 dessertspoon Balsamic vinegar (optional)

To serve:

200g cooked pasta
Fresh Parmesan cheese
Fresh parsley or basil

Equipment

sharp knife, board, scissors, teaspoon, pot stand, tablespoon, wooden spoon, saucepan, serving dish.

Dicing onion

Idea!
Wheat intolerant? Serve Bolognese with wheat-free pasta made from maize or rice or use quinoa (see page 98).

Steps — Method

Gather equipment, collect/weigh ingredients, set worktop.

1 If serving with pasta, cook as on page 84.

2 Meanwhile, peel onion and halve lengthways. Slice, first following the lines on onion and then slice into fine dice.

3 Smash garlic sharply with the flat side of a large knife to help remove skin, then dice finely or crush.

4 Use scissors to cut rashers into short strips (see Chef's Tip and diagram, page 89).

5 Heat oil in saucepan and then gently soften bacon, onion and garlic for 5 minutes. Add diced/grated carrot and chopped mushrooms.

6 Turn up the heat, add meat and cook to develop flavour, stirring all the time. Add remaining ingredients.

7 Bring to a **simmer** (see page 86) and stir. Reduce heat, cover and simmer gently for 20-25 minutes.

8 Thin with 1-2 tablespoons water or stock if the sauce is too thick; if too thin, boil with the lid off until it thickens.

9 Taste and add more seasoning if necessary.

Garnish with chopped fresh herbs and grated fresh Parmesan or other hard Italian cheese.

Serve hot with pasta, freshly-tossed salad and garlic bread.

Variation

Vegetarian: Use 300g Quorn mince instead of meat.

Vegan: Use 30g vegan cheese, Quorn mince, beans or lentils.

Food Fact!
Mycoprotein is the main ingredient in Quorn products. It is a meat-free form of protein derived from an edible fungus. It is low in fat and saturates, contains no cholesterol or trans fats and is a good source of dietary fibre.

Vegetarian Bolognese Sauce

VARIATION

Ingredients

1 x Bolognese Sauce (page 90) but omit the meat
1 small courgette
1 stick celery
1 tin Puy lentils or beans of choice

To serve:

200g cooked pasta
Fresh Parmesan cheese
Fresh parsley or basil

Chef's Tip!
Add a pinch of sugar to tomatoes when cooking as it brings out the flavour.

Vegetarian Bolognese and Spelt Pasta

Preparing mushrooms

Steps **Method**

1 Follow the Bolognese Sauce recipe from Steps 1 to 3 on page 90.

2 Wash vegetables, peel and grate carrot, dice celery and courgette. Wash and slice mushrooms.

3 Heat oil, sauté the onion, add carrot and celery, sauté to develop flavour.

4 Finally add the remaining vegetables. Continue through Steps 7 to 9 on page 90.

Serve hot, garnished with chives and chopped parsley.

Idea!
Try adding a tablespoon of soy sauce or balsamic vinegar for a lovely flavour in this recipe.

Bolognese-Stuffed Tortilla

VARIATION

Ingredients

1 x Bolognese Sauce (meat or vegetarian)
1 carton hummus (170g)
Packet tortillas (8)
75g Cheddar cheese

In a hurry!
Warm in a microwave instead of an oven.

Steps **Method**

Preheat oven to 180°C/Fan 170°C/Gas Mark 5.

1 Make Bolognese Sauce following the method on page 90 or 91.

2 Spread the tortillas with a thick layer of hummus (page 21) and then a layer of Bolognese sauce. Roll up, tucking in each end.

3 Place in a shallow, greased casserole and sprinkle with grated cheese.

4 Put in oven until cheese melts and tortillas are cooked through.

Lasagne

ITALY

Cooking Time: 55-60 minutes

Serves: 3-4

Ingredients

- 1 x Bolognese Sauce (see pages 90/91)
- 8-9 sheets pre-cooked lasagne

Cheese sauce

- 150g Cheddar cheese
- 50g butter
- 50g flour
- ½ teaspoon dry mustard
- Salt and pepper
- 700ml milk

Garnish: parsley

Equipment

sharp knife, board, scissors, teaspoon, pot stand, wooden spoon, saucepan, grater, plate, small bowl, tablespoon, square or oblong ovenproof dish.

In a hurry! Use flour tortillas instead of lasagne.

Steps **Method**

Preheat oven to 190°C/Fan 180°C/Gas Mark 4-5.

1. Make a quantity of Bolognese Sauce using the recipe on pages 90/91.
2. Grate cheese. Grease ovenproof dish.
3. **Cheese Sauce:** Whisk the milk, butter, flour, mustard, pepper and salt in a saucepan and heat until it boils and thickens. Simmer for 3 minutes, remove from heat and add ⅔ of the cheese.
4. Place a layer of meat sauce followed by a layer of lasagne followed by a layer of cheese sauce in the dish. Repeat the layering, finishing with a layer of cheese sauce. Thin the cheese sauce a little with milk or water if necessary.
5. Sprinkle with remaining cheese. Bake until golden (20-30 minutes).

Serve with garlic bread and a tossed green salad.

Freezing: This freezes well. Freeze after topping with cheese. Wrap, label, cool and freeze.

To reheat, thaw and then bake as above. See page 95.

Quick Lasagne

VARIATION

Ingredients

- 1x Bolognese Sauce (see pages 90/91)
- 8-9 sheets lasagne
- 450g-500g cottage cheese
- 200g mozzarella, grated

Chef's Tip!
Lasagne is often made this way in America. It is quick to make and a nice change. However, it is more expensive.

Steps **Method**

1. Mix ⅔ of the mozzarella with the cottage cheese and use this mixture instead of the cheese sauce above.
2. Follow the method for Lasagne. Cover top with remaining mozzarella

Sour Cream Pasta Bake

BERMUDA

Cooking Time: 40 minutes

Serves: 3-4

Ingredients

- 1 x Bolognese Sauce (see pages 90/91)
- 150g spaghetti or other pasta
- 1 scallion or use cottage cheese with chives
- 1 onion
- 250g cottage cheese
- 50g Cheddar cheese
- 170g-200g sour cream or crème fraîche
- **Garnish:** 1 tomato

Equipment

sharp knife, board, scissors, pot stand, teaspoon, grater with large holes, tablespoon, wooden spoon, saucepan, plate, bowl, ovenproof dish.

In a hurry!
Use noodles instead of pasta. Soak in boiling water and they are ready to use. Just as delicious!

Food Fact!
Soured Cream: This is made by growing a culture of bacteria that makes lactic acid in the cream. It has a tangy flavour and is used in dips, dressings, sauces and on baked potatoes.

Look Up!
Cottage cheese, sour cream and crème fraîche.

Steps **Method**

Preheat oven to 190°C/Fan 180°C/Gas Mark 4-5.

Gather equipment, collect/weigh ingredients, set worktop.

1 Cook pasta as on page 84 and make one quantity of Bolognese Sauce (pages 90/91).
2 Grease ovenproof dish.
3 Chop onion very finely. Grate Cheddar cheese.
4 Combine pasta, cottage cheese, sour cream and scallion.
5 Layer ½ the Bolognese sauce, ½ the pasta followed by remaining Bolognese and then remaining pasta.
6 Sprinkle with Cheddar cheese.
7 Bake until golden. This will take about 20 minutes.

Garnish with thinly sliced tomato wedges.

Serve with garlic bread and a green salad tossed in Orange Dressing (see page 37).

Buy Local, Buy Irish!
Ireland is a top producer of all dairy products, e.g. milk, cream, cheese, butter, etc.

BAKING — COOKING METHOD

Baking means cooking food in hot air in a ventilated oven. If food is covered, it partially cooks in its own steam and stays moist.

Potato-Topped Bolognese

Cooking Time: 40-45 minutes

Serves: 4

Ingredients

1 x Bolognese Sauce (see pages 90/91)

4-5 medium potatoes

Salt and pepper

25g butter or oil for top

Garnish: chopped parsley

Equipment

sharp knife, board, scissors, pot stand, tablespoon, saucepan, lid, fork, bowl, wooden spoon, colander, teaspoon, potato masher, peeler, ovenproof dish.

Dicing onion

Steps **Method**

Preheat oven to 190°C/Fan 180°C/Gas Mark 4-5.

1 Wash, peel and quarter potatoes. Boil until soft (see page 64).

2 Follow recipe for bolognese, meat or vegetarian (pages 90/91).

3 Grease ovenproof dish, pour in the bolognese. Keep warm in oven.

4 Drain potatoes, season, mash and beat in enough potato water to make a soft, spreadable mixture.

5 Use a teaspoon to spoon potato over the bolognese. Spread gently, score with a fork. Dot with butter or brush with olive oil. Bake for 20-30 minutes until golden on top.

Garnish with chopped parsley.

Serve with cooked broccoli, green beans or a tossed salad.

Chef's Tip!
Top the potato with 25g grated cheese for a sizzling top.

Healthy Hint!
Add a tin of butter beans or mixed beans (drained) to the Bolognese sauce to increase the protein and fibre content of the dish.

In a hurry!
Replace potato with 4-5 sweet potatoes as they cook more quickly or see Quick Cook Diced Potato Topping recipe on page 109.

Food Fact!
Sweet potatoes are a great source of Vitamin A (beta carotene), Vitamin B and Vitamin C, potassium and fibre.

Idea!
Defrost ½ a packet of puff or shortcrust pastry, roll out and place on top of sauce in pie dish. Decorate with pastry leaves (page 121) and brush with beaten egg. Bake for 30 minutes at 190°C/Fan 180°C/Gas Mark 5.

Chicken Chorizo

Cooking Time: 30 minutes

Serves: 4

Ingredients

- 200g pasta, fusilli or penne
- 2 chicken breasts
- 150g chorizo sausage
- 1 onion
- 2 cloves garlic
- 1 red pepper
- 1 teaspoon coriander
- 1 teaspoon paprika
- 1 level teaspoon chilli flakes
- 1 teaspoon sugar
- 1 tin chopped tomatoes
- 170ml cream
- Large sprig of parsley
- 25g grated Parmesan

Equipment

sharp knife, board, teaspoon, scissors, pot stand, tablespoon, wooden spoon, colander, 2 saucepans, measuring jug, serving dish.

Steps **Method**

Gather equipment, collect/weigh ingredients, set worktop.

1 Boil water in kettle for pasta. Cook pasta in boiling, salted water until **al dente**, see page 84. Do not cover.
2 Wash chicken, dry on kitchen paper and cut into cubes. Cut chorizo into 1cm pieces.
3 Wash pepper, halve, deseed and dice. Peel onion and garlic and dice finely.
4 Heat oil, fry chorizo for 2 minutes or until the oil runs. Add chicken, fry for 2 minutes. Add the onion and garlic, fry for 2 minutes.
5 Add peppers, all spices, sugar and tomatoes. Bring to the boil, reduce heat and simmer for 10 minutes.
6 Test texture for **al dente** and drain pasta, see page 84. Cover saucepan to keep warm.
7 Add cream to sauce, reduce heat and simmer uncovered for 8-10 minutes. Do not cover.
8 Wash and chop the parsley, see page 73.
9 Mix the sauce into the pasta. Add chopped parsley.

Serve piled on a serving dish sprinkled with Parmesan cheese.

Food Fact!
Chorizo is a Spanish spiced pork sausage cured and dried with paprika. It is commonly used in Spanish and Mexican dishes.

Healthy Hint!
Too much salt is bad for your blood pressure, heart, kidneys, brain and health. Try replacing salt with herbs, spices, lemon or lime juice instead. Alternatively use low sodium soy sauce.

TO FREEZE FOOD — TECHNIQUE

Dishes or foods must be completely cold. Dishes must be covered and sealed in good-quality freezer wrapping or foil containers.

Label with name of dish, portions/amounts, weight, date of freezing. Turn freezer to low setting and freeze. Follow manufacturer's instructions for your freezer. Remember to return freezer to normal setting afterwards.

REHEATING OF FOOD — TECHNIQUE

Reheating of all foods must be thoroughly done. Stews/casseroles take approximately 15-20 minutes in a microwave or 30-40 minutes in a hot oven. Food should reach 72ºC. Bring liquid quickly to the boil, simmer for 5 minutes. Serve without delay. Tepid food incubates bacteria – micro-organisms can multiply every 20 minutes.

CHICKEN PICASSO

Cooking Time: 60 minutes

Serves: 3-4

Ingredients

120g pasta shapes
25g butter
2-3 chicken fillets
1 small onion
1 clove garlic
50g mushrooms (optional)
1 stick celery
½ red pepper
1 tin chopped tomatoes
1 teaspoon tomato purée
½ teaspoon oregano
1 dessertspoon Worcestershire sauce
75ml cream
50g mozzarella cheese
Salt and pepper
Topping
1 large egg
50g Cheddar cheese, grated
125g carton natural yoghurt
Garnish: parsley

Equipment

2 large saucepans, frying pan, sharp knife, board, grater, tin-opener, whisk, small bowl, tablespoon, garlic crusher, teaspoon, colander, casserole dish.

In a hurry!
Just sprinkle with cheese and bake, omit the topping.

Dicing meat

Steps **Method**

Preheat oven to 170°C/Fan 160°C/Gas Mark 3-4.

Gather equipment, collect/weigh ingredients, set worktop.

1 Cook pasta in a saucepan of boiling water. Drain well (see page 84).

2 Wash, peel and dice all vegetables. Slice mozzarella.

3 Dice chicken into large chunks. Heat butter, add chicken and brown quickly. It should not be cooked through.

4 Add onion, garlic, mushrooms, celery and red pepper. Fry over a low heat for 5 minutes.

5 Add tomatoes, tomato purée, oregano, Worcestershire sauce, salt and pepper. Simmer for 15 minutes.

6 Stir in cream. Spread pasta into casserole dish, cover with sliced mozzarella and then the chicken mixture.

7 **Topping:** Beat egg, add cheese and yoghurt. Spread over chicken mixture. Bake for 35-40 minutes until nicely browned. Cover with tinfoil if necessary.

Garnish with chopped parsley.

Serve hot with a mixed salad and garlic bread.

TO SKIN TOMATOES TECHNIQUE

Boil some water in a saucepan. Put a cross in the bottom of the tomatoes. Drop tomatoes into water. Count to 30 and drain in a colander. Cool and refresh with cold water. The skins should slip off. Under-ripe tomatoes will take a little longer.

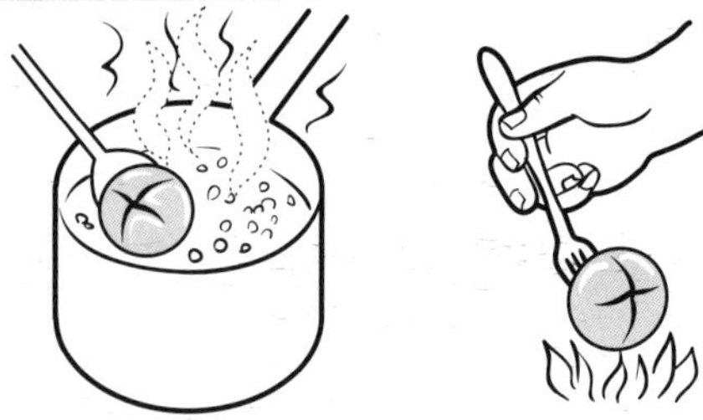

Scald in boiling water for 1 minute or hold on a fork over a low flame.

Carefully pull away the loosened, blistered skin with a sharp knife.

PIZZA

ITALY

Cooking Time: 25-30 minutes

Serves: 4

Ingredients

Base

250g strong white flour

Pinch salt

3g or ½ sachet of fast acting yeast

200ml warm water

1 teaspoon sugar

1 tablespoon olive oil

Sauce

½ onion

1 tablespoon cooking oil

1 tin chopped tomatoes

2 teaspoons tomato purée

Salt and pepper

1 teaspoon herbs (oregano, basil and/or marjoram)

100g grated cheese

Topping (see ideas)

Garnish: chopped parsley

Equipment

sharp knife, board, medium bowl, sieve, tablespoon, teaspoon, saucepan, pot stand, wooden spoon, pizza tin, rolling pin, flour dredger, serving plate.

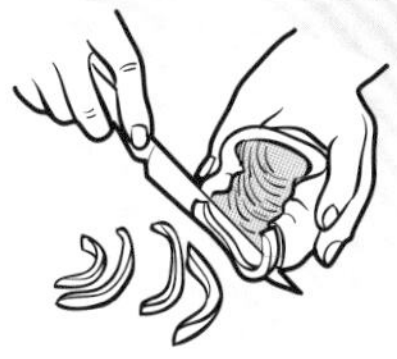

Slicing peppers

Watch Out!
Burns from melting cheese on a hot pizza are very common. Be careful!

Steps — Method

Preheat oven to 190°C/Fan 180°C/Gas Mark 5-6.

Gather equipment, collect/weigh ingredients, set worktop.

1 Sieve flour and salt into bowl. Add the dried yeast, sugar and mix.

2 Add the warm water and oil to the flour mixture, mix well.

3 Knead on a lightly floured board for 10 minutes.

4 Roll out dough into a 25cm circle, place on a baking sheet. Brush with olive oil and cover with cling film. Leave in a warm place for 15 minutes so the dough rises.

5 **Sauce:** Peel and dice onion. Heat oil in saucepan, sauté onion.

6 Add tomatoes, purée, herbs, salt and pepper. Cook for 5 minutes to reduce the liquid.

7 Spread the tomato mixture over the base. Add the prepared topping of choice and cover with the grated cheese.

8 Bake for 20-25 minutes.

Garnish with chopped parsley.

Serve immediately in wedges with a fresh salad.

Topping Ideas

- Chopped cooked ham or bacon and pineapple.
- Sundried tomato, mozzarella and black olives.
- Pepper, tomato and onion.
- Pepperoni or chorizo, pepper and mozzarella.
- Spinach, mushroom and goats cheese.
- Four different cheeses.

Resource Management: Wrap leftover pizza and refrigerate. Reheat pizza slices gently in a frying pan to keep the base crispy.

Couscous

NORTH AFRICA AND MIDDLE EAST

Cooking Time: 5-10 minutes

Serves: 2 (100g per person)

Ingredients

150ml water
¼ teaspoon salt
1 teaspoon oil
100g couscous
15g butter or oil
Garnish: coriander, parsley

Equipment

large saucepan, tight lid or a square of foil, fork, measuring jug, teaspoon, sharp knife, board, serving dish.

Food Fact! Couscous is made from wheat. It has small grains like semolina and is pre-cooked. It is used as an accompaniment for meat, fish or vegetables.

Steps — **Method**

Gather equipment, collect/weigh ingredients, set worktop.

1 Boil the water and add salt. Add couscous, stir once and cover. Remove from heat and allow to swell (fine grain 5 minutes, coarse grain 10 minutes – follow directions on packet).

2 Prepare garnish. Chop herbs or fruits, toast almonds, etc.

3 When time is up, add butter or oil and any other ingredients to be used, swirl through and fluff up with a fork.

4 Tip onto a serving dish and cover with foil to keep warm.

Garnish with chopped fresh herbs before serving.

Garnish Variation: Add poppy seeds, sesame seeds, toasted almonds or chopped dried fruits, e.g. apricots.

Quinoa Pilaf

ALTERNATIVE TO RICE, COUSCOUS OR PASTA

Cooking Time: 15 minutes

Serves: 3-4

Ingredients

225g quinoa
850ml orange juice
100g raisins
1 lemon, zest and juice
1 tablespoon olive oil
Salt
Garnish: fresh parsley, coriander

Equipment

saucepan, wooden spoon, sieve, grater, lemon squeezer, measuring jug, serving dish.

Steps — **Method**

Gather equipment, collect/weigh ingredients, set worktop.

1 Wash, zest (see page 150) and juice the lemon.

2 Heat olive oil, add zest and quinoa. Sauté until quinoa starts to heat and the aroma of the lemon rises. Add salt and dried fruit. Stir to coat

3 Add orange juice, cover and reduce heat to the very lowest for 10 minutes until the juices are absorbed. Add 2-3 teaspoons lemon juice to taste. Turn into serving dish.

Garnish with chopped herbs.

Serve with stir-fries, stews, salads or instead of rice, pasta or couscous.

Food Fact!
Quinoa (pronounced Keen Wah) is a grain from South America. It is a complete protein, containing all eight essential amino acids. It is actually a seed rather than a grain and is gluten-free. It is easy to digest and low in fat. Use instead of couscous or pasta for coeliacs.

Moroccan Lamb Tagine

MOROCCO

Cooking Time: 30 minutes

Serves: 2-3

Ingredients

400g diced lamb

Dry Marinade:

1 heaped teaspoon each of ginger, coriander seeds, turmeric, paprika, cumin, cinnamon.

Sauce:

25g butter or
1 tablespoon oil

1 onion

1 clove garlic

1 carrot

1 small courgette

½ lemon, zest and juice

1 x 230g tin chickpeas

1 tablespoon raisins

1 flat teaspoon salt

400ml stock

50g dried apricots

To serve: 300g couscous

Garnish: ½ lemon, bunch fresh coriander

Equipment

sharp knife, board, saucepan and lid, grater, medium bowl, wooden spoon, teaspoon, measuring jug, juicer.

Chef's Tip!
This is a basic sauce in which any meat, fish or vegetables can be cooked. Serve with couscous.

Look Up!
Tagine.

Steps — Method

Gather equipment, collect/weigh ingredients, set worktop.

1 Mix the **dry marinade*** spices in a bowl. Rub into meat or mix well with a wooden spoon.

2 Wash, peel and dice vegetables. Grate zest of lemon then squeeze (see technique on page 150).

3 Heat oil, **sear*** meat quickly. Add onions, courgette and carrot, sauté for 5 minutes then add all the other ingredients and spices. Add lemon zest and juice.

4 Bring to the boil, lower heat, cover and simmer slowly for 20-30 minutes until meat is tender.

5 Prepare couscous (see page 98), spoon onto a serving dish, flatten the top a little.

6 Wash, dry and chop coriander. Slice lemon.

7 Spoon meat and vegetables onto the couscous to make a cone shape.

8 Boil the juice to reduce if necessary and then pour over the 'mound' so that the couscous absorbs it.

Serve hot and **garnish** with lemon and fresh coriander leaves.

*DRY MARINADE — TECHNIQUE

A dry marinade is a mixture of herbs and spices rubbed into meat and left for a few hours if possible in order to flavour and tenderise the meat.

*SEAR — TECHNIQUE

Sear means to cook food in very hot fat, on all sides, for a short time to seal the outside and therefore keep in the juices. The protein on the outside coagulates in the heat so the juices cannot get out.

RICE

(COOKING METHOD 1) WHITE RICE

Cooking Time: 15 minutes

Serves: 2 (80g uncooked rice = 100g (approximately) cooked rice per person)

Ingredients

2 teaspoons oil or butter

160g long grain rice

400ml water

½ teaspoon salt

Garnish: parsley, paprika, poppy seeds

Equipment

medium or large saucepan covered with a tight lid or tinfoil, fork, teaspoon, measuring jug, wooden spoon, serving dish.

Watch Out!
If the heat is too high, it will burn.

Steps **Method**

Gather equipment, collect/weigh ingredients, set worktop.

1 Boil some water in a kettle.

2 Heat oil or butter in medium or large saucepan and add rice. Stir once to coat the rice.

3 Measure boiling water, add to rice. Add salt. Boil up once and then stir.

4 Cover closely – use foil and lid if lid doesn't fit well. **Reduce heat to the very lowest.** Cook for 15 minutes exactly. Do not stir.

5 After 15 minutes, bite a grain to see if it is tender but not too soft. Tilt the saucepan to check if water has been absorbed; if not, strain through a sieve placed in a bowl in sink.

6 Tip onto serving dish (cover with oiled foil to keep warm). Fluff with a fork or push to the sides of dish to form a ring for curries, etc. Clean dish of any stray rice.

Garnish with parsley or paprika or poppy seeds.

RICE

(COOKING METHOD 2) WHITE RICE

Cooking Time: 12-15 minutes

Serves: 2 (80g uncooked rice = 100g (approximately) cooked rice per person)

Ingredients

160g long grain rice

1 litre water

3 teaspoons salt

Garnish: parsley, paprika, poppy seeds

Equipment

large saucepan, lid, teaspoon, fork, foil, wooden spoon, serving dish.

Steps **Method**

Gather equipment, collect/weigh ingredients, set worktop.

1 Boil water, add salt. When boiled, add rice. Stir once. Reduce heat to simmer. Cover and simmer gently for 12 minutes, see page 86.

2 Bite a grain to see if it is tender but not too soft. Strain through a sieve placed in a bowl in sink.

3 Tip onto serving dish (cover with oiled foil to keep warm). Fluff with a fork or push out to the sides of dish to form a ring for curries, etc. Clean dish of any stray rice.

Garnish with parsley or paprika or poppy seeds.

Idea!.
Rice can be moulded or shaped before serving. Pack it into a wet ramekin, small cup or ring mould. Turn out onto the serving plate. This is ideal for dinner parties.

In a hurry!
Use boil-in-bag rice.

Types of Rice

Brown rice has a nutty flavour. It has more nutrients and fibre and takes longer to cook.
Basmati rice has a delicate flavour and must be washed before cooking.
Arborio rice becomes sticky and is used for making risotto.
Pearl rice has a round grain and is used for puddings. Rice is gluten-free.

Red or Green Rice

Ingredients

- 1 x Rice recipe (page 100)
- 1 red or green pepper
- 2 tablespoons frozen peas or 1 diced tomato
- 1 tomato or 6 sundried tomatoes
- Fresh basil or parsley

1. Cook the rice as in Method 1 on page 100. Wash, deseed and dice pepper and tomato very finely. Wash, dry and chop herbs very finely.
2. When rice is cooked, add pepper, tomato or peas and herbs, fork through the rice. Garnish with green herbs.

Yellow Rice

- 1 x Rice recipe (page 100)
- 1 teaspoon turmeric

Cook rice as in Method 1 on page 100, but add turmeric to the oil or butter before adding the rice. Garnish and serve.

Coconut Rice

- 1 x Rice recipe (page 100)
- 2 teaspoons oil or butter
- 400ml coconut milk
- ½ teaspoon salt
- Fresh parsley or coriander

1. Cook rice as in Method 1 on page 100 – replace water with coconut milk.
2. Wash, dry and chop herbs very finely.

Serve with Indian or Thai curries or with fish, meat or vegetable dishes.

Wild Rice Mix

- 30g wild rice
- 130g long grain rice

1. Cook rice as in Method 2 on page 100 but sprinkle in the wild rice first and cook for 15 minutes. Add white rice, cook for a further 15 minutes.
2. Drain. This black and white rice looks good with light-coloured sauces, white meat or fish.

Brown Rice

- 160g brown rice
- 3 teaspoons salt

Follow Method 2 on page 100 but cook for 30-35 minutes until the grains are soft. Drain and serve. Garnish as required.

Fried Rice

CHINA

Cooking Time: 15 minutes

Serves: 2

Ingredients

200g long grain rice, cooked and chilled

2 teaspoons oil or butter

2 eggs

1 onion or 2 scallions

50g mushrooms

25g frozen peas

Salt and black pepper

2 tablespoons soy sauce

Garnish: flat-leaf parsley or coriander is best

Equipment

plate, sharp knife, board, large frying pan (non stick) or wok, tablespoon, 2 wooden spoons, fork, serving dish.

Chef's Tip!
This is a tasty way of using leftovers. Use cold rice for salads and fried rice. Reheat, covered in a microwave (2 minutes).

Idea!
Add cooked shrimps, diced ham, diced peppers, sweetcorn.

Shredding rolled-up omelette

Steps — Method

Gather equipment, collect/weigh ingredients, set worktop.

1 Peel and slice onion finely. Wash mushrooms and slice. Wash and chop herbs.

2 Beat eggs, salt and pepper.

3 Heat oil or butter in frying pan or wok. Add eggs and fry quickly like an omelette (see page 76) until nicely set. Remove to a plate, roll-up like a swiss roll and shred finely (see diagram on left).

4 Sauté onions and mushrooms using two wooden spoons for 5 minutes.

5 Add peas and sauté for 2 minutes. Remove and place on plate with egg.

6 Add rice to pan, stir-fry over a high heat for 2 minutes.

7 Add vegetables, shredded egg and soy sauce. Stir for 1 minute.

8 Season, pile onto serving dish. Clean dish of any stray rice.

Garnish with parsley or coriander and serve.

Variation

Gluten-free: Soy sauce contains gluten, instead use Tamari sauce. Always read the label.

Vegan: Omit butter and eggs. Use 25g of cashew nuts instead.

RISOTTO

ITALY

Cooking Time: 40 minutes

Serves: 2-3

Ingredients

2 streaky rashers

1 large chicken fillet

1 medium onion

1 clove garlic

1 green pepper

1 red pepper

3 tablespoons olive oil

200g long grain or arborio rice (see Chef's Tip)

500ml stock

100g mushrooms

1 level teaspoon salt

Black pepper

Garnish: 50g cheese (Emmental, fresh Parmesan or mild Cheddar), parsley

Equipment

sharp knife, board, large saucepan with lid, garlic crusher, wooden spoon, measuring jug, kitchen paper, scissors, grater, pot stand.

Chef's Tip!

Italian 'Arborio' rice is best for risotto as it gives a nice, creamy texture. This recipe uses white long grain rice as it is much easier to find in the shops.

Steps — Method

Gather equipment, collect/weigh ingredients, set worktop.

1. Peel, slice and dice onion finely. Peel and crush garlic.
2. Cut pepper, deseed, wash, dry and dice finely. Put a little aside for garnish. Wash and slice mushrooms.
3. Wash, dry and dice chicken fillet into 2cm pieces.
4. Derind the rasher and snip into small pieces. Make stock.
5. Heat oil in saucepan and fry rashers until beginning to brown.
6. Add onions, soften for 1 minute. Add chicken, fry for 3 minutes.
7. Add peppers, mushrooms, garlic, rice and stir over the heat until the rice is covered with oil. Add stock and bring to the boil, stirring all the time.
8. Reduce heat, cover tightly and simmer gently for 25 minutes until the rice is soft and all the stock has been absorbed. Stir the bottom of pot often to prevent sticking. Add hot water if necessary, 50ml at a time.
9. Wash, dry and chop parsley for garnish. Grate the cheese or use Parmesan shavings. Taste the risotto, correct the seasoning and add salt if required.

Serve hot sprinkled with cheese and parsley.

Accompaniment: Crusty garlic bread or a crispy crudités salad (page 20).

VEGETARIAN NUT AND BEAN RISOTTO

VARIATION

Ingredients

1 x Risotto ingredients (see above) but omit rashers and chicken

50g cashew nuts

125g chick peas, drained

Steps — Method

Follow the Risotto recipe, adding cashew nuts instead of rasher and chickpeas (or beans) instead of chicken.

Chapter 6

Fish is a nutritious and natural resource. Fish oil contains good Omega-3 fatty acids that help the brain to develop and reduce the risk of heart disease. Buy fresh, sustainable seafood and consume it on the day of purchase. It is recommended to eat oily fish, such as salmon, mackerel, trout or tuna at least twice a week.

Fish fillets, darnes or culets are often cooked in a simple way because the flesh is tender and has a delicate flavour. Buy it as fresh as possible. **Poach, grill, fry or roast fish**. Serve it with a sauce (page 42 or 47) or a flavoured mayonnaise (page 39).

To grill or roast: Preheat grill or preheat oven to 220°C/Fan 210°C/Gas Mark 7, line grill or roasting pan with oiled foil. Brush fish with oil or butter, season with pepper and salt, grill or roast for 10-15 minutes depending on thickness. See Kinsale Kebabs on page 107.

To poach: Boil water in saucepan, add 2 teaspoons salt. Add fish, cover and poach on a low heat (the water should barely move). Cook for 6-10 minutes depending on thickness. See **Poaching** page 75.

To fry: Dust fish with flour or dip fish in batter, see page 80.

Key Words and Skills

- flake
- roast
- knead
- sweat
- poach
- accompaniment
- marinate
- preheat
- de-seed
- zest
- sauté
- bake
- parboil
- grill
- steam

Other suitable recipes:

Fish in Batter (page 80), Smoked Seafood Pâté (page 21), Seafood Chowder (page 29).

Evaluation! See pages 223 and 224.

- Did you meet the brief and did you refer to the specific requirements of the task or dish/dishes?
- Discuss the results of your finished dish/dishes including the presentation, colour, taste and texture.
- What aspects were done well and what aspects could be improved?
- Did you correctly cost and budget for all ingredients?

Parmesan Roast Fish with Wedges and Peas

Cooking Time: 20 minutes

Serves: 2

Ingredients

2 x 180g fish fillets (hake or cod)

Salt and pepper

1 tablespoon oil

Topping

2 tablespoons mayonnaise

1 dessertspoon chopped parsley

½ lemon or lime

4 tablespoons white breadcrumbs

2 tablespoons grated Parmesan

To serve: 2 large potatoes

1 tablespoon olive oil

Salt and pepper

50g frozen peas

½ lemon or lime

Equipment

sharp knife, board, grater, tablespoon, teaspoon, small saucepan, sieve, kitchen paper, 2 small bowls, 1 plastic bag, non-stick parchment paper, baking tray, pot stand, shallow ovenproof dish.

Idea!
Use dill in place of parsley – it's delicious!

Chef's Tip!
See instructions for making breadcrumbs, page 119.

Resource Management:
Save fuel and time by roasting potatoes, vegetables and fish in the oven together so that everything can be cooked at the same time.

Steps / Method

Preheat oven to 200°C/Fan 190°C/Gas Mark 6.

Gather equipment, collect/weigh ingredients, set worktop.

1 Scrub potatoes and cut in half. Cut each half lengthways into 4-5 pieces to make wedges, see page 71. Put wedges into a plastic bag with pepper, salt and oil and toss to coat. Microwave for 5 minutes in a plastic bowl covered with a plate (or parboil for 10 minutes and drain). Allow to cool. Place the parchment on the baking tray, spread the potatoes on top. **Roast** on top shelf (see page 71).

2 Oil the ovenproof dish lightly. Wash fish, dry with kitchen paper, place on dish and season with salt and pepper.

3 Wash and halve the lemon or lime. **Grate** the zest from one half, then juice it. **Sprinkle** the juice over the fish. **Slice** the remainder and use for garnish. Wash and chop the parsley. Grate the cheese if necessary, see page 87.

4 Mix the mayonnaise and parsley in a bowl. Spread mixture over the fish with the back of a spoon.

5 Mix the breadcrumbs with cheese, zest, pepper and salt. Spoon this evenly on top of the fish.

6 **Roast** on the second shelf for 15-20 minutes until golden and the fish flakes easily with a fork.

7 **Cook** the peas in boiling water for 5 minutes, drain.

8 Remove fish from oven and rest for 5 minutes before lifting onto the serving plate.

Garnish fish with lemon slices.

Serve with wedges, peas and the salsa from page 43. Use lemony kale salad (page 140) in place of peas.

Variation

Dairy-free: Omit the cheese. Add 1 tablespoon of Dijon mustard to the mayonnaise.

Spanish Salmon or Mackerel Bake

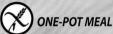

ONE-POT MEAL

Cooking Time: 30 minutes

Serves: 2

Ingredients

2 salmon darnes or 1 mackerel fillet

8-10 baby potatoes

2 tablespoons olive oil

1 onion

1 clove garlic

½ red pepper

130g courgette

1 tin cherry tomatoes

1 teaspoon oregano

¼ teaspoon nutmeg

Salt and pepper

25g Cheddar cheese

Parsley to garnish

Equipment

sharp knife, board, tablespoon, colander, fish slice, deep frying pan or skillet, large ovenproof dish.

Healthy Hint!
This is an economical, one-pot meal suitable for gluten-free and pescatarian diets.

In a hurry!
Use a packet of frozen Mediterranean vegetable mix.

Food Fact!
Oily fish such as salmon, mackerel and trout are rich in healthy Omega-3 oils that are good for the heart.

Steps — Method

Preheat oven to 180°C/Fan 170°C/Gas Mark 5.

Gather equipment, collect/weigh ingredients, set worktop.

1. Wash and scrub potatoes, cut in half or quarters, if necessary. **Parboil** (page 70) for 10 minutes in salted water or **microwave** (page 134) for 6 minutes.
2. Peel and dice the onion and garlic. Wash courgette, dice or slice very thinly. Wash, deseed and dice the pepper finely, see page 124.
3. **Wash and skin the fish**, see page 111. Dry on kitchen paper and remove any bones. Season with salt and pepper.
4. **Sauté:** Heat oil in pan, sauté onion and garlic for 2 minutes (see page 60). Add all the vegetables, tomatoes, oregano, nutmeg, salt and pepper, and simmer gently for 10 minutes.
5. Drain the potatoes. Place into the large ovenproof dish.
6. Pour the vegetable mixture from the pan over the potatoes. Place the fish on top of the potatoes; scatter the cheese over the fish and vegetable mixture.
7. Bake (see **Baking** page 68) for 15-20 minutes or until the fish is cooked and the cheese melted.

Garnish with chopped fresh parsley.

Serve with a green salad.

Variations

Vary the vegetables: Add chopped mushrooms, sliced green beans and celery.

Vary the fish: Use haddock, hake or plaice fillets.

Vary the topping: Use Crunchy Topping from page 113 or mix 30g breadcrumbs in with the cheese.

Kinsale Kebabs

GRILLED
TURKEY, MIDDLE EAST, NORTH AFRICA

Cooking Time: 10 minutes

Serves: 3 kebabs

Ingredients

400g thick white fish fillet or smoked fish

Salt and pepper

1 pepper – orange or red

1 small onion

Marinade

½ lemon, juice and zest

1 tablespoon parsley

2 tablespoons olive oil

2 teaspoons light soy sauce

To serve: 225g boiled rice, couscous or quinoa (page 98)

Garnish: ½ lemon, parsley

Equipment

3 skewers, kitchen paper, sharp knife, board, large bowl, tablespoon, grater with small holes, juice squeezer, teaspoon, foil, brush, pot stand, tongs or 2 forks, serving dish.

Chef's Tip!
Metal skewers are best for kebabs. If wooden ones are to be used, soak first in warm water for 20 minutes so that they won't scorch during cooking.

Kinsale Kebabs, Tandoori Style

Steps **Method**

Gather equipment, collect/weigh ingredients, set worktop.

1 If using wooden skewers, soak them in warm water (see Chef's Tip).

2 Wash fish, dry on kitchen paper, skin. Remove bones. Cut into large chunks. Place on a plate.

3 Wash, zest and juice ½ lemon (see page 150). Wash and chop parsley.

4 **Marinade:** Sprinkle the fish with salt, pepper, lemon juice, parsley, oil and soy sauce. Toss or brush into fish to coat. Marinate for 10 minutes.

5 **Cook rice** as on page 100, couscous or quinoa as on page 98.

6 Skin onion, quarter then separate into layers.

7 Cut pepper lengthways into quarters, deseed, cut each piece across to make two squares. Thread pepper, fish and onion alternately onto skewers. Brush the kebabs with remaining marinade.

8 Preheat grill, see **grilling** on page 127. Remove grid from grill pan, line pan with foil, grease the foil. Place fish on foil and grill for 2 minutes. Turn using tongs or forks.

9 Reduce heat to medium and cook for 5 minutes until fish is cooked.

Garnish with lemon wedges and parsley.

Serve on a bed of rice with the juices from the grill pan accompanied by grilled pepper salsa (page 43), coleslaw (page 49) or a crisp green salad (page 50).

Tandoori Kebabs

MARINADE VARIATION

Ingredients

Omit soy sauce in marinade, and replace with 3 teaspoons Tandoori spice mix.

Steps **Method**

Follow the recipe for kebabs and add the spices with the oil at Step 4.
Serve with rice (page 100) or couscous (page 98) with a salsa (page 43), yoghurt dressing or raita (page 129).

Quick Light Fish Curry

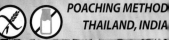

POACHING METHOD
THAILAND, INDIA

Cooking Time: 15 minutes

Serves: 3

Ingredients

400g chunky fish fillet
1 tablespoon olive oil

Base Sauce

1 onion
1 clove garlic
3cm fresh root ginger
½ red pepper
50g mangetout
200ml coconut milk
2 teaspoons cornflour
Salt and pepper
¼ cucumber
Small bunch fresh coriander or parsley
1 green apple, diced
6 cherry tomatoes
2-3 teaspoons Thai green curry paste
or
3 teaspoons mild curry powder

To serve: rice, see page 100

Equipment

sharp knife, board, vegetable peeler, teaspoon, tablespoon, wooden spoon, grater, measuring jug, 2 plates, kitchen paper, sieve, 2 medium saucepans and pot stands, 2 bowls to serve.

Buy Local, Buy Irish!
Choose good-quality, in season, organic produce when possible.

Steps — Method

Gather equipment, collect/weigh ingredients, set worktop.

1 Cook the rice using cooking method 1 on page 100.

2 Wash the fish and dry using kitchen paper. **Remove skin** and bones, see page 111. Cut fish into cubes and season well using pepper and salt. Wash and chop the coriander or parsley as on page 70.

3 Peel the ginger and grate. Peel and finely dice the onion, apple and cucumber. Wash, **deseed** and **dice** the pepper as on page 128. Wash and slice the mangetout.

4 Warm the oil in a saucepan. Add the curry powder **or** Thai curry paste and gently cook for 1 minute. Stir in the pepper, ginger, onion and garlic. Allow to sauté for 2 minutes.

5 Mix the cornflour and coconut milk together and add to the saucepan of vegetables. Simmer gently for 2 minutes and stir. Add the fish, apple, cucumber, tomato, mangetout and half the chopped coriander. Cover and allow **poach** (see page 75) very gently for 5 minutes until the fish is just cooked. Turn off heat.

6 Check rice, drain if necessary.

Serve the curry and rice in two separate bowls.

Garnish with coriander or basil. Serve with naan bread and fresh green salad.

Chef's Tip!
Add the juice of ½ a lemon or lime for a sharp taste. Serve with the zest sprinkled on top.

In a hurry!
Try noodles instead of rice and use freeze-dried ginger if there is no fresh ginger available.

Creamy Leek and Fish Pie

ONE-POT MEAL
FRESH OR SMOKED FISH

Cooking Time: 40 minutes

Serves: 4

ngredients

500g smoked cod, haddock or coley with the skin removed

Sauce

25g butter

1 tablespoon vegetable oil

1 large leek

1 onion

25g flour

250ml milk

Salt and pepper

½ lemon, zest and juice

2 teaspoons Dijon mustard

75g frozen peas

Topping

450g baby potatoes

Knob butter or oil

Salt and pepper

Garnish: ½ lemon, fresh parsley

quipment

harp knife, board, tablespoon, ›lastic bowl, plate, teaspoon, vooden spoon, grater, spatula, 1 nedium saucepan, 1 pot stand, ›venproof pie dish.

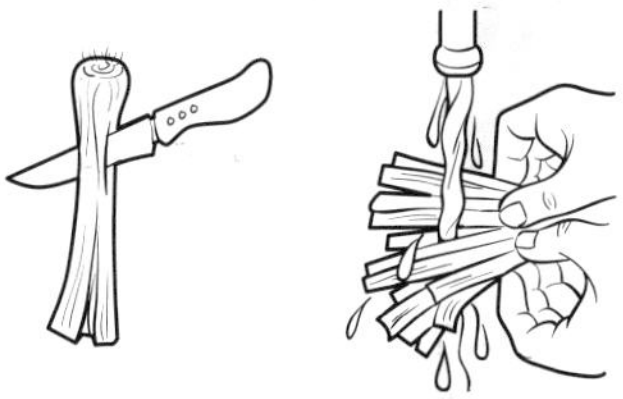

Preparing and washing a leek

Idea!
Add 2 sliced, hard-boiled eggs at Step 5 with the fish.

Steps — Method

Preheat oven to 190°C/Fan 180°C/Gas Mark 5-6.

Gather equipment, collect/weigh ingredients, set worktop.

1 **Diced Potato Topping:** Wash and dice potatoes and put in plastic bowl. Add knob of butter, salt and pepper, cover with a plate and microwave for 2 minutes. Then, stir, microwave for further 3 minutes and allow to stand, see page 134.

2 Wash and zest ½ the lemon, (page 150) then juice. Wash fish and dry using kitchen paper. Skin and bone (page 111) if necessary and cut into 3cm chunks.

3 Trim part but not all of the strong green top from the leek, and make two long cuts through the leaves from the root end to the green ends – see diagram. Wash between all the leaves in fresh, cold water. Shake to dry, and slice each into 1cm slices. Peel and dice onion.

4 **Sauce:** Heat oil and butter in saucepan, sauté the onion and leek until soft for 5 minutes. Stir in the flour, pepper and salt and continue to cook for 1 minute. Remove from heat and stir in the peas. Slowly stir in the milk, gradually beating out all the lumps. Bring to the boil while stirring. Simmer for 5 minutes to cook and thicken.

5 Add the lemon juice, zest and mustard to the sauce. Add the fish to the sauce and stir once to coat.

6 Pour the sauce and fish into the casserole dish, using a spatula. Spoon the diced potato over the pie and season with salt and pepper. Bake for 15-20 minutes and use a skewer to check if the fish and potato are soft.

Garnish with lemon slices and parsley.

Serve with a lettuce and tomato salad.

In a hurry!
For topping use ½ packet (100g) of thawed pastry and follow the method in Steps 2 and 3 on page 61, Ratatouille Pastry Pie.

Chef's Tip!
Coeliacs could thicken this sauce with cornflour instead of wheat and omit the mustard.

Thai Fish Cakes

FRYING METHOD
THIS RECIPE USES A FOOD PROCESSOR

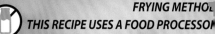

Cooking Time: 10 minutes

Serves: 4

Ingredients

400g thick white fish fillet
50g green beans
1 clove garlic
Grated zest 1 lime or lemon
2 slices white bread
2 teaspoons red curry paste
1 tablespoon Thai fish sauce (nam pla)
1 egg
Few coriander leaves
Oil for frying
Garnish: coriander, rocket leaves or parsley

Equipment

food processor, sharp knife, board, tablespoon, teaspoon, spatula, grater with small holes, frying pan, pot stand, fish slice, serving platter.

Chef's Tip!
Use Thai green curry paste for a 'cooler' taste and a change of flavour.

Thai Fish Cakes and 'Bites' with Fresh Tomato Sauce

Steps **Method**

Gather equipment, collect/weigh ingredients, set worktop.

1 Assemble and plug in the food processor.
2 Peel the garlic, grate the zest from lime or lemon.
3 Cut the bread into pieces. Wash the beans and cut finely.
4 Wash, skin and remove bones from fish, put into processor with the beans, egg, bread, zest, curry paste, fish sauce and garlic. Put on the cover. Buzz a few times to chop and mix all ingredients.
5 Turn onto a plate. Clean out the processor with a spatula.
6 Heat the oil. Wet hands and form the fish mix into 8 even-sized cakes. Place directly onto pan. Fry on both sides until golden and cooked through. Drain on kitchen paper.

Garnish with coriander leaves or parsley.

Serve with rice (pages 100/101) and a salsa (page 43) or sweet chilli sauce (page 45) and a green salad.

Food Fact!
Nam pla or fish sauce is an essential ingredient in Thai and Vietnamese cooking. It is a fermentation of small fish and is quite salty but nicely pungent. Use Soy sauce as an alternative.

Cocktail Fish Bites

VARIATION

Ingredients

Use basic Thai Fish Cakes ingredients

Equipment

deep-fat fryer and oil, slotted spoon.

Steps **Method**

Follow Steps 1-5 above. Form the fish mix into 14-16 small balls (see diagram on page 117). **Deep-fat fry** (page 80) until just golden. Spear with cocktail sticks and serve with a dipping sauce or salsa (page 43) or Tahini Sauce, page 141.

***FRYING** COOKING TERM

Frying can be deep or shallow. Food is in direct contact with hot fat or oil at a temperature between 150°C and 195°C. Food should be dry before frying, see page 80.

QUICK FISH FRITTATA 🗝

ITALY

Cooking Time: 40 minutes

Serves: 4-6

Ingredients

- 400g white fish fillet or smoked fish
- Sea salt and pepper
- 1 potato
- 2 tablespoons oil
- 1 small onion
- 100g frozen peas
- 100g sweetcorn
- 4 medium eggs
- 1 clove garlic
- **Garnish:** 1 tomato, chives

Equipment

sharp knife, board, potato peeler, whisk, medium frying pan, tablespoon, pot stand, wooden spoon, scissors, medium bowl, grill, serving dish.

Chef's Tip!
To turn a frittata: Turn the frittata out onto an oiled plate, heat 1 tablespoon oil on the pan and then slip the frittata back onto the pan to cook the second side.

To skin a fish:
Hold skin in one hand and use salt to help you grip. Hold the knife at a 45° angle. Use a sawing action to cut flesh from the skin while pushing away from you.

Steps — Method

Gather equipment, collect/weigh ingredients, set worktop.

1. Wash and skin fish, remove bones, cut into cubes, sprinkle with salt.
2. Wash, peel, halve and slice potato **very thinly**.
3. Peel onion and garlic, dice finely.
4. Heat 1 tablespoon oil in frying pan, add potato, cook on medium heat for 5 minutes. Stir from time to time.
5. Add onion and garlic, cook for 5 minutes. Add peas and sweetcorn, cook for 5 minutes. Season with salt and pepper.
6. Beat eggs, mix in the fish and all vegetables from pan and stir.
7. Heat 1 tablespoon oil in frying pan, turn egg mix into the pan, spread out the ingredients evenly. Lower heat and continue cooking slowly for 15 minutes. **It shouldn't burn underneath.**
8. Heat grill, put the frittata under grill to cook the top or turn, (see Chef's Tip). Wash and slice tomato for garnish. Slide out of pan onto a plate. Cut into wedges.

Garnish with sliced tomatoes and fresh snipped chives.

Serve with a salad and fresh bread or rolls.

Variations using 🗝 recipe for Frittata

Vegetarian: Add a drained tin of cooked beans instead of fish. Use butter beans, black eye beans, flageolet beans or a tin of mixed beans. Sauté 100g mushrooms with the onions for added flavour. Top with cheese to increase protein.

Coeliacs, Wheat or Milk Allergies: This recipe is suitable for people with milk or wheat allergies. Serve with red or green rice (page 101), rice salad (page 55) or baked potatoes (pages 68/69).

Resource Management: Upcycle Leftovers. Use cooked meats or sausage instead of fresh fish in this recipe. The vegetables can be varied also, try adding cooked broccoli or mangetout, sautéd to soften before adding to the egg.

Dingle Quiche

Cooking Time: 40-45 minutes

Serves: 4

Ingredients

Pastry

100g flour

Salt

50g butter

Cold water

Filling

300g fish fillet (fresh, smoked or a mixture)

Oil to grease tin

1 tomato

25g mild cheese

1 tablespoon oil

2 eggs

Sea salt, pepper

Large pinch nutmeg

150ml milk

Garnish: parsley

Equipment

mixing bowl, knife, fork, measuring jug, pot stand, baking tray, rolling pin, sharp knife, board, grater with large holes, plate, 20cm quiche tin, whisk, serving dish.

Dingle Quiche *Salmon and Broccoli Quiche*

Steps — Method

Preheat oven to 170°C/Fan 160°C/Gas Mark 4.

Gather equipment, collect/weigh ingredients, set worktop.

1. **Pastry:** Make Shortcrust pastry (see page 167). Chill.
2. **Filling:** Wash fish, place on a greased baking tray skin side up, bake for 10-15 minutes.
3. Wash and dice tomato. Grate cheese using large holes on grater.
4. Beat eggs, milk, pepper, salt and nutmeg.
5. Remove fish from oven. Remove skin and bones and then flake. Add to eggs with the cheese and tomatoes and stir gently.
6. Roll pastry and line quiche tin. Do not stretch. Trim. Place on a baking tray. Pour egg mixture into pastry case. Bake on the baking tray for 30 minutes until golden brown and set.

Garnish with a sprig of parsley.

Serve with a colourful fresh salad or some green vegetable accompaniments from page 140.

Salmon and Broccoli Quiche

VARIATION

Ingredients

1 x 100g Shortcrust pastry (page 167)

Use 200g salmon fillet instead of white fish and 100g broccoli (fresh or frozen) instead of tomato.

Use all other filling ingredients.

Steps — Method

Blanch the broccoli florets first in boiling, salted water for 5 minutes. Drain and chop roughly. Continue to make and cook as in the quiche recipe above.

Chef's Tip!
Spinach is also good instead of broccoli in this recipe.

Buy Local, Buy Irish!
Buy free-range eggs.

In a hurry!
Use ½ packet or 150g frozen shortcrust pastry, thawed.

Crunchy Seafood Pasta

Cooking Time: 30 minutes

Serves: 3

Ingredients

- 400g thick fish fillet (cod, salmon, smoked cod or coley)
- 100g pasta
- ½ onion
- 1 red pepper
- 25g butter
- 75g cheese, grated
- 2 eggs
- 250ml milk
- 1 dessertspoon wholegrain mustard
- 1 dessertspoon parsley
- Salt and pepper

Crunchy Topping

- 25g butter, melted
- 50g cornflakes, crushed

Garnish: sprig fresh parsley

Equipment

sharp knife, board, 2 saucepans, bowl, grater, fork, whisk, colander, kettle, ovenproof dish.

Idea!
The topping can be varied. Try 50g grated cheese and 50g breadcrumbs mixed or use a packet of cheese and onion crisps instead of cornflakes.

Steps — Method

Preheat oven to 180°C/Fan170°C/Gas Mark 5.

Gather equipment, collect/weigh ingredients, set worktop.

1. Boil water in kettle. Pour boiling water into saucepan, add pasta and 2 teaspoons salt. Boil gently for 10 minutes. Grease ovenproof dish.
2. Wash fish, put into saucepan skin side up (cut to fit if necessary). Barely cover with boiling water and poach very gently for 3-4 minutes. Cover and remove from heat. Set aside.
3. Wash, deseed and dice the pepper finely, peel and grate the onion. Grate the cheese. Wash and chop parsley.
4. Drain fish, gently remove the skin and any bones using a knife and fork. Drain the pasta.
5. Melt butter in saucepan, sauté onion and pepper for 2-3 minutes.
6. Using a large bowl, whisk eggs, milk, mustard, parsley and seasoning. Add the pasta, fish, cheese, onion and red pepper and mix very gently. Spoon into a buttered ovenproof dish.
7. **Crunchy Topping:** Melt butter, add crushed cornflakes and mix. Sprinkle over the pasta mix. Bake for 20-25 minutes until just browned and crunchy.

Garnish with a sprig of fresh parsley.

Serve with a green salad (page 50).

Crunchy Tuna or Chicken Pasta

VARIATION

Ingredients

Use 1 tin tuna or 200g cooked chicken pieces instead of fish.

Follow recipe above. Omit Steps 2 and 4.

Resource Management: Buy sustainable and responsibly sourced fish. Store fish covered in the fridge. Fish is best used on the day of purchase.

Chapter 7 Meat

Irish beef and lamb are prized throughout the world because the animals are mostly grass fed and reared outdoors. When possible, buy Irish meat and poultry products that carry the Bord Bia Quality Assurance label. Always check the date stamp and choose the correct cut of meat for the dish being cooked and the method of cooking. Cover raw meat and store in the fridge on the bottom shelf to prevent cross-contamination. Use within 2/3 days.

Key Words and Skills

- stew
- de-rind
- grill
- cross-contaminate
- reheat
- sear

Other suitable recipes:

Chicken and Pasta Bake (page 89), Bolognese Sauce (page 90), Lasagne (page 92), Chicken Picasso (page 96), Crunchy Chicken Pasta (page 113), Chicken or Lamb Korma (page 139).

Evaluation! See pages 223 and 224.

- Did you meet the brief and did you refer to the specific requirements of the task or dish/dishes?
- Discuss the results of your finished dish/dishes including the presentation, colour, taste and texture
- What aspects were done well and what aspects could be improved?
- Did you correctly cost and budget for all ingredients?

Beef Stew (or Casserole)

TRADITIONAL

Cooking Time:
Stew 1-2 hours
Casserole 2 hours

Serves: 3-4

Ingredients

- 400g round or rib beef
- 1 large onion
- 2 carrots
- 1 clove garlic, crushed
- 1 stick celery (optional)
- 1 tablespoon oil
- 25g flour or cornflour
- 400ml stock or water
- 1 teaspoon Worcestershire sauce
- 1 teaspoon tomato purée (optional)
- Salt and pepper
- **To serve:** potatoes
- **Garnish:** fresh parsley

Equipment

sharp knife, board, vegetable peeler, teaspoon, wooden spoon, heavy saucepan with tight-fitting lid, wire whisk, draining spoon, casserole dish to serve.

Chef's Tip!
"A stew boiled is a stew spoiled". Use a wooden spoon to sauté as it doesn't get too hot and it is safer. It is also used with non-stick saucepans and frying pans.

Cutting meat

Steps **Method**

Preheat oven to 170°C/Fan 160°C/Gas Mark 3-4.

Gather equipment, collect/weigh ingredients, set worktop.

1 Wash vegetables, peel thinly, slice. Put aside. Wipe meat, trim fat, cut into cubes.
2 Heat oil in saucepan on high heat, brown ½ the meat quickly. Remove to a plate and repeat with remaining meat.
3 Sauté onion for 2 minutes, reduce the heat and add flour or cornflour. Stir to absorb the fat. Remove from heat.
4 Whisk in the stock, purée and seasoning and bring to the boil (to thicken), stirring with a wooden spoon.
5 Add vegetables and meat and **stew*** very gently with a tight lid until meat is tender – about 1 hour (minimum).
6 Stir occasionally to prevent sticking or turn into a casserole dish, cover and cook in oven for 2 hours.
7 Scrub the chopping board to prevent cross-contamination.
8 Prepare the accompaniment.
9 When meat is tender, correct the seasoning.

Serve with mashed potatoes (page 64).

Garnish with chopped fresh parsley.

Reheating of stew must be thoroughly done. This will take 15-20 minutes in a microwave or 30-40 minutes in a hot oven.

***STEWING** — COOKING METHOD

Stewing means long, slow cooking of food at 85°C to 90°C in a small amount of liquid in a tightly-covered saucepan or casserole. Stewing tenderises meat by slowly converting the white connective tissue called collagen into gelatine. The addition of an acid, e.g. tomatoes, purée, lemon juice, cider or wine, will speed up this process.

Irish Stew

TRADITIONAL ONE-POT MEAL

Cooking Time: 1 hour minimum

Serves: 3

Ingredients

- 400g gigot lamb chops
- 1 large onion
- 2 carrots (optional)
- 1 stick celery (optional)
- 500ml water or stock
- 1 sprig fresh thyme or ¼ teaspoon dried thyme
- 1 tablespoon fresh parsley with stalks or 2 teaspoons dried parsley
- 1 level teaspoon salt
- Pepper
- 6 potatoes
- **Garnish:** fresh parsley

Equipment

sharp knife, board, vegetable peeler, heavy saucepan with tight-fitting lid, teaspoon, wooden spoon, casserole dish to serve.

Chef's Tip!

This is a quick method for making Irish stew. Cooking for longer greatly improves the flavour and tenderises the meat. Remember, a stew boiled is a stew spoiled.

Watch Out!

Reheating of stew must be thoroughly done. This will take 15-20 minutes in a microwave or 30-40 minutes in a hot oven.

Buy Local, Buy Irish!

Support local farmers.

Steps — Method

Gather equipment, collect/weigh ingredients, set worktop.

1 Wipe meat, trim fat but not bone, cut into large pieces.

2 Put into saucepan, add salt, pepper, thyme, chopped parsley and the water or stock. Cover and begin cooking on a moderate heat.

3 Wash potatoes and peel thinly. Dice 2 potatoes very finely and add to pot. Quarter the other 4 potatoes and add to pot.

4 Peel and slice the onion. Wash and slice carrots and celery if using. Add to the pot, stir and bring to the boil. Lower heat, cover and **simmer** (see page 29) for 1 hour (minimum) until tender.

5 When meat is tender, lift potatoes onto a serving dish. Give the stew a good stir to break up the chopped potatoes to thicken the sauce.

6 Thicken with a little instant potato powder (*Smash*) if it is too watery. Stir in only one teaspoon at a time.

Serve in a casserole dish garnished with chopped, fresh parsley.

Dumplings are also good with this (see page 117).

Healthy Hint!

Include more fresh vegetables in your diet. You can add extra carrots, celery, leeks and parsnips to stews.

In a hurry!

Cook stews in pressure cooker at high pressure for 15 minutes but reduce the water/stock by half. Always follow the instructions for using your pressure cooker.

Lamb Hot Pot

VARIATION – ENGLAND

Cooking Time: 1-1½ hours

Serves: 3

Ingredients

1 x Irish Stew ingredients (page 116)
25g flour or cornflour
25g butter/oil
To serve:
fresh parsley, chopped

Equipment

casserole dish with cover.

Potatoes overlapping in casserole

Steps	Method

Preheat oven to 190°C/Fan 180°C/Gas Mark 5.

1 Wipe meat, trim and cut into cubes. Toss in flour, put into casserole with the sliced onion, carrot, celery and the 2 finely-diced potatoes.

2 Slice the 4 remaining potatoes very thinly and arrange them 'overlapping' over the casserole. Add water or stock, dot with butter, season well, cover, cook in oven for 1-1½ hours until meat is tender.

3 Remove cover and brown the top (use the grill if in a hurry).

Serve with lots of chopped, fresh parsley. This reheats well.

Dumplings

ONE-POT MEAL

Ingredients

80g self-raising flour
Large pinch salt, pepper
35g butter
1 teaspoon parsley
¼ teaspoon thyme
1 sliced onion (optional)
1 small egg, beaten

Chef's Tip!
Dumplings are easy to make and are delicious to serve instead of potatoes.

Steps	Method

1 Wash and chop parsley finely. Peel and dice onion finely.

2 Sieve flour, rub in butter. Add salt, pepper, parsley, thyme and onion. Add enough beaten egg to bind and form a stiff dough.

3 Shape into 8-10 small balls, carefully put into the simmering stew for last 20 minutes. Do not stir. Cover and cook for 20 minutes until swollen.

4 Lift onto a plate. Serve around any stew or ragoût.

Variation

Gluten-free: Use cornflour to thicken and gluten-free breadcrumbs for dumplings.

Idea!
Cook dumplings in simmering stock, soup or water for use with other meals.

Resource Management: Stews freeze and reheat well. To Freeze: Place in suitable casserole or container. Cool. Seal, label and freeze. To Reheat: If frozen, allow to thaw and then reheat, covered in a moderate oven for 30 minutes until heated through to the middle.

BURGERS

USA

Cooking Time: 20 minutes

Serves: 4 burgers

Ingredients

400g lean minced beef, lamb or turkey

1 small onion

½ teaspoon salt

Pepper

1 teaspoon chopped parsley

¼ teaspoon dried thyme

1 teaspoon tomato ketchup or soy sauce

1 tablespoon breadcrumbs (optional)

1 tablespoon cooking oil

Garnish: Select some from this list – lettuce, tomato, coleslaw, cheese, tomato ketchup or mayonnaise.

To serve: 4 sesame buns

Equipment

sharp knife, board, medium bowl, teaspoon, tablespoon, fish slice or tongs, grill pan, frying pan, serving dish.

Idea!
Use polythene disposable gloves to shape the meat.

Chef's Tip!
Always cook mince quickly and thoroughly. There must be no trace of 'pink' as it can cause food poisoning.

Idea!
When shaping, place a cube of cheese into the centre of the burger. Seal all around and cook.

Dressed Burger

Steps **Method**

Preheat grill if using. (It is better to grill rather than fry.)

Gather equipment, collect/weigh ingredients, set worktop.

1 Peel onion and dice very finely or grate.

2 Combine all ingredients. Use the tablespoon to cut through the meat and blend the mixture well.

3 Wet hands and divide the meat into four portions. Shape into flat discs or shape using a little flour or cornflour. The burgers should be flat in the centre and the same diameter as the buns. This allows the centres to be thoroughly cooked.

4 Cover grill rack with oiled tinfoil to prevent burgers sticking to it. Heat the **grill** (page 127) or heat the oil in a frying pan, put the burgers onto pan or grill pan. See shallow frying on page 119.

5 Wash your hands and **all** utensils immediately in hot soapy water.

6 Use a moderate heat to cook burgers for about 8-10 minutes each side or until all traces of 'pink' are gone from the centre of the burgers. Check by cutting through the middle and looking inside.

7 Wash utensils to prevent cross contamination of harmful bacteria.

Serve in a soft sesame bun.

Garnish the burger according to taste.

Watch Out!
Minced meat can harbour micro-organisms that can cause illness, e.g. E.coli 0157. Keep meats CLEAN, COLD and COVERED and use within one day of purchase. Wash hands and all utensils thoroughly after use. Separate cooked meats from uncooked ones to avoid cross contamination.

Curry or Pesto Burgers

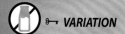

VARIATION

Ingredients

1 x Burgers ingredients (page 118)

1-2 heaped teaspoons curry paste or powder **or** 2 teaspoons green or red pesto

Look Up! Umami.

Buy Local, Buy Irish! Look for a Bord Bia Quality Assurance label when buying meat.

Curry Burgers

Meatballs

Steps **Method**

1 Make burger mixture (page 118).

2 Add curry paste or powder or pesto to the mince mixture and continue as for burger recipe. This is very tasty made with minced lamb.

Serve with naan bread and a salad tossed with Raita (page 129).

Meatballs

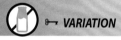

VARIATION

Ingredients

Use ½ the quantity of the Burgers ingredients (page 118)

Healthy Hint! Enhance your dishes by using natural alternatives to salt, such as ginger, herbs and spices. Too much salt in a diet can be bad for your health, blood pressure, heart, brain and kidneys.

Steps **Method**

1 Make burger mixture (Steps 1 and 2, page 118).

2 Shape the mince mixture into 8 even-sized balls. Fry or grill until thoroughly cooked.

Serve with a sauce of your choice, e.g. tomato, curry, barbecue or sweet and sour. The type of sauce should complement the meat used.

Make breadcrumbs from leftover bread

Food processor: Use pulse action to make breadcrumbs. To make stuffing in one go, add the following ingredients: parsley, chopped nuts and sautéed onion.

Liquidiser: Drop small bits of bread onto the running blades through the opening in the lid. Make in small batches so the blades won't clog.

Grate or crumble stale bread into crumbs by rubbing down on a sharp metal grater.

If buying pre-made breadcrumbs check the date and refrigerate.

See how to use liquidisers, processors, bullets and blenders on page 15.

Resource Management: Freeze breadcrumbs for later use. See page 154.

SHALLOW FRYING

COOKING METHOD

Use the minimum amount of oil and always heat the pan and oil first. Dry the food, fry the food on each side, turning down the heat so that the oil doesn't smoke, burn or go on fire. Do not stir continuously so that the food can brown. Drain on kitchen paper.

SAVOURY MINCE

Cooking Time: 20-30 minutes

Serves: 3-4

Ingredients

- 200g minced beef
- 2 tablespoons oil
- 1 small onion
- 1 carrot
- 2 tablespoons frozen peas (optional)
- 50g mushrooms
- 1 clove garlic
- Salt and pepper
- 25g flour or cornflour
- 1 tin chopped tomatoes
- 1 level teaspoon sugar
- 100ml water or stock
- 1 teaspoon fresh herbs
- 1 teaspoon ketchup
- **Garnish**: 1 tomato, parsley

Equipment

tablespoon, teaspoon, sharp knife, board, saucepan, pot stand, wooden spoon, serving dish.

Chef's Tip!
Quorn (see Food Fact, page 90) or all varieties of minced meats can be used, e.g. beef, lamb, pork, chicken and turkey.

Savoury Mince and Pastry-Topped Pie

Steps **Method**

Gather equipment, collect/weigh ingredients, set worktop.

1 Peel and grate carrot. Peel and dice onion. Wash and slice mushrooms. Peel and crush garlic.

2 Heat oil, fry (page 119) meat on one side for 5 minutes. Turn over, add onions, continue to fry for 5 minutes. Do not stir too often, as the meat and onion need to brown slightly to develop a good flavour.

3 Add carrot, mushrooms, garlic, salt and pepper and cook for 2 minutes.

4 Stir in flour, remove from heat. Add all the remaining ingredients.

5 Bring to the boil, stirring all the time. Add more water to make a juicy consistency if necessary.

6 Lower heat, cover and simmer for 15 minutes.

Garnish with chopped parsley and tomato wedges.

Serve with mashed potatoes (page 64) or baked potatoes (pages 68/69), boiled rice (page 100), pasta (page 84) or quinoa (page 98).

Chef's Tip!
This dish can be easily modified for gluten-free diets.

PASTRY-TOPPED SAVOURY MINCE

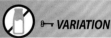

VARIATION

Ingredients

- 1 x Savoury Mince ingredients
- 100g frozen puff pastry (thawed)

Steps **Method**

1 Make Savoury Mince as above. Turn into a greased casserole.

2 Roll out pastry, cover pie with puff pastry, decorate with pastry leaves (page 121), egg wash and bake for 40 minutes at 190°C/Fan 180°C/Gas Mark 5.

Serve with a fresh salad.

Shepherd's Pie

VARIATION

Serves: 3

Ingredients

1 x Mashed Potato (page 64)

1 x Savoury Mince (page 120)

Milk

Equipment

pastry brush, casserole dish.

Piping potato on top

Brushing pie with milk

Shepherd's Pie *Cottage Pie*

Steps **Method**

Preheat oven to 180°C/Fan 170°C/Gas Mark 4.

1 Cook and mash potatoes (page 64) to a very soft consistency.

2 Make Savoury Mince and turn into a greased casserole dish.

3 Using a teaspoon, spoon the mashed potato on top of the mince. Lightly brush with milk and score with a fork or piped potatoes for a special effect – see diagram.

4 Brown in oven for 30 minutes.

Garnish with parsley.

Serve with broccoli or minted peas.

Idea! For the topping, replace mashed potato with mashed sweet potato.

Cottage Pie

VARIATION

Ingredients

1 x Mashed Potato (page 64)

1 x Savoury Mince (page 120)

200g diced mixed vegetables

Steps **Method**

1 Cook and mash potatoes (page 64) to a very soft consistency.

2 Add the diced mixed vegetables to the Savoury Mince recipe at Step 2.

3 Top with mashed potato and bake as for Shepherd's Pie above.

To Make Pastry Leaves

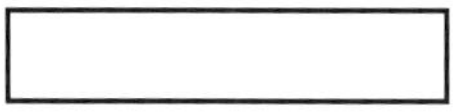

Roll pastry into thin strips

Cut at an angle

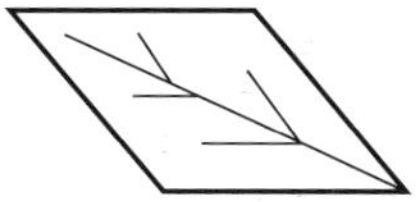

Mark with a knife

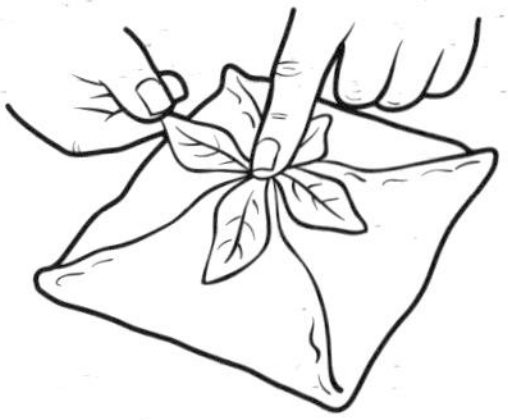

Pastry leaves

Chilli Con Carne

MEXICO

Cooking Time: 30 minutes

Serves: 3-4

Ingredients

400g minced beef
1 tablespoon oil
1 medium onion
2 cloves garlic
1 green or red pepper
1 tin chopped tomatoes
1 level teaspoon sugar
Salt and pepper
1 teaspoon chilli powder or 1 fresh chilli
2 teaspoons tomato purée
½ tin red kidney beans or baked beans
To serve: rice (page 100)
Garnish: 1 tomato, fresh parsley or coriander

Equipment

sharp knife, board, garlic crusher, tablespoon, wooden spoon, teaspoon, large saucepan, tight lid, tin opener, serving dish.

Chef's Tip!
Use 'unflavoured' tins of tomatoes as the flavour is more authentic.

Steps **Method**

Gather equipment, collect/weigh ingredients, set worktop.

1 Peel and dice onion. Peel and crush garlic. Wash, deseed and slice pepper and fresh chilli if using.

2 Heat oil, fry onion until just golden. Add garlic and pepper and stir for 2 minutes.

3 Add mince, fry on medium heat until there is no raw pink colour.

4 Add chopped tomatoes, sugar, salt, pepper, chilli, tomato purée and kidney beans. Cover and simmer for 20 minutes.

5 Cook the rice (page 100).

6 The chilli sauce should be nice and thick. If not, boil rapidly while stirring for 3 minutes to reduce the liquid.

7 Wash tomato and herb for garnish. Cut tomato into 8 wedges. Chop the parsley or coriander for garnish.

Serve on a bed of rice accompanied by a side salad.

Garnish with fresh herbs and tomato.

Idea!
Serve with 2 tablespoons of natural yoghurt swirled onto the sauce, sprinkled with paprika.

Vegetarian Chilli

VARIATION

Ingredients

1 x Chilli Con Carne ingredients
Use 1 can of mixed beans or lentils instead of beef

Steps **Method**

1 Follow the recipe for Chilli Con Carne but omit Step 3.

2 Drain the beans, add with the other ingredients at Step 4. Simmer gently without lid for 15 minutes.

3 Finish and serve as in the Chilli Con Carne recipe.

Chilli Tacos

VARIATION

Serves: 3-4

Ingredients

- 1 x Chilli Con Carne ingredients (page 122)
- 4-6 taco shells
- 6 leaves shredded lettuce
- 100ml soured cream
- 25g grated mild Cheddar

Idea!
Serve on a bed of rice (pages 100/101).

Chef's Tip!
When using chilli, never touch your face as the juice will burn your skin. If you do, use milk, natural yoghurt or oil to relieve the pain. Use ½ a chilli if you prefer less of the hot spice or use ½ a red pepper instead for colour.

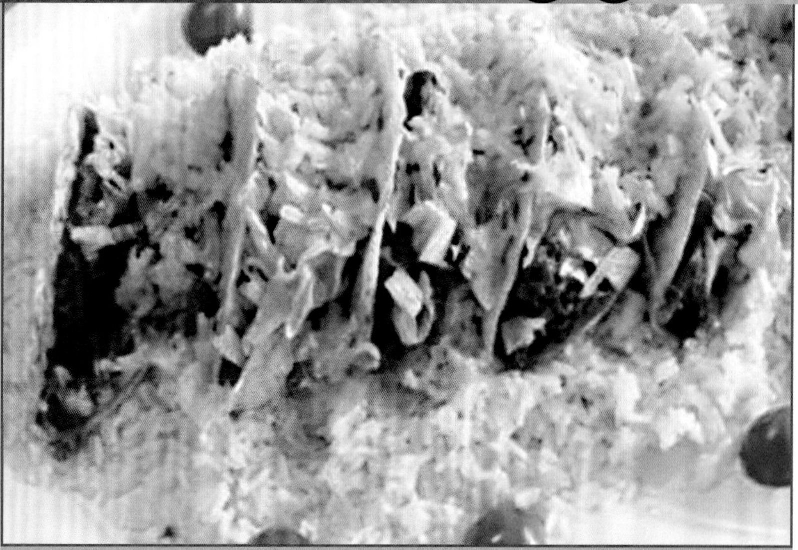

Steps **Method**

1 Follow the recipe for Chilli Con Carne or Vegetarian Chilli.
2 Follow instructions from packet for using tacos or heat in microwave on high for 1 minute.
3 To fill, hold shell in one hand, put in some lettuce, a spoon of chilli and top with soured cream and grated cheese.

Burritos or Enchiladas

VARIATION

Serves: 3-4

Ingredients

- 1 x Chilli Con Carne (page 122)
- 4 large or 8 small soft flour tortillas
- 100g Cheddar cheese
- 100ml crème fraîche

Chef's Tip!
Less meat! Add the whole tin of beans and use less meat.

Buy Local, Buy Irish!
Choose good-quality, in season, organic produce when possible.

Steps **Method**

Preheat oven to 180°C/Fan 170°C/Gas Mark 4.

1 Follow the recipe for Chilli Con Carne or Vegetarian Chilli.
2 Grate cheese using large holes on grater.
3 Follow instructions from packet for rolling up and baking burritos or enchiladas, topped with crème fraîche and grated cheese.

Serve with a salsa (page 43).

Flour Tortillas: Soft Mexican-style flat bread (pancake) made from wheat, used for wrapping around food. Large or small, they are suitable for vegetarians but not for coeliacs.

Taco: This is a Mexican corn tortilla (pancake) that is folded or rolled around a filling. Bought as shells, they can be heated, filled and served.

Tortilla Chips/Corn Chips: These are pieces of corn tortilla or pancake used for dipping into a dip or salsa. They can be plain or flavoured.

Salsa: This is a Mexican chunky sauce. It often contains chilli, coriander and lime juice. Choose a salsa to complement the dish (see page 43).

Chilli-Stuffed Peppers

Cooking Time: 30-40 minutes

Serves: 3-4

Ingredients

400g minced beef
1 tablespoon oil
1 medium onion
2 cloves garlic
4 red or green peppers
1 tin chopped tomatoes
1 level teaspoon sugar
Salt and pepper
1 teaspoon chilli powder or 1 fresh chilli
2 teaspoons tomato purée
½ tin red kidney beans or baked beans
To serve: rice (page 100)
Garnish: 1 tomato, fresh parsley or coriander

Equipment

sharp knife, board, garlic crusher, tablespoon, wooden spoon, teaspoon, large saucepan, tight lid, tin opener, small casserole or ovenproof dish with foil lid.

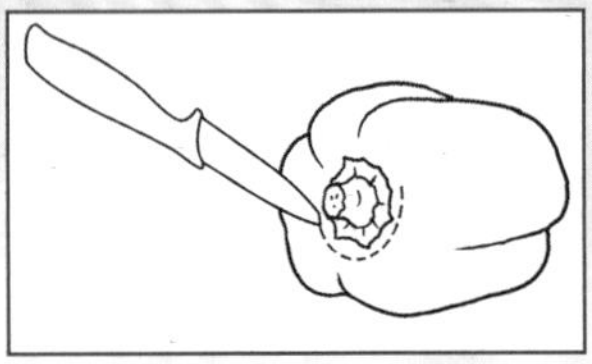

Removing the stalk

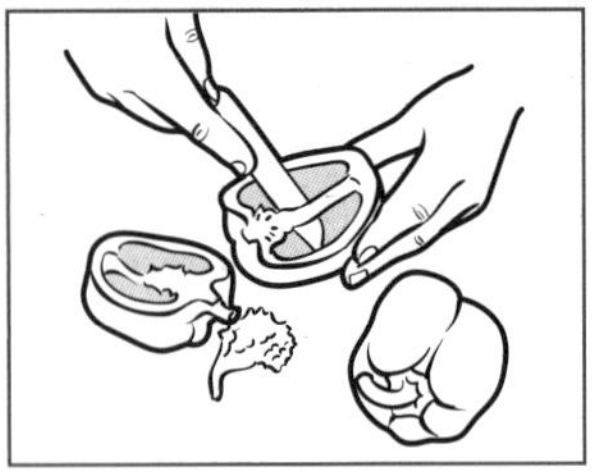

Preparing peppers

Steps **Method**

Preheat oven to 180°C/Fan 170°C/Gas Mark 4.

Gather equipment, collect/weigh ingredients, set worktop.

1 Peel and dice onion. Peel and crush garlic. Wash, deseed and slice pepper and fresh chilli if using (see Chef's Tip on page 123).

2 Heat oil, fry onion until just golden. Add garlic and pepper and stir for 2 minutes.

3 Add mince, fry on medium heat until there is no raw pink colour.

4 Add chopped tomatoes, sugar, salt, pepper, chilli, tomato purée and kidney beans. Cover and simmer for 10 minutes.

5 Cut each pepper in half through stalk from top to bottom. Deseed and wash to remove every seed. See diagrams and Resource Management box.

6 Fill with chilli mixture, sit them in a small casserole, add 3 tablespoons water to the casserole, cover and bake for 30-40 minutes until peppers are soft.

7 Cook the rice (page 100).

Serve on a bed of rice.

Garnish with fresh coriander or parsley.

Healthy Hint!
Chilli dishes are very suitable for women, teenagers and people with anaemia as iron is found in both beef and beans. Vitamin C is found in (a) the capsicum family (peppers and chilli) and (b) lime or lemon juice and fruits as in a salsa. Vitamin C is necessary for the absorption of iron into our bodies.

Resource Management: Buy organic vegetables when possible and wash before use. To reduce waste, prepare peppers carefully removing the centre stalk and hard surround first. Then, halve from top to bottom to remove the membrane and seeds. Store leftovers in the fridge.

Chicken Casserole

Cooking Time: 45-50 minutes

Serves: 4

Ingredients

- 4-6 chicken joints or 3-4 chicken breasts
- 50g bacon/rasher
- 1 onion
- 1 clove garlic
- 2 sticks celery
- 100g mushrooms
- 1 tablespoon oil/fat
- 25g flour or cornflour
- 250ml stock or water
- 1 tin chopped tomatoes
- Salt and pepper
- **To serve:** potatoes, broccoli
- **Garnish:** fresh parsley

Equipment

vegetable peeler, whisk, sharp knife, scissors, board, kitchen paper, pot stand, frying pan, wooden spoon, draining spoon, casserole dish with lid.

Chef's Tip!
Wipe chicken with kitchen paper. It should be cooked quickly and thoroughly with no 'pink' in the flesh or juice (internal temp 80°C). Wash all utensils after use.

Idea!
Chicken joints are very economical and can be substituted in all the recipes given in this section.

Buy Local, Buy Irish!
Choose good-quality, in season, organic produce when possible.

Steps — Method

Preheat oven to 180°C/Fan 170°C/Gas Mark 4.

Gather equipment, collect/weigh ingredients, set worktop.

1 Peel and dice onion and garlic.

2 Wash celery and mushrooms, slice finely. Put aside.

3 Wipe meat with kitchen paper, trim skin but not bone.

4 Derind the bacon and cut into strips.

5 Heat oil and fry bacon for 2 minutes. Add onion and celery and fry for 2 minutes. Add garlic and mushrooms and fry for 1 minute. Remove all to casserole dish with draining spoon. Cover and place in the oven.

6 Fry chicken on both sides over a medium heat until golden. Add to the casserole.

7 Add flour or cornflour to the pan and cook for 1 minute. Remove from heat, stir in stock using a whisk, add the tomatoes, pepper and salt to taste. Boil for 1 minute, pour over chicken, cover and cook for 40–45 minutes.

8 Boil, bake or mash potatoes (pages 64). Prepare garnish.

Garnish with chopped parsley.

Serve with potatoes and steamed broccoli.

Reheating of casserole must be thoroughly done, 15–20 minutes in a microwave or 30–40 minutes in a hot oven.

Watch Out!
Prevent cross-contamination – wash everything very well!

Healthy Baked Chicken or Pork

SALT-FREE

Cooking Time: 1 hour

Serves: 2-3

Ingredients

2-3 chicken fillets/joints or pork chops/sliced pork steak

Basic Marinade (page 107)

2 tablespoons oil

Pepper

½ lemon

1 teaspoon fresh ginger

1 clove garlic

Garnish: lemon

Marinade Variations (optional)

(1) Tandoori Marinade
2 tablespoons yoghurt
1 tablespoon Tandoori spice mix

(2) Paprika Marinade
1 teaspoon paprika
½ teaspoon chilli powder

Equipment

kitchen paper, tongs, sharp knife, scissors, board, grater, garlic crusher, small bowl, shallow casserole dish, pot stand, teaspoon, tablespoon, lemon squeezer, serving dish.

Chef's Tip!
This is lovely served with Cheese and Potato Pie (page 87) or Macaroni Cheese (page 87) and a crisp salad. Never salt the surface of meat before grilling or barbecuing as salt draws out the juices and the meat will not brown well. Brush food with oil before cooking to protect it.

Steps — Method

Preheat oven to 190°C/Fan 180°C/Gas Mark 5-6.

Gather equipment, collect/weigh ingredients, set worktop.

1. **Marinade:** Peel garlic and crush. Peel and grate ginger on medium holes of grater.
2. Juice and zest ½ lemon. Mix oil, lemon juice, zest, pepper, garlic and ginger in a bowl. Add Tandoori or Paprika Marinade ingredients if using and mix well. See marinade technique on page 57.
3. Wash meat, dry and trim skin/fat if necessary. Make shallow cuts in the flesh. Put into bowl with marinade and mix to coat meat. Allow to 'marinate' and absorb the flavours. Refrigerate for 30 minutes.
4. Prepare the accompaniment – rice (page 100), baked potato (page 68) or pasta (page 84).
5. Put meat into greased casserole dish. Bake uncovered for 30 minutes. Turn and continue cooking for another 15–20 minutes. Test by cutting into a thick part to see if it is fully cooked through. (Grill for 5 minutes if not done.)

Garnish with ½ lemon cut into fine wedges.

Serve with green vegetables, salad or whipped cauliflower (page 140).

Food Fact!
Chicken is a good source of high, biological-value protein and is easily digested. Chicken is a low-fat meat as most of the fat is found in the skin. Look for the Bord Bia Quality Assurance label and try to purchase Irish free range chicken and always check the use-by or best before date. Store at bottom of fridge and use as soon as possible.

CHICKEN OR PORK SATAY

INDONESIA

Cooking Time: 20 minutes

Serves: 4

Ingredients

400g pork fillet or
3 chicken fillets

Peanut Sauce

2 tablespoons peanut butter (crunchy)

1 tablespoon peanuts

2 tablespoons soy sauce

1 tablespoon brown sugar

1 tablespoon lemon juice

2 tablespoon vegetable oil

Dash of Worcestershire sauce

100ml water

Garnish: chopped parsley

Equipment

sharp knife, board, saucepan, wooden spoon, plastic bag, rolling pin, pastry brush, tablespoon, small bowl, 8-10 skewers, pot stand, serving plate.

Healthy Hint!
Eat two servings from the protein group each day. Three servings daily are necessary during pregnancy.

Watch Out!
Be careful when using peanuts as some people can be allergic to them; they can suffer anaphylactic shock. Never serve them in food at a party. Never give peanuts to toddlers or young children as peanuts can easily get stuck in their windpipes and cause choking!

Steps — Method

Gather equipment, collect/weigh ingredients, set worktop.

1 Put peanuts into a plastic bag and crush with rolling pin.

2 Put the sauce ingredients into saucepan, stir over a moderate heat to make a creamy consistency. Add a little more water if necessary.

3 Preheat the grill. Thread the pork/chicken pieces onto the skewers (see page 107) and brush with the sauce mixture all over.

4 **Grill*** for 8-10 minutes, turning twice to cook through. Brush occasionally with sauce during cooking.

5 Heat any remaining sauce and serve with the satays.

Serve on a bed of red or green rice (page 101) or use noodles with roasted root vegetables (page 57) or garlicky greens (page 139).

Garnish with chopped parsley.

Chef's Tip!
Coeliacs or those on gluten-free diets should check the labels on all purchased sauces for traces of wheat, e.g. Worcestershire sauce. Use Tamari in place of soy sauce.

GRILLING — COOKING METHOD

Grilling means cooking food under or over radiant heat. As this method does not tenderise food, only tender meat should be grilled. Food should be at room temperature before grilling. Food is often marinated first to tenderise and moisten it. Dry frying on a ridged pan or using a contact grill is a form of grilling or griddling. It leaves seared lines on the surface of food and the fat runs off.

SWEET AND SOUR PORK OR CHICKEN

CHINA

Cooking Time: 40 minutes

Serves: 3-4

Ingredients

250g pork pieces **or**
3 pork chops **or**
2 chicken fillets

1 onion

1 clove garlic

1 green or red pepper

1 carrot (optional)

1 tablespoon oil

2 heaped teaspoons cornflour or arrowroot

½ tin pineapple in own juice

1 tablespoon soy sauce

1 tablespoon vinegar

1 teaspoon brown sugar

1 teaspoon tomato purée

¼ teaspoon salt, pepper

To serve: rice

Garnish: fresh flat-leaf parsley or coriander

Equipment

sharp knife, board, 2 heavy saucepans with lids, wooden spoon, pot stand, teaspoon, tablespoon, serving dish.

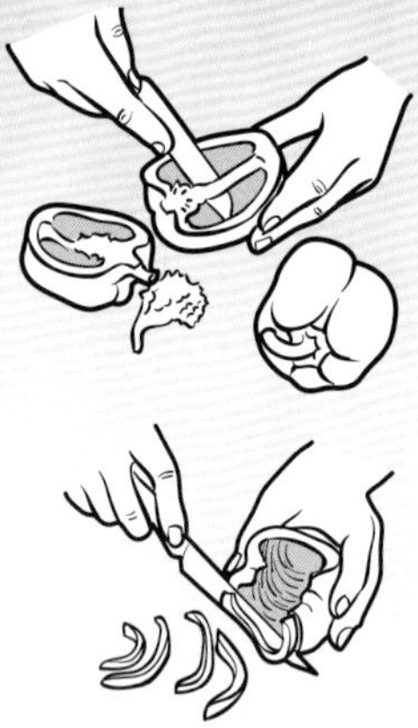

Slicing peppers

Steps — Method

Gather equipment, collect/weigh ingredients, set worktop.

1 Wash pepper, halve, deseed and dice. Peel onion and slice finely.

2 Peel garlic and crush. Peel carrot and cut into thin strips.

3 Wipe meat, trim fat, cut into pieces. Heat oil and **sear*** the meat quickly. Remove to a plate, repeat with remaining meat.

4 Add onion, carrot and garlic and sauté for 2 minutes. Return meat to saucepan, add pepper and cover.

5 Measure pineapple juice and make it up to 400ml with water. Blend with cornflour, add to saucepan with all other ingredients, stir and boil.

6 Cover tightly then simmer very gently until meat is tender – 30 minutes. Stir occasionally to prevent sticking. (Cook in a casserole dish in oven if desired for 1½ hours.)

7 Cook rice (page 100) and prepare garnish.

Serve with boiled rice (page 100).

Garnish with flat-leafed parsley or coriander.

Reheating of dish must be thoroughly done. This will take 10-15 minutes in a microwave or 20-30 minutes in a hot oven.

Resource Management: Buy organic vegetables when possible and wash before use. To reduce waste, prepare peppers carefully removing the centre stalk (page 124) and hard surround first. Then, halve from top to bottom to remove the membrane and seeds, see diagram. Store leftovers in the fridge.

*SEAR — COOKING TECHNIQUE

Sear means to cook food in very hot fat, on all sides, for a short time to seal the outside and therefore keep in the juices. The protein on the outside coagulates in the heat so the juices cannot get out.

Chicken Curry (Beef or Lamb)

INDIAN

Cooking Time: 35-40 minutes (depends on meat)

Serves: 3-4

Ingredients

- 3 chicken fillets or 300g lean beef or lean lamb
- 25g butter
- 2 tablespoons oil
- 1 onion
- 1 clove of garlic
- 25g flour
- 2 tablespoons curry paste or powder – mild/medium/hot
- 1 level teaspoon salt
- 400ml stock or water
- 1 tablespoon tomato purée
- 1 tablespoon chutney
- 1 tablespoon lemon juice
- 1 dessert apple

To serve: rice (page 100)

Garnish: parsley

Equipment

sharp knife, board, tablespoon, wooden spoon, large perforated spoon, saucepan, pot stand, whisk, serving dish.

Idea!
For a creamier sauce, add 1 small can (165ml) coconut milk.

Food Fact!
Turmeric gives curry its yellow colour. Turmeric is a root of the ginger family. Both are powerful antioxidants and anti-inflammatory when used with oil/butter and black pepper. See Smoothie idea on page 15.

Steps — Method

Gather equipment, collect/weigh ingredients, set worktop.

1. Wash meat, trim fat, cut into cubes.
2. Peel and chop onion, garlic and apple.
3. Heat oil and butter, **sear** ½ the meat quickly, remove to a plate and repeat with remaining meat (see technique page 128).
4. Sauté onion and garlic for 2 minutes. Add flour, salt and curry paste or powder. Cook for 1 minute, remove from heat.
5. Whisk in the water or stock and bring to the boil, stirring all the time.
6. Add the meat, tomato purée, chutney, lemon juice and chopped apple. Correct the seasoning if necessary.
7. Cover and simmer over a very gentle heat until the meat is tender – chicken 30 minutes, beef and lamb 1 hour.

Serve with boiled rice and a variety of **sambals*** and poppadums (page 139).

Garnish with parsley and toasted almonds (optional).

Variation

Vegetarian Curry: Omit the chicken, add 1 sliced pepper, 1 diced carrot, 1 small head broccoli florets and 25g peanuts or cashews at Step 4.

Dairy-free: omit the butter and use extra oil.

*SAMBALS

Sambals are accompaniments served with curries, e.g. tomato, cucumber, poppadams (page 139), naan breads, chutney, crème fraîche, toasted flaked almonds, sliced banana tossed with lemon juice or Raita (see below).

*RAITA

Grate 10cm of cucumber. Discard the juice. Mix with 125g natural yoghurt, 2 teaspoons fresh mint or 1 teaspoon dried mint, a pinch of sugar and salt. Garnish with paprika. This is very cooling with a curry.

Thai Green Pork or Chicken Curry

Cooking Time: 40 minutes

Serves: 4

Ingredients

- 1 pork fillet or 3 chicken fillets
- 2 tablespoons olive oil
- 1 onion
- 1 clove garlic
- 1 carrot
- 1 red pepper
- 5 mushrooms (optional)
- 50g mange tout
- 50g sweetcorn
- 1 tin/300ml coconut milk
- 2-4 teaspoons Thai green curry paste*
- 1 tablespoon cornflour
- 1 lime
- 50g cream cheese (optional)
- Small bunch coriander
- **Garnish:** fresh coriander

Equipment

sharp knife, board, tablespoon, wooden spoon, juicer, 2 saucepans or 1 wok and 1 saucepan, pot stand, colander, serving bowls.

Watch Out!
Too much salt is bad for your health. Look for low sodium substitutes. Try replacing salt with herbs, spices, lemon or lime juice instead.

Look Up!
Salt in the diet.

Steps — Method

Gather equipment, collect/weigh ingredients, set worktop.

1. Wash meat and dry on kitchen paper, cut into cubes. Peel and chop the onion and garlic. Wash, dry and dice the coriander. Juice the lime.
2. Peel and finely slice the carrot. Wash and finely slice pepper and mushrooms, wash and diagonally slice the mange tout in two.
3. Heat oil, **sear** (page 128) ½ the meat for 2 minutes, remove and place on a plate. Sear the remaining meat. Add the carrot, onion, garlic and sauté for 2 minutes. Add the peppers, mushrooms, remaining meat and sauté together for 5 minutes.
4. Stir in beans, sweetcorn, **curry paste***, cornflour. Finally, add the lime juice and coconut milk and bring to the boil. Simmer chicken for 20 minutes and pork for 25 minutes. Cook the rice now, as on page 100.
5. Remove curry from heat. Stir in half the coriander and cream cheese, if using.

Serve Thai curry and rice in two separate bowls.

Garnish with fresh coriander.

Variation

Use French beans in place of mange tout and brown rice or noodles instead of white rice.

Vegetarian: Omit meat, use Quorn (see Food Fact, page 90) chickpeas or butter beans instead.

Food Fact!
CURRY PASTE*
Thai green paste is mostly made from green chillies, garlic, basil, coriander, shallots, lemongrass, ginger, salt, lime zest and juice. Depending on the brand you use, the heat can vary, so add 2 teaspoons to begin, taste, and add more if you wish.

Chicken, Leek and Tarragon Pie

Cooking Time: 45 minutes

Serves: 4-5

Ingredients

- 4 chicken fillets
- 25g butter
- 1 tablespoon olive oil
- 1 onion
- 2 cloves garlic
- 1 leek
- 100g mushrooms
- 2 medium carrots
- 200ml stock (see Healthy Hint below)
- 100ml white wine (optional)
- 25g flour
- 3 tablespoons crème fraîche
- 1 tablespoon fresh tarragon or 1 heaped teaspoon, dried
- Salt and pepper
- 1 packet puff pastry, fresh or frozen and defrosted

Equipment

sharp knife, board, tablespoon, wooden spoon, large saucepan, pot stand, ovenproof casserole dish, rolling pin, pastry brush.

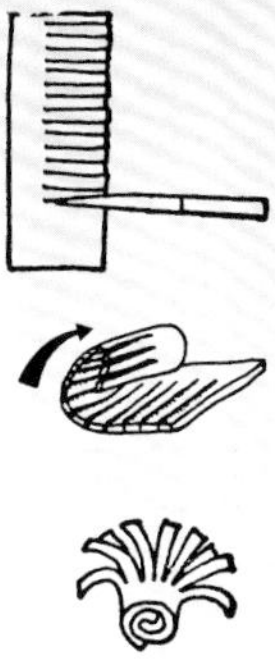

Pastry tassels

Idea!
See pastry leaves on page 121.

Steps — Method

Preheat oven to 190°C/Fan 180°C/Gas Mark 5.

Gather equipment, collect/weigh ingredients, set worktop.

1. Wash meat, dry on kitchen paper and cut into cubes. Peel and chop onion and garlic.
2. Wash and chop leek, see page 25. Wash, peel and dice carrots. Wash and dice mushrooms. Wash and chop tarragon, if fresh. Dissolve the stock cube in 200ml boiling water and stir well.
3. Heat oil and butter, **sauté** chicken until nicely brown. Put into a casserole dish.
4. Sauté onion, garlic and leek for 2 minutes, add mushrooms and carrots and cook for 1 minute. Add flour to make a **roux*** sauce (see page 41), cook for 1 minute. **Remove from heat**, slowly stir in stock and wine if using. Return to heat, bring slowly to the boil to thicken, stirring all the time. Add the crème fraîche and tarragon.
5. Pour over chicken and allow to cool a little.
6. Roll out the pastry, place over the filling/dish and trim round the edges. Make a small hole in the centre to allow steam to escape and decorate with pastry tassels or leaves. Brush with milk or egg to **glaze*** (see page 167) and cook for 15 minutes. Reduce the heat and continue cooking 15-20 minutes, until nicely browned

Garnish with parsley.

Serve with roasted root vegetables (page 57) or a fresh salad.

Chef's Tip!
Pastry needs a hot oven for the first 10 minutes to burst the starch grains so they absorb the fat quickly. This makes the pastry nice and light. Reduce the heat and continue cooking until cooked through.

Healthy Hint!
Use homemade stock where possible (see page 24) or only half of a low-salt, organic stock cube.

Chinese Stir-Fry (Meat or Vegetarian)

Cooking Time: 20-25 minutes

Serves: 2-3

Ingredients

- 200g meat – chicken fillet, lean lamb, pork fillet or lean beef
- 1 small carrot
- 1 red pepper
- 1 clove of garlic
- 1cm piece root ginger (optional)
- 4 mushrooms
- 4 scallions or ½ onion
- 1 small courgette
- 50g sweetcorn (optional)
- Small head broccoli (optional)
- 50g bean sprouts (optional)
- 25g peanuts/cashew nuts
- 2 tablespoons vegetable oil
- 2 tablespoons soy sauce or Tamari (see Chef's Tip)
- 2 tablespoons sherry (optional) or water
- 1 rounded teaspoon cornflour
- ¼ teaspoon salt

Equipment

sharp knife, board, wok or frying pan, 2 wooden spoons, 1 tablespoon, 1 teaspoon, colander, scissors, tin opener, pot stand, serving plate.

Chef's Tip!
Food to be stir-fried is cut into thin strips so that it can be eaten with chopsticks.

Steps — Method

Gather equipment, collect/weigh ingredients, set worktop.

1. Prepare accompaniment – rice or noodles.
2. Wash and dry meat and cut into matchstick-like strips.
3. Wash and prepare all vegetables according to type, crush garlic, cut the carrot into thin batons, the pepper into strips and the broccoli into florets. Peel ginger and dice finely.
4. Thinly slice mushrooms, courgette and scallions and drain the sweetcorn.
5. Heat oil, cook the meat on medium heat for 10 minutes, then add the garlic, ginger and carrot and cook for a further 5-6 minutes. Use two wooden spoons to stir the stir-fry. See **al dente**, page 84.
6. Add the broccoli and pepper. Cook for 5 minutes and finally add the remaining vegetables and nuts. Continue to stir-fry until vegetables are cooked but still crisp.
7. Dissolve the cornflour in 2 tablespoons water and soy sauce. Add to the wok with the sherry and seasoning. Stir to coat the vegetables and cook the cornflour.

Serve at once with boiled rice (page 100) or Chinese noodles.

Vegetarian Stir-Fry – omit the meat but be sure to add some nuts or beans for protein.

Chef's Tip!
Use light soy sauce with chicken, pork and fish dishes and dark soy sauce with beef and lamb. Use tamari for gluten-free diets.

Healthy Hint!
Eating a variety of fresh, brightly coloured fruit and vegetables is important for your health. They contain lots of vitamins, minerals and live enzymes.

Chicken – Italian Style

Cooking Time: 40 minutes

Serves: 4

Ingredients

3 chicken fillets
1 tablespoon olive oil
1 onion
2 cloves garlic
1 yellow pepper
1 small courgette
6 mushrooms
1 tin chopped tomatoes
Salt and pepper
1 teaspoon oregano
¼ teaspoon nutmeg
150ml water
25g grated Parmesan cheese
Garnish: flat-leaf parsley or basil

Equipment

sharp knife, chopping board, wooden spoon, teaspoon, large saucepan, shallow casserole dish with cover or foil, pot stand.

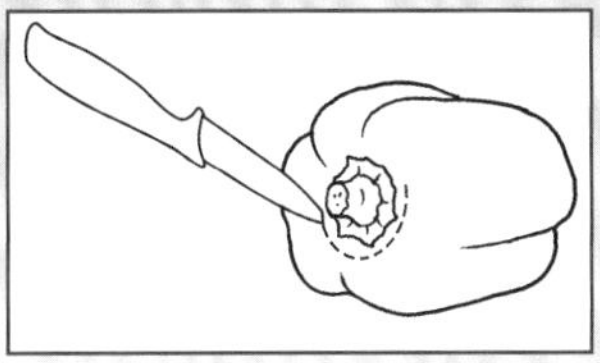

Removing the stalk

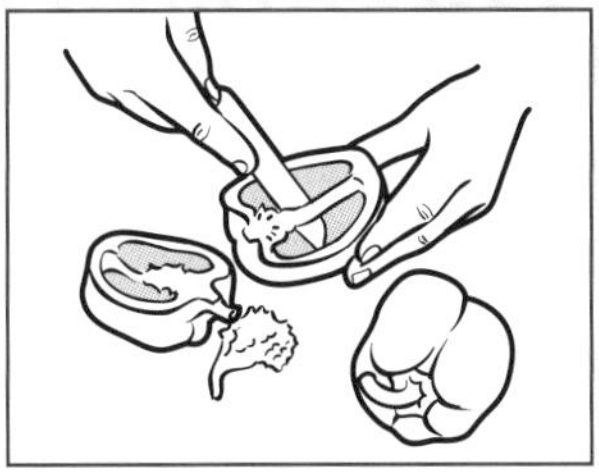

Preparing peppers

Steps — Method

Preheat oven to 190°C/Fan 180°C/Gas Mark 5.

Gather equipment, collect/weigh ingredients, set worktop.

1 Wash meat, dry on kitchen paper, cut each fillet lengthways in two.

2 Peel and dice onion and garlic. Wash mushrooms, courgette and pepper – chop roughly.

3 Heat oil in saucepan, **sauté*** (see page 70) onion and garlic for 2 minutes. Add courgette, pepper and mushrooms, sauté for 2 minutes. Add the water, tomatoes, oregano and nutmeg. Season with salt and pepper. Bring to the boil, simmer for 2 minutes and transfer to an ovenproof dish.

4 Heat oil in the same saucepan, **sear*** (see page 128) the chicken fillets for 2 minutes on each side.

5 Place the chicken fillets on top of the vegetables and cover with lid or foil. **Bake*** (see page 68) for 20 minutes.

6 Remove from the oven and scatter the Parmesan on top. Bake for 10 minutes until just golden.

Garnish with basil leaves or flat-leaf parsley.

Serve with mashed potato (page 64) or baked potato (page 68), pasta (page 84) and green salad.

Buy Local, Buy Irish!
When buying chicken or poultry products, choose Irish reared poultry with the Board Bia Quality Assurance label. Buy free-range if possible, look for traceability and always check the best before date.

Microwave Cooking – Tips and Techniques

The type and wattage of a microwave cooker can mean a difference of 2-3 minutes plus or minus in cooking times. Always test to see if food has cooked through and allow to 'stand' before serving.

STANDING TIME is a necessity, not an option. Food needs to 'rest' for a time inside or outside the microwave to finish cooking before serving.

REHEATING FOODS: Reheat in small quantities. Microwave for 2 minutes. Turn or stir food. Test and stand for 2 minutes.

Idea!
To soften crystallised honey: Spoon into a suitable bowl, microwave on HIGH for 30 seconds at a time until runny. Look at it after each 30 seconds as it can burn easily.

Watch Out!
Foods with a high sugar or fat content can burn easily or go on fire in a microwave.

Microwaves are electromagnetic waves of energy that cause food particles to vibrate against each other. This friction produces the heat that cooks the food. Microwave cooking is economical and a quick way to cook small portions of food.

- Always follow the **instruction booklet** for your microwave.
- Use **microwaveable cooking dishes**, e.g. Pyrex.
- Cut food into **equal-sized pieces** to cook evenly.
- Place the **thickest parts** of foods to the outer edge of the dish. **Arrange the food in circles.**
- **Pierce** foods that have skins, e.g. apples, tomatoes, jacket potatoes, to prevent bursting.
- **Cover foods** to speed up cooking and keep the oven clean.
- Some foods should be **stirred often** during cooking
- **Turn** foods that are more than 2cm thick.
- When **reheating**, check the food is **reheated** in the centre.

Ideas for using a microwave

Scrambled Eggs: Put 15g butter, 2 beaten eggs, 2 tablespoons milk, salt and pepper into a bowl. Cook for 1 minute, stir. Cook for 30 seconds, stir, repeat and stir. Stand for 30 seconds.

Poached Egg: Break egg into a ramekin dish. Add 1 tablespoon water. Pierce white and yolk in 4 places, cover and cook for 40-50 seconds. Stand for 1 minute.

Porridge: Mix ½ cup porridge oats in a bowl with 1 cup milk or water. Cook for 1 minute, stir and repeat. Stand for 30 seconds.

Stewed Apple/Fruits: Place prepared fruits in a dish, cover, cook for 2 minutes and stir. Cook for 1 minute, check and repeat as required. Stand for 2 minutes.

Potatoes or Sweet Potatoes: see pages 68 and 69.

Quick Cook Diced Potatoes: for topping, see page 109.

Rice: Put 1 cup rice into a bowl with 2 cups boiling water, 1 teaspoon oil and ½ teaspoon salt. Cook for 5 minutes, stir and repeat. Stand for 5 minutes. Serves 2.

Melting: Melt butter, sugar and syrup ('melted mixtures') for 1 minute and stir. Stand for 1 minute before using.

Poppadums: Cook three at a time, see page 139.

Reheating foods: Reheat in small quantities, turn or stir each after 2 minutes. Test the centre with a clean finger and stand for 2 minutes.

Chapter 8 Special, Functional Recipes for Health and Wellbeing

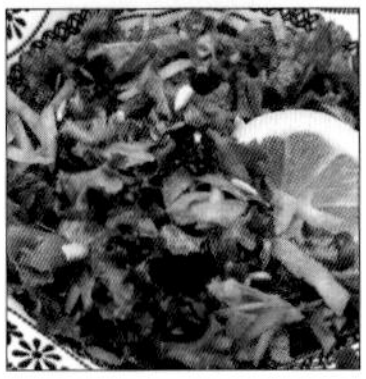

Our wellbeing centres around our mind, our attitude, our gratitude and our food.

Factors affecting **wellbeing** include health status, home and work environments and socio-economic influences. The type, quality and quantity of the food consumed, combined with regular exercise is a major factor in determining our health and wellbeing.

As individuals, we can improve our health through the foods we choose to consume. It is advised to reduce your intake of sugars and refined carbohydrates, and to avoid 'trans' fats. Eat foods that are fresh, easily digested, good quality and free from toxic, artificial chemicals.

A healthy gut and immune system is promoted by the regular intake of prebiotics (green vegetables, fibre and pulses), probiotics and live enzymes.

For **optimal wellbeing**, we need to be conscious of our general health. The functional recipes in this chapter provide a starting point for further research into foods that strengthen the immune system, combat stress- and diet-related diseases.

Key Words and Skills

- pulse
- drizzle
- trans fats
- buzz
- sauté
- prebiotics
- fold in
- marinade
- probiotics
- Modified Atmosphere Packaging (MAP)

Other suitable recipes:

Healthy Smoothies (page 14), Fresh Melon (pages 16, 17), Avocado (pages 18, 19), Crudités (page 20), Hummus (page 21), Seafood Chowder (page 29), Salsas (page 43), Waldorf Salad (page 51), Roast Vegetables (page 59), Quick Ratatouille (page 60), Quick Light Fish Curry (page 108), Stir-Fry (page 132).

Evaluation! See pages 223 and 224.

- Did you meet the brief and did you refer to the specific requirements of the task or dish/dishes?
- Discuss the results of your finished dish/dishes including the presentation, colour, taste and texture.
- What aspects were done well and what aspects could be improved?
- Did you correctly cost and budget for all ingredients?

Healthy Granola

BREAKFAST OR SNACK

Cooking Time: 30 minutes

Serves: 2

Ingredients

- 150g gluten-free porridge oats
- 2 tablespoons olive or coconut oil
- ½ teaspoon cinnamon
- 1 teaspoon vanilla extract
- 50g desiccated coconut
- 50g chopped nuts
- 50g mixed seeds
- 50g dried apricots
- 50g raisins or cranberries
- 25g linseeds/flaxseeds

Optional ingredients

- 1 tablespoon chia seeds
- 25g goji berries

Equipment

sharp knife, board, scissors, large bowl, wooden spoon, teaspoon, large roasting tin, airtight storage container.

Steps — Method

Preheat oven to 170°C/Fan 160°C/Gas Mark 3-4.

Gather equipment, collect/weigh ingredients, set worktop.

1 Snip the apricots using a scissors. Chop any large nuts, e.g. almonds and walnuts. If using coconut oil, allow to melt.

2 Mix all ingredients, except the raisins and optional ingredients, in a bowl. Spread on the roasting tin and bake for 15 minutes. Stir and coo for a further 10 minutes. Add raisins, stir and cook for 5 minutes.

3 Cool in tin. Stir in the optional ingredients and store in an airtight container.

Serve with diced apple and live unsweetened bio yoghurt.

Variations

Add various types of nuts: almonds, walnuts, hazelnuts, cashews or pecans.

Look Up! Goji berries.

Chia Pots

BREAKFAST OR DESSERT

Serves: 2

Ingredients

- 1 tablespoon chia seeds
- 175ml non-dairy milk
- 3 drops vanilla extract
- 1 teaspoon honey (optional)

Equipment

jug, whisk, little pots, spatula.

Look Up! Inulin, probiotic, prebiotic, microbiome.

Steps — Method

Gather equipment, collect/weigh ingredients, set worktop.

1 Whisk all ingredients together in a jug for 2 minutes. Allow to chill for 30 minutes.

2 Whisk again and pour into little pots. Chill for 1 hour or overnight.

Serve with any combination of the following toppings: raspberries, blueberries, strawberries, chopped nuts, porridge oats, coconut pieces, chia seeds or sunflower seeds.

Food Fact!

Chia seeds are tiny, black seeds that are rich in fibre, protein and antioxidents. They release their energy very slowly. When steeped, they form a thick gel-like liquid and are ideal for thickening desserts, soups and stews.

RED LENTIL DAL

INDIA

Cooking Time: 30 minutes

Serves: 3-4

Ingredients

150g red lentils

200ml water

1 tin chopped tomatoes

1 star anise

Sauté

1 tablespoon coconut or olive oil

1 red onion

1 garlic clove

1 teaspoon fresh ginger

¼ teaspoon red chilli flakes

1 teaspoon curry powder

To serve:

100g baby spinach (optional)

Salt and pepper to season

Garnish: 1 teaspoon poppy seeds or chopped coriander

Equipment

sharp knife, board, sieve, grater, teaspoon, frying pan, saucepan with lid, measuring jug, serving bowl.

Idea!
Dal freezes well.

Steps — Method

Gather equipment, collect/weigh ingredients, set worktop.

1 **Lentils:** Put lentils in a sieve and wash with cold water. Place in saucepan with water, add tomatoes and star anise. Bring to the boil, lower heat and cover. **Simmer** (page 29) very gently for 20 minutes.

2 Peel and dice onion and garlic, peel and grate ginger. Heat oil in frying pan. **Sauté** onion (see page 28), cook over a low heat for 5 minutes, stirring occasionally, until softened. Add garlic, ginger, chilli and curry powder. Cook for 2 minutes.

3 **Assembly:** Tip the sautéd vegetables into the lentils, reduce heat and cover. Cook for 10 minutes or until lentils are tender.

4 Taste and season. Remove the star anise. Gently stir in the washed spinach, if using.

Serve on a warm dish with boiled rice or quinoa.

Garnish with poppy seeds, coriander and Raita (page 129) or Tahini sauce (page 141) or salsa (page 43), naan bread and a salad.

Variations

Nutty Dal: Add 30g chopped nuts with the spices and garnish with 20g nuts, toasted on a dry frying pan.

Vegetable Dal: Add 1 diced carrot or courgette with the tomatoes.

COMFORTING KITCHARI

CLASSIC INDIAN CLEANSER

Ingredients

1 x Dal ingredients

Replace lentils with 100g basmati rice and 50g mung beans (soaked for 12 hours in cold water)

Replace tomato with 600ml cold water

25g butter or ghee (optional)

Look Up! Kitchari and ghee.

Steps — Method

Gather equipment, collect/weigh ingredients, set worktop.

1 Wash the mung beans and bring to the boil in 600ml of water in a covered saucepan. Simmer for 10 minutes until tender or 30 minutes, if not previously soaked. Rinse the rice, add to the beans and simmer for 10 minutes.

2 **Sauté:** Follow Step 2 as above. When the sauté is cooked, add to the rice and beans. Pour in a little water if the mix becomes too dry.

3 **Assembly:** When beans are soft, add spinach and butter or ghee, if using.

Chickpea Patties

Cooking Time: 20 minutes

Makes: 8

Ingredients

3 tablespoons olive oil
1 onion
2 cloves garlic
2 teaspoons ground cumin
1 teaspoon curry powder
½ teaspoon salt
Pinch chilli powder
1 x 400g tin chickpeas
130g courgette
30g porridge oats
1 tablespoon coriander or kale

Equipment

sharp knife, board, tablespoon, wooden spoon, teaspoon, mixing bowl, palette knife, sieve, juicer, frying pan, food processor.

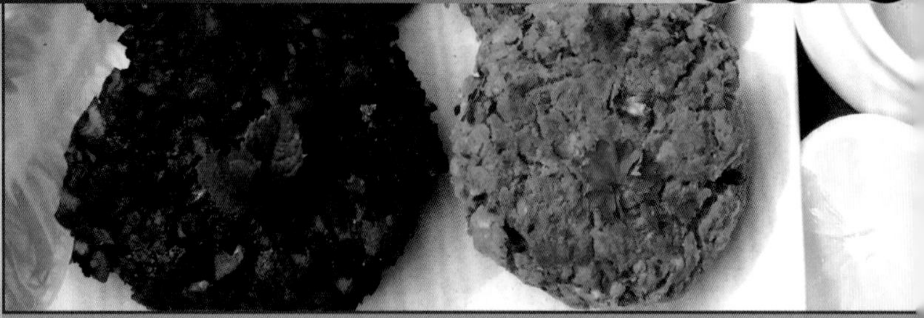

Beetroot Burgers *Chickpea Patties*

Steps **Method**

Gather equipment, collect/weigh ingredients, set worktop.

1 Peel and chop onion and garlic, wash and roughly chop the courgette. Pulse vegetables in processor until just chopped.

2 Heat 2 tablespoons oil in frying pan, add the vegetables and **sauté** (page 28) for 5 minutes. Add the salt and spices, sauté for 2 minutes. Turn off heat.

3 Drain chickpeas in a sieve and pulse in processor with the oats and coriander or kale. Add the vegetables from the frying pan and pulse briefly to mix.

4 Heat remaining oil in frying pan. Using either a dessertspoon or teaspoon, take a piece of mixture and form a ball with your hand. Flatten slightly and place on the frying pan. Cook for 5 minutes on both sides until browned. Turn using a palette knife.

Serve with a green salad (page 50) and a salsa (page 43) or Riata (page 129) or Tahini Sauce (page 141) or add to a Bento Box (page 141).

Beetroot Burgers

RICH IN NUTRIENTS

Cooking Time: 25 minutes

Makes: 6

Ingredients

270g uncooked beetroot
2 spring onions
40g mature grated Cheddar
50g feta cheese
50g mixed nuts
2 teaspoons honey
2 tablespoons olive oil
2 tablespoons mint
60g porridge oats
½ lemon, juice only
Salt and pepper

Equipment sharp knife, board, tablespoon, wooden spoon, teaspoon, mixing bowl, palette knife, sieve, juicer, frying pan, food processor, baking tray, grater.

Steps **Method**

Preheat oven to 200°C/Fan 190°C/Gas Mark 6.

Gather equipment, collect/weigh ingredients, set worktop.

1 Wash beetroot and grate or use a processor. Finely chop the spring onions, grate the Cheddar and crumble the feta. Chop the nuts.

2 Heat oil in frying pan, add beetroot and spring onions. **Sauté** (page 28) for 5 minutes, stirring over a medium heat.

3 Put the beetroot mixture into a bowl with the remaining ingredients and mix well using your hands. Form into 6 flat burgers and place on baking tray. Bake for 25 minutes, turn carefully after 12 minutes.

Serve with rice, salad and Raita (page 129) or Tahini sauce (page 141).

Chicken or Lamb Korma

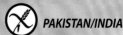

PAKISTAN/INDIA

Cooking Time: 30 minutes

Serves: 2

Ingredients

- 2 chicken fillets
- **Marinade** (page 107)
- 100ml natural yoghurt
- 1 clove garlic
- 1-2 teaspoons turmeric
- **Korma Sauce**
- 25g butter
- 1 onion
- 2cm piece fresh ginger
- ¼ teaspoon chilli powder
- ½ teaspoon cumin
- 3 cloves
- ¼ teaspoon salt
- Big pinch black pepper
- 150ml coconut milk
- **Garnish:** fresh coriander
- 15g flaked almonds

Equipment

saucepan, sharp knife, board, medium bowl, teaspoon, saucepan with lid, pot stand, tablespoon, grater with medium holes.

Dicing an onion

Steps — Method

Gather equipment, collect/weigh ingredients, set worktop.

1. **Marinade:** Peel and crush the garlic. Mix garlic, yoghurt and turmeric in bowl. Wash the chicken, dry on kitchen paper, cut into 3cm cubes and mix into marinade. Cover and marinate for 15 minutes.
2. **Garnish:** Heat saucepan, add the almonds and dry roast for 2 minutes until slightly browned. Allow to cool.
3. **Sauce:** Peel and finely dice the onion. Peel and grate the ginger. Melt butter in the saucepan and sauté onion for 3 minutes. Add ginger, cloves, cumin and chilli powder, sauté for 5 minutes. Stir in the coconut milk, chicken and marinade, bring to the boil, reduce heat, cover and **simmer** for 20 minutes. Remove the three cloves and add half of the toasted almonds. Season to taste.
4. Boil rice (see page 100). Wash and chop the coriander for garnish.

Serve with boiled rice and poppadums (below) and sambals (page 129).

Garnish with the remaining toasted almonds and chopped fresh coriander.

Variations

Lamb Korma: Use 250g diced lamb and allow to stew gently for 40 minutes, see page 115. This tenderises the lamb.

Dairy-free Korma: Use lemon juice instead of yoghurt in marinade.

Chef's Tips!

Cook three Poppadums in a microwave at a time, placed standing up against the sides of a deep plastic bowl. Cook on high for 1-2 minutes until they are fully puffed up. Leave to stand for 3-4 minutes until cool and crisp.

Garlicky Greens

EASILY DIGESTED, ANTI-VIRAL, ANTI-BACTERIAL

Ingredients

- 1 tablespoon coconut oil
- 2 cloves garlic
- 100g kale
- Salt and pepper

Steps — Method

1. Peel and crush garlic. Wash kale, remove the centre rib, chop the leaves.
2. Heat oil in saucepan, add garlic and sauté for 1 minute. Add the kale, pepper and salt, and stir until wilted.

Serve with lamb korma or chickpea patties (page 138).

Creamed Spinach

Cooking Time: 12 minutes

Makes: 2

Ingredients

- 100g fresh spinach
- 2 tablespoons olive oil
- 1 onion
- 2 cloves garlic
- 40g cashews or almonds
- Pinch chilli flakes
- ½ lemon, juice only
- Pinch nutmeg
- Salt

Equipment

processor, saucepan, sharp knife, board, tablespoon, serving dish.

Creamed Spinach, Whipped Cauliflower and Lemony Kale, Carrot and Avocado Salad

Steps **Method**

Gather equipment, collect/weigh ingredients, set worktop.

1 If possible, soak nuts for 1 hour in 1 cup of water. Peel and dice the onion and garlic. Wash and chop the spinach.

2 Heat oil in large saucepan, sauté onion and garlic for 5 minutes.

3 Put onion and garlic, chilli flakes, lemon juice, nutmeg, nuts and water into processor and buzz until creamy. Return the sauce to saucepan and simmer for 5 minutes. Add spinach to the sauce. Simmer for 1 minute until soft and add salt to taste.

Whipped Cauliflower

GENTLE ON THE STOMACH

Ingredients

- 1 small cauliflower
- Small bunch parsley
- Butter or olive oil
- Salt

Equipment

See Creamed Spinach recipe above.

Steps **Method**

Gather equipment, collect/weigh ingredients, set worktop.

1 Boil water in kettle. Wash and cut cauliflower into florets and place in saucepan. Cover florets with boiling water, simmer for 8 minutes.

2 Wash parsley. Drain cauliflower in a sieve and transfer to processor. Add parsley, butter or oil, salt and buzz until smooth in texture, resembling mashed potato.

Lemony Kale, Carrot and Avocado Salad

NUTRIENT RICH, GOOD DETOX

Ingredients

- 1 lemon, juice only
- 1 tablespoon olive oil
- 100g kale
- 1 carrot
- 1 avocado
- 25g raisins
- 25g sunflower seeds
- Salt

Equipment See Creamed Spinach recipe above

Steps **Method**

Gather equipment, collect/weigh ingredients, set worktop.

1 Wash kale, remove the central rib and chop leaves finely. Toss in a large bowl with the lemon juice. Add salt, oil and toss again.

2 Peel and grate carrot. Remove stone, peel and dice the avocado. Toast the sunflower seeds in a dry frying pan until just beginning to brown. Add all the ingredients to the kale and mix gently. Refrigerate for 1 hour before eating.

3 Store in a fridge in a covered container for up to 5 days – eating a little every day is detoxing and cleansing.

Buddha Bowl, Salad Jar and Bento Box

- **Buddha (or Macro) Bowl:** is a meal in a bowl – a simplified form of balanced eating. Fill the bowl with a variety of small portions of colourful, healthy foods. Cover the bowl, if transporting.
- **Salad Jar:** similar to the Budda Bowl. Made by layering salad ingredients starting with the dressing at the bottom and adding 4 to 5 layers of vegetables and protein, finishing with leaves at the top. The jar is closed for transport to ensure the leaves stay crisp and tossed before eating.
- **Bento Box:** an airtight container with a lid and individual compartments for different foods.

Watch Out!
Containers should always be spotlessly clean before use. Food should be prepared in a hygienic way and not handled too much. Once ready, store in a refrigerator, transport in a cool bag and keep away from radiators or out of the sun. Use within 24 hours.

Lunchboxes should contain all the macronutrients: protein, fat and the three carbohydrates (fruit, vegetables and starches). Always include a dressing to add texture and flavour, oil is important to balance the diet.

Protein
Cooked meats
Salmon, tuna
Fish Frittata, **page 111**
Chickpea Patties, **page 138**
Beans, lentils
Red Lentil Dal, **page 137**
Eggs, Spanish Tortilla, **page 77**
Cheese
Nuts and seeds

Fruits
Tomatoes
Apples
Pineapple
Blueberries
Mango
Avocado, **pages 18, 19 and 22**
Dried fruits

Vegetables
Salads, **page 51**
Cucumber, radish
Broccoli, Crudités, **page 20**
Whipped Cauliflower, **page 140**
Beetroot Burger, **page 138**
Coleslaw, **page 49**
Carrot Salad, **page 54**
Onion, peppers, Lemony Kale Salad, Creamed Spinach, **page 140**

Starches
Rice, **page 100**
Pasta Salad, **page 55**
Potato Salad, **page 52**
Quinoa, **page 98**
Couscous, **page 98**
Bread
Scones, **page 182**

Dressings
Tahini Sauce/Dressing, **below**
Hummus, **page 21**
Vinaigrette, **page 36**
Mayonnaise, **page 38**

Tahini Sauce/Dressing

Ingredients
1 tablespoon tahini
1 lemon
½ clove garlic
1 teaspoon honey
1 tablespoon oil
Salt or miso
2-3 tablespoons water

Method

Steps

1. Juice the lemon, crush the garlic and mix with the tahini in a small jar with a teaspoon.
2. Add the water and a dash of miso or salt to taste and shake. Use on its own or mix with natural yoghurt. This is very nutritious and versatile.

Serve cold with salads or hot with vegetables, meats or fish.

Beetroot and Walnut Tray Bake

Cooking Time:
25-30 minutes

Ingredients

3 free range eggs
150ml olive oil
50g soft brown sugar
150g plain flour
1 tablespoon cocoa
2 teaspoons mixed spice
1 teaspoon baking powder
Pinch salt
120g raw beetroot
60g walnuts
60g sultanas (optional)
Icing (optional)
125g icing sugar
1 dessertspoon milk

Equipment

bowl, small bowl, sieve, wooden spoon, sharp knife, board, grater, teaspoon, dessertspoon, tablespoon, electric beater, wire tray, baking parchment, 20cm x 3cm high square tin.

Chef's Tip!
Decorate with commercial beetroot or vegetable crisps.

Steps	Method

Preheat oven to 190°C/Fan 180°C/Gas Mark 5.

Gather equipment, collect/weigh ingredients, set worktop.

1. Grease and line the square tin with baking parchment. Grate the beetroot and chop walnuts.
2. Whisk eggs, oil and sugar until light and smooth. Sieve in the flour, cocoa, baking powder and salt, mix gently. Fold in the beetroot, walnuts and sultanas, if using.
3. Pour mixture into tin, level the surface and bake for 25-30 minutes. Allow to cool in the tin for 10 minutes. Remove onto a wire tray and cool.
4. **Icing:** Sieve the icing sugar into a small bowl. Beat in the milk until it forms a thick but spreadable consistency. Spread or drizzle evenly over the cold cake. Cut into 16-18 even pieces.

Serve on a plate with a doyley. Store in an airtight container.

Idea!
Serve as a dessert with Nut Cream, below or Coconut Cream, page 152.

Vegetarian Nut Cream

Ingredients

100g cashew nuts
125ml non-dairy milk
1 tablespoon coconut oil
½ orange zest (optional)
honey (optional)

Step	Method

Soak cashew nuts in water for 1 hour. Drain and buzz in a blender with non-dairy milk and 1 tablespoon coconut oil, until smooth. Add honey and/or orange zest and chill. Serve as a vegetarian cream or dip.

Variation

Vegan: Substitute honey with Stevia or sugar.

Oatmeal Chocolate Cookies

Cooking Time: 12 minutes

Makes: 10-12

Ingredients

1 egg
60g almond butter
150g sugar
25g coconut oil
¼ teaspoon bread soda
½ teaspoon vanilla extract
25g dark chocolate, chopped
30g sunflower seeds
140g gluten-free oats

Equipment

electric beater, bowl, teaspoon, dessertspoon, wooden spoon, baking tray, parchment paper, wire tray.

Steps — Method

Preheat oven to 170°C/Fan 160°C/Gas Mark 4.

Gather equipment, collect/weigh ingredients, set worktop.

1 Grease the baking tray and line with parchment paper.
2 Use electric beater to cream the egg, almond butter, sugar, vanilla and coconut oil together until smooth.
3 Stir in the bread soda, chocolate, sunflower seeds and oats.
4 Drop a dessertspoon of batter onto the parchment paper leaving 5cm of space between each.
5 Bake for 12 minutes until cookies are brown around the edges but still soft in the middle. Remove from oven and cool a little before lifting onto a wire tray.

Store in an airtight container.

Chocolate Avocado Pots

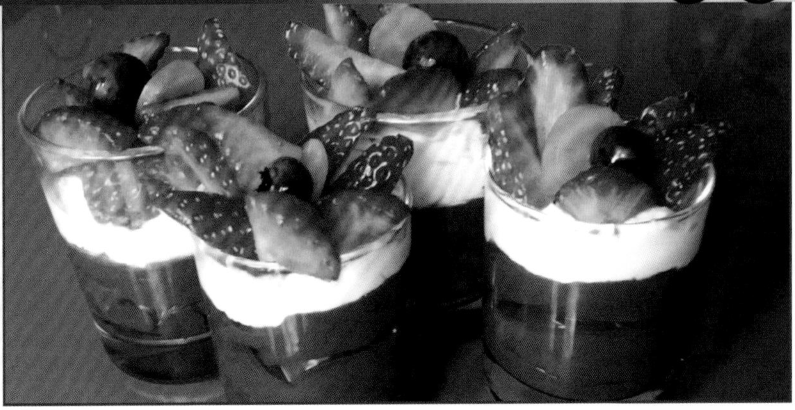

Ingredients

1 very ripe avocado
25g cocoa
2 tablespoons sugar or 1 tablespoon Stevia
Pinch salt
2 ½ tablespoons non-dairy milk
4 drops vanilla extract

Equipment

tablespoon, spatula, hand/stick or bullet blender, bowl.

Look Up! Stevia.

Step — Method

Gather equipment, collect/weigh ingredients, set worktop.

Buzz the ingredients until smooth. Taste and add a little more sugar or Stevia, if necessary and chill for 1 hour. **Serve** in little pots or shot glasses with Nut Cream (page 142) or dairy-free coconut yoghurt and fruit.

Idea! Use this vegan-friendly recipe to ice and fill cakes.

Chapter 9

Puddings, Desserts and Sweet Sauces

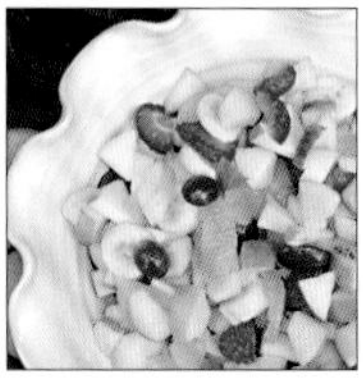
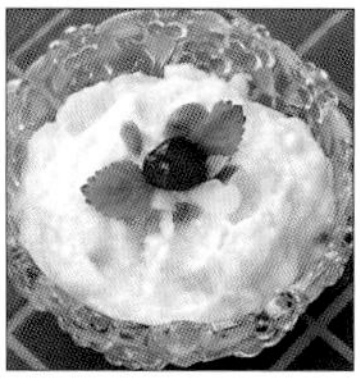
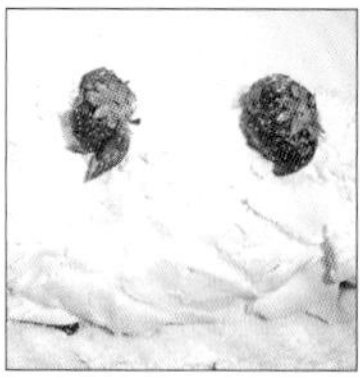
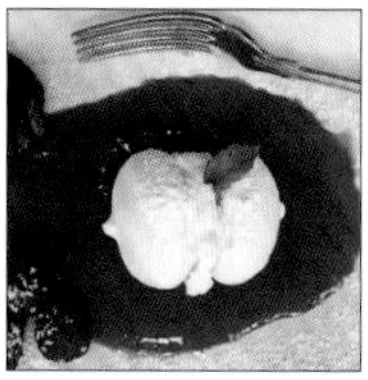

Enjoy the colour, flavour, texture and taste of fresh fruits. Use as much fresh fruit as possible when making and serving desserts. Traditionally, desserts and puddings are served at the end of a meal. Desserts should complement a meal nutritionally and contrast with its previous textures and flavours. Use fruits to sweeten puddings as too much refined sugar can lead to tooth decay, weight gain and Type 2 Diabetes. Eat at least three portions of fresh fruit every day and keep desserts with a high sugar content for special occasions.

Key Words and Skills

❖ core	❖ curdle	❖ blend
❖ grease	❖ meringue	❖ separate
❖ segment	❖ decorate	❖ dredge
❖ whisk	❖ garnish	❖ coagulate

Other suitable recipes:

Sweet Stuffed Pancakes (page 79), Fruit Fritters (page 80), Chocolate Avocado Pots (page 143), Baked Raspberry Cheese Cake (page 173).

Evaluation! See pages 223 and 224.

- ❖ Did you meet the brief and did you refer to the specific requirements of the task or dish/dishes?
- ❖ Discuss the results of your finished dish/dishes including the presentation, colour, taste and texture.
- ❖ What aspects were done well and what aspects could be improved?
- ❖ Did you correctly cost and budget for all ingredients?

Fresh Fruit Salad

Serves: 4

Ingredients

1 pear
1 orange
1 apple
1 banana
2 kiwis
6 green grapes
6 red grapes
Juice of ½ a lemon

Syrup

250ml water
50g sugar

To decorate:
fresh mint leaves

Equipment

sharp knife, board, saucepan, tablespoon, kitchen paper or tea towel, pot stand, serving bowl, apple corer.

Chef's Tip!
Pears, apples and bananas are dipped in lemon juice to prevent enzymic browning.

Idea!
For a special occasion, serve in a melon basket with a doyley on a plate.

In a hurry!
For special diets or a change of flavour, use 200ml fresh orange or apple juice instead of the syrup.

Steps **Method**

Gather equipment, collect/weigh ingredients, set worktop.

1 **Syrup:** Heat sugar and water in a saucepan and stir until dissolved. Boil for 5 minutes without stirring. Allow to cool.
2 Wash fruit, dry with tea towel or kitchen paper.
3 Remove skin and pith from oranges, cut into small bite-sized pieces or segments (see diagram) and save the juice. Put into serving bowl.
4 Peel and slice kiwis and banana. Add to bowl.
5 Cut grapes in half and remove seeds. Add to bowl.
6 Core pear and apple, cut into small bite-sized pieces or segments, dip in lemon juice. Add to bowl with cooled syrup. Mix gently.

Decorate with mint leaves.

Serve with pouring cream, natural yoghurt or vegetarian nut cream (page 142).

Variation

Very Berry: In place of grapes, use a selection of fresh berries for colour, texture, extra vitamins and antioxidants.

Segmenting an orange

Use a serrated knife to remove the rind and pith. Scrape off remaining white pith. Cut the flesh into segments, leaving the membrane behind.

Stewed Apple or Rhubarb

Cooking Time: 8-10 minutes

Serves: 2-3

Ingredients

400g cooking apples or rhubarb

50g-75g sugar

100ml water

2 cloves (optional)

Equipment

sharp knife, board, small saucepan and lid, wooden spoon, peeler, pot stand, apple corer, serving dish.

Chef's Tip!
A squeeze of lemon juice added to apples while stewing is good to keep them nice and white.

Steps **Method**

Gather equipment, collect/weigh ingredients, set worktop.

1 Wash, quarter, peel, core and slice apples or wash and chop rhubarb into 2cm lengths.

2 Put all the ingredients into a saucepan and **stew** (see page 115) very gently over a low heat until fruit is soft but still keeps its shape.

Serve with custard or ice cream or use to make apple sauce from page 156

In a hurry! Microwave fruit at Step 2, see page 134.

Fruit Fool

Cooking Time: 8-10 minutes

Serves: 2-3

Ingredients

3 cooking apples or 5-6 sticks of rhubarb

1 tablespoon water

Sugar to taste – 50g approximately

125ml cream

250ml readymade custard

To decorate: mint leaves, cherry (optional)

Equipment

sharp knife, board, peeler, apple corer, saucepan, wooden spoon, pot stand, liquidiser or hand whisk, spatula, small bowl, tablespoon, serving bowl.

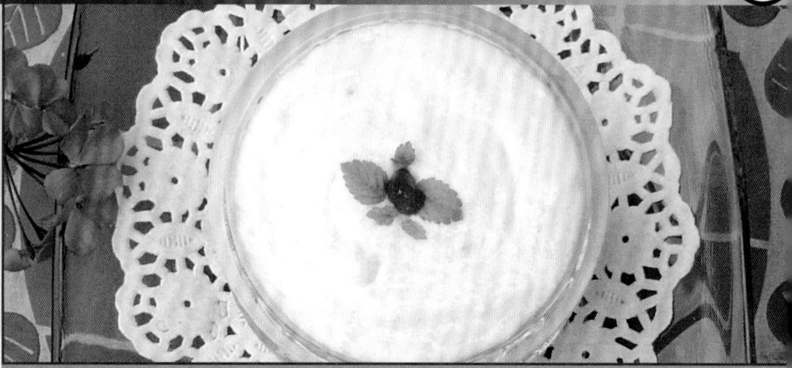

Steps **Method**

Gather equipment, collect/weigh ingredients, set worktop.

1 Follow Steps 1 and 2 for Stewed Apple or Rhubarb and allow to cool.

2 Blend in a liquidiser or beat to a pulp with a hand whisk.

3 Mix the custard into the fruit purée.

4 Whip cream, fold into the fruit mixture with spatula.

5 Pour into the serving bowl or individual glasses or dishes. Chill.

Decorate with a mint leaf and a piece of cherry.

Serve with some small homemade biscuits.

Stuffed Baked Apples

Cooking Time: 30 minutes

Serves: 3-4

Ingredients

3 medium cooking apples
1 orange
100ml water
Butter for greasing

Filling

25g butter
½ teaspoon cinnamon
25g mixed nuts
25g dried fruit – raisins, cranberries, dried blueberries
25g brown sugar

Equipment

sharp knife, board, apple corer, teaspoon, small Pyrex dish, tablespoon, pot stand, small bowl, wooden spoon, zester, juicer, fork.

Steps — Method

Preheat oven to 180°C/Fan 170°C/Gas Mark 5.
Gather equipment, collect/weigh ingredients, set worktop.

1 Grease the dish. Zest and juice the orange. Add juice to the water.
2 **Filling:** Mix all filling ingredients together and add the orange zest.
3 Wash apples and remove cores. Make a cut into the skin around the equator of each apple.
4 Stand the fruit in the small dish. Spoon and pack filling into the cavity of each, pour water and juice over and around the apples.
5 Bake for 30 minutes until soft. Remove from oven and test with a skewer. Use a knife and fork to remove the top skin only from the apple.

Serve warm with juices spooned over the fruit and fresh, bio live yoghurt or cream.

Baked Nectarine, Peach or Plum

VARIATION

Ingredients

1 x Stuffed Baked Apples above but replace apples with nectarine, peach or plum

Filling

1 x filling above
1 egg white
25g ground almonds or desiccated coconut

Step — Method

Wash and halve the fruit of choice. Remove stone using a sharp knife – but be careful. Mix all filling ingredients together and continue as in Step 4 of the above recipe, spooning filling into the apple pit cavities. Bake for 20-25 minutes.

Serve with Greek yoghurt, crème fraîche and shortbread biscuits (page 208).

Variations

Vegan: Use coconut oil for filling.

Dairy-free: Serve with vegan coconut yoghurt.

In a hurry!
Use 1 tablespoon of Christmas mincemeat in place of filling in either recipe.

Trifle

Cooking Time: 10 minutes

Serves: 4-6

Ingredients

Sponge base

1 packet of sponge cake or basic whisked sponge (page 193)

2 tablespoons jam

Fruit

1 tin fruit of choice (pears, peaches, fruit cocktail)

6 tablespoons sherry

Custard

1 tablespoon custard powder

1 tablespoon cornflour

375ml milk

1 dessertspoon sugar to sweeten

Topping

250ml cream to decorate

Decoration: cherries, cream, chocolate flake bar

Equipment

sharp knife, board, table knife, tablespoon, tin opener, wooden spoon, saucepan, pot stand, medium bowl, whisk, serving dish.

In a hurry! Use readymade custard.

Chef's Tip! For a traditional sherry trifle, use homemade custard sauce (page 155).

Buy Local, Buy Irish! Support Irish fruit growers.

Steps — Method

Gather equipment, collect/weigh ingredients, set worktop.

1 **Sponge Base:** Split the sponge, spread with jam and sandwich together before cutting into thin slices and line the base of the serving bowl.

2 Drain the fruit. Mix the juice with the sherry. Spread the fruit over the sponge. Pour half of the juice over the fruit.

3 Cover with the remaining sponge and soak with the remaining juice. Press down with a tablespoon.

4 **Custard:** Blend cornflour and custard powder with 5 tablespoons of milk. Heat milk and blended custard powder together, bring to the boil, stirring for 1 minute. Sweeten with sugar. Cool slightly.

5 Pour over the soaked sponge and chill.

6 **Topping:** Whip cream and sweeten to taste if desired.

Decorate with cream, crushed flake bar and cherries.

Variations

Omit tin of fruit and juice. Sprinkle sherry over the sponge.
Replace juice and fruit with one of the following:

Rhuberry Trifle: Use stewed rhubarb (page 146) and mix with 1 punnet of sliced strawberries.

Banberry Trifle: Use 400g raspberries and 1 large sliced banana.

Look Up!
Different varieties of cream available in the shops.

STRAWBERRY MERINGUE ROULADE

Cooking Time: 25 minutes

Serves: 6

Ingredients

Meringue

3 large eggs

150g caster sugar

½ teaspoon white vinegar

½ teaspoon cornflour

Filling

170ml whipping cream

Punnet strawberries

25g caster sugar

Equipment

large and small bowl, knife, spatula, electric beater, Swiss roll tin, tin foil, tablespoon, teaspoon, sharp knife, piping bag and rose pipe.

Chef's Tip!
Adding 100g mascarpone cheese to the cream gives it a nice flavor and texture.

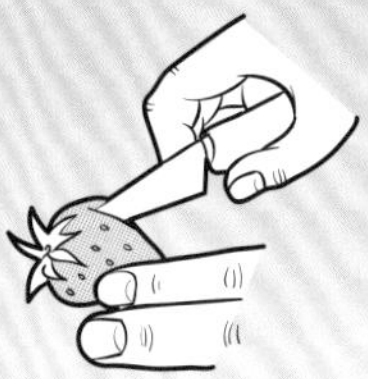

Fanning strawberries

Rolling meringue

Steps **Method**

Preheat oven to 150°C/Fan 140°C/Gas Mark 3-4.

Gather equipment, weigh ingredients, set worktop.

1 Prepare tin by lining it with tinfoil and secure it well around the edges. Oil it very well, especially along the sides.

2 **Meringue:** Separate the eggs carefully. Using an electric beater, whisk the egg whites in a clean bowl until they stand in peaks (see Chef's Tip on page 175).

3 Whisk in 1 tablespoon sugar and beat again until it stiffens. Continue with this until only half the sugar remains. Stop beating now. Fold in the vinegar, cornflour and the remaining sugar. Do not overdo this. Pour into the prepared tin, smooth over and spread into the corners.

4 Bake for 25 minutes, leave to cool completely in the tin.

5 **Filling:** Whip cream until it stands in peaks. Wash and slice the strawberries, keeping 4 for decoration.

6 Place a sheet of tinfoil on the table and turn out the meringue on top, carefully removing the lining paper.

7 Spread over the cream, arrange sliced fruit on top, roll up. Fan the remaining strawberries (see diagram).

Decorate with fanned strawberries and a dusting of icing sugar.

Separating Yolks from Whites

1 Have two bowls ready. Crack egg shell sharply in middle with knife.

2 Hold one egg shell upright over bowl so that egg yolk will stay in it and carefully remove the other half. Most of the white will fall into the bowl.

3 Very carefully, transfer yolk from shell to shell, allowing white to drain away. Take care that the sharp edges of the shell do not break the yolk.

4 Place yolk in second bowl.

Safer way for beginners:

Break egg onto saucer. Place egg cup over yolk and turn saucer sideways so that white falls into bowl placed below.

Eve's Pudding

ALL-IN-ONE METHOD

Cooking Time: 40-45 minutes

Serves: 4

Ingredients

Victoria Sponge

100g caster sugar

100g butter at room temperature

2 large eggs

125g self-raising flour

Fruit Base

2 large cooking apples

1 tablespoon water

2 tablespoons sugar

To decorate: 1 tablespoon caster sugar

Equipment

mixing bowl, electric beater, wooden spoon, sieve, tablespoon, spatula, peeler, sharp knife, board, bowl, pot stand, ovenproof dish, apple corer.

Idea!
Add the zest and juice of ½ lemon to the Victoria Sponge mixture to make Lemony Eve's Pudding.

Zesting a lemon

Chef's Tip!
See apple varieties on page 153.

Steps — Method

Preheat oven to 170°C/Fan 160°C/Gas Mark 3-4.

Gather equipment, collect/weigh ingredients, set worktop.

1. Grease the dish. Wash, quarter, peel, core and slice apples. Put into the greased dish with water. Sweeten with the sugar.
2. Make the all-in-one sponge method, beating the butter, sugar, eggs and flour for 2 minutes with a wooden spoon or 1 minute with electric beater. Spoon it over the apples.
3. Bake for 40-45 minutes until the pudding is cooked. Test with a skewer – it should come out clean from the sponge.
4. Dredge with caster sugar.

Serve with custard (page 155) or cream.

Variations

Apple and Blackberry Sponge Pudding:
Add 125g of blackberries to the apples in Step 1.

Plum and Apple Sponge Pudding:
Replace ½ the apple with 4 chopped and stoned fresh plums.

Rhubarb Sponge Pudding:
Use 4-5 sticks rhubarb, finely chopped, and ½ teaspoon cinnamon instead of apples.

Rhubarb and Banana Sponge Pudding:
Replace apples with 4-5 sticks of rhubarb and 2 bananas.

Resource Management: Use a **vegetable peeler** to peel the apples thinly. Use a **spatula** to scrape the mixture out of the bowl so nothing is wasted and the wash up is easier.

***ZEST** — TECHNIQUE

To zest means to grate finely the yellow part of the skin. This contains the essence and oils of the fruit. Do not grate down into the white pith as it is bitter.

Apple Crumble

USE RHUBARB, GOOSEBERRIES OR BLACKBERRIES TO MAKE OTHER DELICIOUS CRUMBLES

Cooking Time: 30 minutes

Serves: 3-4

Ingredients

2 large cooking apples
4 tablespoons water
30g sugar to taste

Crumble
100g flour
50g porridge oats
75g butter
30g sugar, brown or white
1 teaspoon cinnamon
25g chopped mixed nuts (optional)
To serve: whipped cream or crème fraîche.

Equipment

sharp knife, board, sieve, saucepan and lid, wooden spoon, peeler, mixing bowl, tablespoon, pot stand, ovenproof dish.

Chef's Tip!
To reduce sugar, add 5-6 fresh plums to the apples. For added fibre, do not peel the apples.

In a hurry!
Use frozen berries.

Healthy Hint!
Substitute sugar for 50g raisins and use eating apples to reduce sugar content.

Steps — Method

Preheat oven to 180°C/Fan 170°C/Gas Mark 4-5.

Gather equipment, collect/weigh ingredients, set worktop.

1. **Crumble:** Sieve flour and rub in butter until it resembles breadcrumbs. Mix in sugar, oats, cinnamon and nuts, if using.
2. Grease the pie dish.
3. Wash, peel, quarter and core the apples. Slice **very** thinly. See Resource Management below. Put into the dish with the water and 30g sugar.
4. Turn the crumble onto the apple, spread out evenly.
5. Bake for 30 minutes until golden on top.

Serve with whipped cream, crème fraîche or custard (page 155).

Crumble Variations

High-fibre: Use 100g wholemeal flour and 25g chopped mixed nuts (optional).
Muesli: Substitute the porridge oats and nuts for 100g of muesli.
Vegan, Dairy-free: Use coconut oil in place of butter and serve with Nut Cream (page 142) or vegan coconut yoghurt.

Filling Variations

Wild Blackberry and Apple: Add 300g-400g of blackberries to apple recipe above.

Garden Rhubarb and Strawberry: Substitute cooking apples for 300g of garden rhubarb and 150g of strawberries.

Fresh Rhubarb and Banana: Replace apples with 300g of rhubarb and 1 large banana.

Resource Management: Do not be wasteful when preparing apples. Wash, peel, half and quarter the apple and remove core from the centre of each quarter. Place in a bowl of cold water to prevent enzymic browning, see page 18. Slice thinly. Compost all fruit peelings and trimmings.

Chocolate Vegan Dessert Cake

Cooking Time: 35 minutes

Serves: 8-10

Ingredients

300g plain flour

30g cocoa powder

1½ teaspoons baking powder

1 teaspoon bread soda

200g caster sugar

100ml sunflower oil

1½ teaspoons white wine vinegar or cider vinegar

1½ teaspoons vanilla extract

200ml water

Frosting

1 ripe avocado

25g cocoa powder

2 tablespoons maple syrup

4 drops vanilla extract

1-2 tablespoons non-dairy milk

Pinch salt

Equipment

mixing bowl, small bowl, measuring jug, sieve, teaspoon, wooden spoon, spatula, skewer, electric beater, parchment paper, wire rack, hand or bullet blender, 18cm square or 20cm round cake tin, serving plate.

Steps — Method

Preheat oven to 170°C/Fan 160°C/Gas Mark 3-4.

Gather equipment, collect/weigh ingredients, set worktop.

1 Grease tin and line the base with parchment paper.

2 Sieve the flour, bread soda, cocoa and baking powder into the bowl. Stir in sugar.

3 Mix the oil, vinegar, vanilla and water together in a small bowl.

4 Add the wet mix to the dry ingredients and stir well.

5 Pour mixture into the tin. Bake for 35 minutes until a skewer inserted comes out clean. Allow to cool in the tin for 10 minutes. Loosen the edges with a knife and turn out onto a wire rack. Allow to cool fully.

6 **Frosting:** Beat all the ingredients until smooth, taste and add more syrup, if necessary. Spread on top of the cold cake. Refrigerate for 20 minutes.

Decorate and serve with strawberries.

Serve as a dessert with Coconut Cream.

Variation

Add the zest and juice of 1 orange to the cake mixture at Step 4. Serve with orange segments or slices.

Decorate with crushed pistachios and serve with raspberries.

Coconut Cream

Ingredients

1 small tin coconut cream

1 tablespoon almond butter

1 tablespoon maple syrup

Equipment

bowl, bullet or hand/stick blender.

Step — Method

Blitz all ingredients using a bullet or hand/stick blender.

Chef's Tip!
Chill tin of coconut cream in the fridge overnight, if possible.

Yummy Apple Cake

Cooking Time: 30 minutes

Serves: 6

Ingredients

Base

200g plain flour

75g butter, cubed

75g caster sugar

1 egg

150ml milk

Fruit

2 medium cooking apples

Topping

1 tablespoon granulated sugar

1 level teaspoon cinnamon

To serve: whipped cream

Equipment

sharp knife, board, bowl, wooden spoon, sieve, measuring jug, tablespoon, 18cm-20cm sandwich tin, spatula, serving plate.

Chef's Tip!

Sliced rhubarb or plums can be used instead of apples.

Rubbing in method

Healthy Hint!

To increase fibre content use 100g brown flour and 100g white flour.

Steps — Method

Preheat oven to 190°C/Fan 180°C/Gas Mark 5.

Gather equipment, collect/weigh ingredients, set worktop.

1. Grease tin with butter even if non-stick.
2. **Base:** Sieve flour and rub in butter until it resembles breadcrumbs. Add egg, milk and sugar and beat to a very soft consistency. Spoon into the tin.
3. **Fruit:** Wash, peel, core and slice apples very thinly, see **Resource Management** page 151. Arrange the apples over the top of the mixture. Avoid piling too much in the centre.
4. **Topping:** Sprinkle evenly with the cinnamon and granulated sugar.
5. Bake for 30-35 minutes until the top is brown and the cake is cooked through.

Serve hot straight from the tin or cool a little, loosen and turn out onto a plate. Serve with cream or ice cream.

Dessert Apples: Pink Lady

Dessert Apples: Braeburn

Dessert Apples: Royal Gala

Cooking Apples: Bramley

Tart Baking Apples: Granny Smith

Trendy Bread and Butter Pudding

UPCYCLED BREAD

Cooking Time: 25 minutes

Serves: 4

Ingredients

50g butter

8 slices white bread

Nutmeg to sprinkle

1-2 tablespoon granulated sugar

25g sultanas (optional)

50g chocolate (optional)

Custard

350ml milk

2 tablespoons sugar

2 eggs

1 orange, zest only

Equipment

saucepan, pot stand, sharp knife, board, tablespoon, whisk, small bowl, knife, grater with medium holes, baking tray, pie dish or ovenproof dish.

Chef's Tip!
For a change, use barm brack, panetone or croissants instead of white bread. Use white chocolate instead of milk chocolate - delicious!

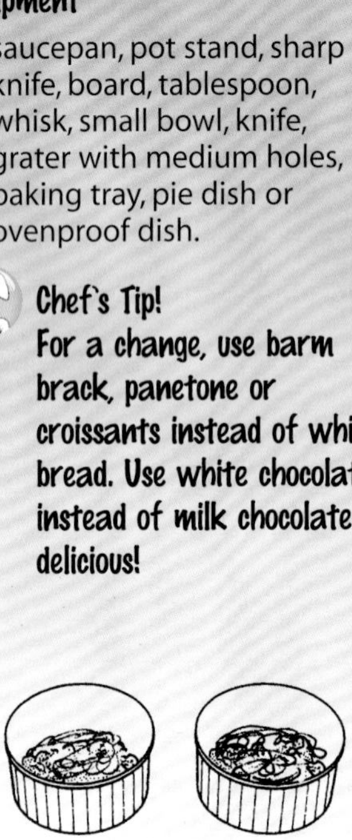

Ramekins

Steps — Method

Preheat oven to 190°C/Fan 180°C/Gas Mark 5.

Gather equipment, collect/weigh ingredients, set worktop.

1 Wash and **zest** (page 150) the orange using the medium holes of grater. Chop chocolate if using.

2 Lightly butter each slice of bread, remove only the black crusts, cut into fingers. Line the bottom of the ovenproof dish, buttered side facing downwards. Sprinkle with sultanas or chocolate.

3 Repeat until all the bread is used finishing with a layer of bread, buttered side facing upwards.

4 **Custard:** Heat milk, sugar and zest in saucepan until quite hot but do not allow to boil. Beat eggs and stir in the hot milk. Pour over the bread.

5 Grate or sprinkle a little nutmeg on top, sprinkle with granulated sugar, place on a baking tray and bake for 25-30 minutes.

Decorate with sieved icing sugar.

Serve with cream or crème fraîche.

Individual Bread and Butter Puddings

Use a scone cutter to cut bread into circles. Fit into ramekins and layer as above. Cook for 15-20 minutes.

Food Fact!
Raisins, sultanas and currants are forms of dried grapes. Use the washed, seedless variety when baking.

Resource Management: Use stale, leftover bread to make breadcrumbs (see page 119), and freeze for use later. Use for stuffed tomatoes (page 56), burgers (page 118), coating fish (page 105) and making stuffing for chicken or vegetables.

Custard Sauce

THIS CUSTARD IS A REAL LUXURY MADE WITH ½ MILK AND ½ CREAM, WONDERFUL FOR SPECIAL OCCASIONS

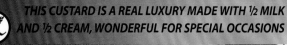

Cooking Time: 20 minutes

Serves: 4-6

Ingredients

2 eggs
400ml milk
2 teaspoons sugar
Vanilla pod or essence

Equipment

small bowl, sieve, fork or mini whisk, double saucepan, wooden spoon, teaspoon, pot stand, sauce boat.

Chef's Tip!
If the custard curdles, it can be rescued by emptying it at once into a cool, clean bowl and whisking until smooth.

Food Fact!
Egg white coagulates at 60°C.
Egg yolk coagulates at 65°C.
Egg yolk and white mixed coagulate between 63°C and 65°C.

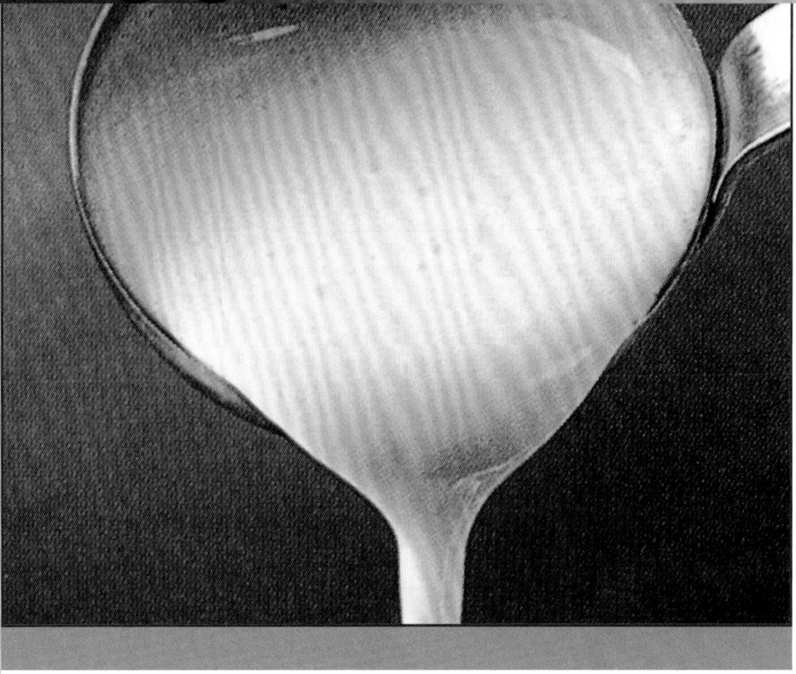

Vanilla Pod

Buy Local, Buy Irish!
Support your local farm providers.

Steps / Method

Gather equipment, collect/weigh ingredients, set worktop.

1. Beat eggs and sugar in bowl using fork or whisk.
2. Heat milk and vanilla pod until steam begins to rise. It should not be allowed to boil. Pour warm milk over beaten eggs, stirring all the time.
3. Strain into saucepan and stir over a gentle heat until custard thickens. You will know when it is cooked as it will be thick enough to coat the back of a wooden spoon (this is never as thick as commercial custard).
4. Add vanilla essence if using and serve at once.

Use **hot fresh custard sauce** to pour over sponge puddings, hot gingerbread, fruit puddings and chocolate ice cream. Hot custard can be used to make traditional trifle (page 148).

Use **cold fresh custard sauce** to make Fruit Fool (page 146).

Food Fact!
A vanilla pod is the long, thin seed pod of the vanilla plant. Both the pod and seeds have a wonderful flavour and are often used in baking and cooking. Vanilla extract and vanilla bean paste are natural and are far superior to vanilla essence, which is a synthetic and cheaper product.

***CURDLING** — COOKING TERM

A mixture is said to curdle when it begins to separate and change from a smooth texture to a grainy texture. Curdling happens when egg dishes are cooked at too high a temperature. For curdled custard see Chef's Tip, above.

Fresh Berry Coulis

Serves: 4

Ingredients

- 100g raspberries
- 100g strawberries
- 1 tablespoon lemon juice
- 1 tablespoon icing sugar

Equipment

liquidiser, spatula, sieve, tablespoon, jug to serve.

Chef's Tip!
Make sauce ahead of time. Store in a jar in fridge.

Buy Local, Buy Irish!
Support Irish fruit growers.

Steps **Method**

Gather equipment, collect/weigh ingredients, set worktop.

1 Liquidise everything together, then pass through a sieve to take out the seeds. Check taste.

Serve with ice cream, fruit desserts and meringues.

When using tinned fruit, drain the fruit, liquidise with 1 tablespoon lemon juice and 3-4 tablespoons of the juice. Pass through a sieve if necessary. Sweeten with 1-2 teaspoons icing sugar. Add 2-3 drops of food colouring to improve the colour.

Apple Sauce

Ingredients

- 400g cooking apples
- 25g-35g sugar
- 125ml water
- 15g butter, softened
- 2 cloves (optional)

Equipment

liquidiser, spatula, sieve, tablespoon, jug to serve.

In a hurry!
Use a microwave to cook the apples, see page 134.

Resource Management:
See page 151.

Steps **Method**

1 Wash, peel, quarter, core and slice apples. Put all ingredients into saucepan. Cook until fruit is soft. Remove cloves if using.

2 Beat apples to a smooth pulp with butter using a liquidiser.

Serve hot or cold with pork dishes.

Toblerone Sauce

Cooking Time: 10 minutes

Serves: 4-6

Ingredients

- 200g Toblerone
- 25g butter
- 100ml whipping cream

Equipment

heatproof bowl, sharp knife, board, small saucepan, pot stand, measuring jug, wooden spoon, serving dish.

Ice Cream with Toblerone Sauce

Chef's Tip!
Use butter when making sauces.
It gives a great flavour.

Steps **Method**

Gather equipment, collect/weigh ingredients, set worktop.

1 Cut the Toblerone into small pieces. Melt in a heatproof bowl over a saucepan of simmering water.

2 Add butter, allow to melt, then stir in the cream.

Serve with ice cream or on pancakes (page 78).

Fudge Sauce

Cooking Time: 25-30 minutes

Serves: 4-6

Ingredients

- 200ml milk
- 2-3 drops vanilla essence
- 50g butter
- 75g brown sugar
- 1 tablespoon golden syrup
- 2 rounded teaspoons cornflour
- 1 tablespoon lemon juice

Equipment

measuring jug, teaspoon, 2 small saucepans, wooden spoon, pot stand, 2 tablespoons, sauce boat.

Steps **Method**

Gather equipment, collect/weigh ingredients, set worktop.

1 Melt the sugar and syrup in saucepan, stirring over a gentle heat. Boil for 30 seconds. Remove from heat. Stir in the butter. Be careful as it will bubble up. Now stir in half the milk.

2 Whisk the cornflour into the remaining cold milk. Whisk this into the fudge mixture and return to heat. Stir and boil up once until thickened. Add the lemon juice and essence.

Serve in a sauce boat. Delicious with ice cream, bananas or sponge.

Chapter 10

Bread and Pastry

Products baked at home have a better flavour than commercial products and are additive free. Baking allows for creativity and can be very satisfying, while dietary requirements and needs can be catered for, e.g. sugar and salt can be reduced and recipes can be adjusted for coeliacs and those with lactose intolerance. Buy the best-quality ingredients for home baking. Always check the use-by dates and store baked goods in airight containers in a dry place. Use butter, olive or coconut oils and avoid unhealthy trans fats in margaines.

Key Words and Skills

- preheat
- raising agent
- whisk
- rub in
- bake blind
- knead
- roll out
- rolling pin
- glaze
- sieve
- pastry leaves
- dice

Other suitable recipes:

Dingle Quiche (page 112) and Salmon and Broccoli Quiche (page 112).

Evaluation! See pages 223 and 224.

- Did you meet the brief and did you refer to the specific requirements of the task or dish/dishes?
- Discuss the results of your finished dish/dishes including the presentation, colour, taste and texture.
- What aspects were done well and what aspects could be improved?
- Did you correctly cost and budget for all ingredients?

Lining Baking Tins

A./B. Lining a round or square tin

- Place tin on parchment/ greaseproof paper.
- Pencil all round the tin.
- Cut a strip of parchment/ greaseproof paper long enough to go round the tin and a little deeper. Make 1cm snips at bottom edge of paper. Cut a circle or square to fit the base.
- Fit the strip inside the tin and finally fit the circle or square inside.
- When lining a sandwich tin just pencil all round the base. Cut the circle a little smaller than the tin and use a little oil to keep it in place – no need to line the sides.

C. Lining a swiss roll tin or tin with sloped sides

- Snip paper diagonally at corners and fold to fit the tin.

D. Lining a loaf tin

- Measure the length and width of the tin and add twice the tin's depth to each of these measurements. Cut a piece of greaseproof paper to this size and position the tin in the centre of the oblong. Make a cut at each corner as shown.
- Grease the tin and fold the paper to fit the tin.

E. When breads and cakes are cooked properly

- **Bread:** hollow sound underneath when tapped.
- **Cake:** Insert a dry skewer, it should come out clean.
- **Sponges:** Surface springs back when lightly pressed with finger.

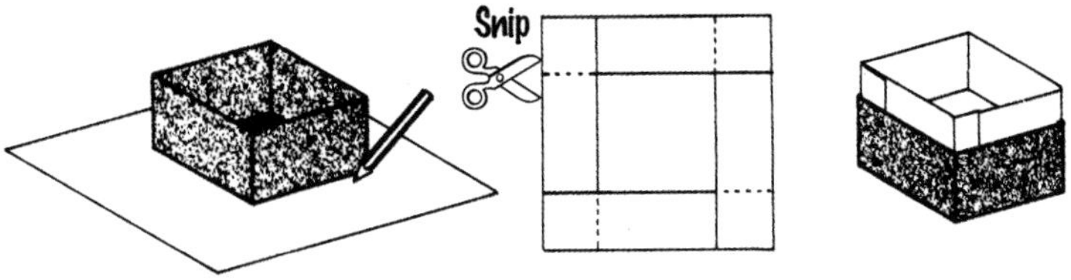

A. Square Tin (Simple method)

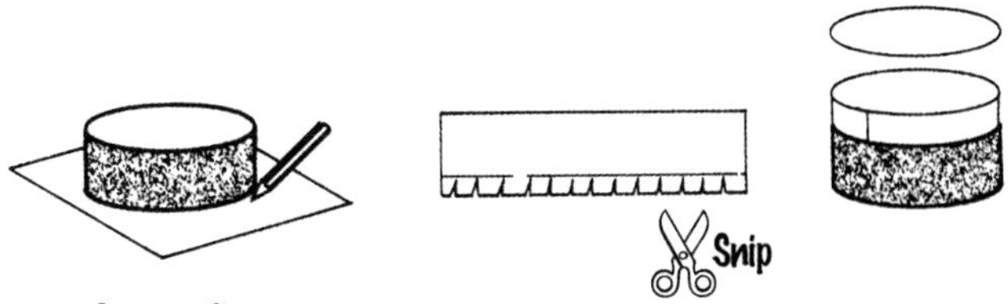

B. Round or Square Tin

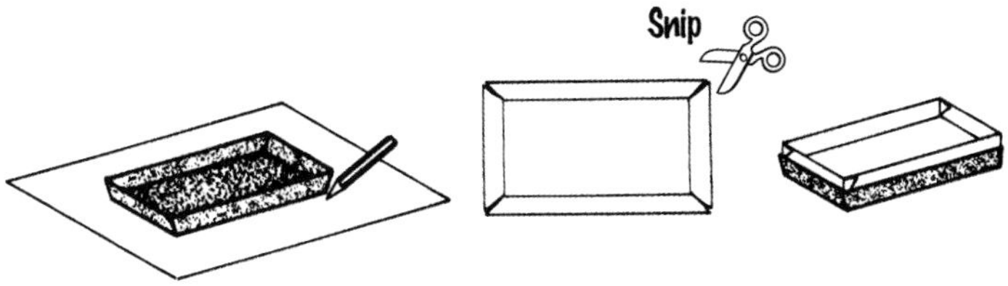

C. Swiss Roll Tin

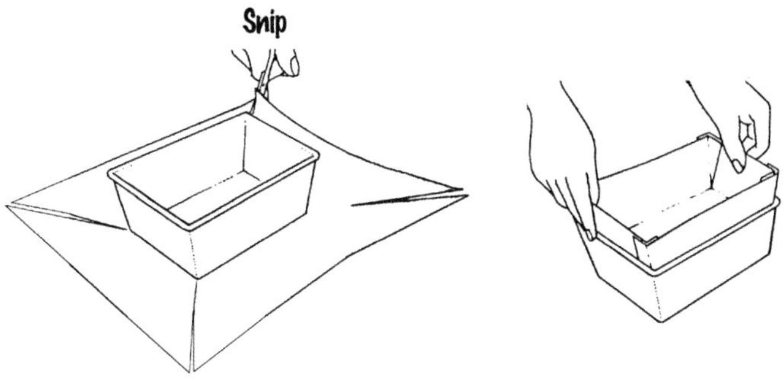

D. Loaf Tin

E. Testing Bread and Cakes to see if they are cooked

Irish White Soda Bread (Wet Mix)

Cooking Time:
40 minutes round tin;
45 minutes loaf tin

Ingredients

400g plain flour
1 level teaspoon salt
1 level teaspoon bread soda
2 rounded teaspoons sugar
50g butter
350ml buttermilk
1 egg
Butter or white fat and kitchen paper for greasing

Equipment

round sandwich tin (18cm-20cm) or 1kg/2lb loaf tin, teaspoon, mixing bowl, sieve, knife, spatula, wooden spoon, measuring jug, pot stand, wire rack, serving board or plate.

Chef's Tip!
Non-stick tins are the best to use as there is no need to grease them.
Other tins are best greased with butter or white fat. Spread it over the tin with a small piece of kitchen paper. Avoid using oil as it can be difficult to clean from the tins afterwards.

Spatula

Resource Management: Always use a spatula to scrape the mixture out of the mixing bowl, so nothing is wasted and the wash up is easier.

Steps — Method

Preheat oven to 210°C/Fan 200°C/Gas Mark 7.

Gather equipment, collect/weigh ingredients, set worktop.

1 Grease tin. Beat egg with milk.

2 Sieve flour, salt and bread soda into bowl.

3 Lightly rub in the butter. Add sugar, mix well.

4 Pour all the milk into flour and mix to a soft, sticky consistency. Turn into tin, scrape bowl with spatula but keep the top of the tin clean. Flatten and wet the top with back of knuckles.

5 Bake for 40-45 minutes on middle shelf. Cover for last 20 minutes if getting too brown.

6 Remove from tin using oven mitts. Test by tapping the bottom of the loaf. It will sound hollow if it is cooked (see page 159).

7 Cool on a wire rack. It is best to cut it when cold.

Serve for breakfast, with soup or salads or just for a snack.

Variation White Fruit Loaf: Add 100g raisins, sultanas or cranberries to the recipe at Step 3 and mix with the sugar.

Food Fact!
Buttermilk is the liquid left behind after cream is churned into butter. It is a 'cultured' low-fat milk product made slightly acidic with lactic cultures.
Bread soda or sodium bicarbonate is an alkali and when combined with an acid and liquid, produces CO_2. When heated, CO_2 expands and the dough rises.

Irish White Soda Bread

TRADITIONAL KNEADED METHOD

Ingredients

400g plain flour
1 level teaspoon salt
1 level teaspoon bread soda
2 rounded teaspoons sugar
50g butter
300ml buttermilk
1 egg
Butter or white fat and kitchen paper for greasing

Equipment

round sandwich tin (18cm-20cm) or 1kg/2lb loaf tin, teaspoon, mixing bowl, sieve, knife, spatula, wooden spoon, measuring jug, pot stand, wire rack, serving board or plate, baking tray, flour dredger.

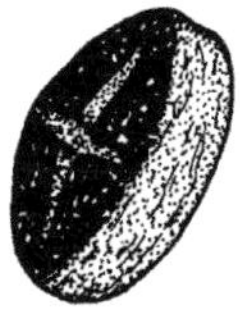

Testing bread

Buy Local, Buy Irish!
Buy Irish dairy produce.

Steps — Method

Preheat oven to 210°C/Fan 200°C/Gas Mark 7.

Gather equipment, collect/weigh ingredients, set worktop.

1. Flour baking tray or grease tin. Beat egg with milk.
2. Sieve flour, salt and bread soda into bowl.
3. Lightly rub in the butter. Add sugar, mix well.
4. Gradually add enough milk to form a dough that is soft but not too sticky. Gather it into a ball, flour table, knead lightly 8-10 times only.
5. Put the dough on the floured tray and flatten the top just a little. Brush with milk, cut a cross right through.
6. **Bake*** for 40 minutes. Bread should be well risen and nicely browned. It should sound 'hollow' when tapped gently on the bottom.
7. Cool on a wire rack.

Serve on a bread board with a bread knife for cutting.

Variations

Fruit Loaf: Add 100g sultanas to the dry mix at Step 3.

Cheese and Chive Bread: At Step 3 add 100g grated Cheddar cheese, 2 tablespoons fresh or dried chives and 1 teaspoon of mustard powder to the dry mix.

Tomato Pesto Soda: Add 8 chopped sundried tomatoes and 8 chopped, pitted black olives to the dry mix. Add 1 tablespoon of green basil pesto to the milk.

Spelt Bread: Replace plain flour with spelt flour.

> **Resource Management:**
> Always use a spatula to scrape the mixture out of the mixing bowl, so nothing is wasted and the wash up is easier.

BAKING — COOKING METHOD

Baking means cooking food in hot air in a ventilated oven. If food is covered, it partially cooks in its own steam and stays moist.

Irish Brown Soda Bread (Wet Mix)

Cooking Time:
40 minutes round tin;
45 minutes loaf tin

Ingredients

- 250g wholemeal flour
- 100g plain white flour
- 60g porridge oats
- 1 level teaspoon salt
- 2 rounded teaspoons sugar
- 1 heaped teaspoon bread soda
- 375ml buttermilk
- Butter or oil and kitchen paper for greasing
- **Topping:** 2 teaspoons pinhead oatmeal or flaked oats

Equipment

round sandwich tin (18cm-20cm) or 1kg/2lb loaf tin, pastry brush, mixing bowl, sieve, spatula, wooden spoon, measuring jug, teaspoon, knife, wire rack, serving board or plate.

Steps — Method

Preheat oven to 210°C/Fan 200°C/Gas Mark 7.

Gather equipment, collect/weigh ingredients, set worktop.

1. Grease tin. Put wholemeal flour, oats and sugar into bowl. Sieve in white flour, salt and bread soda and mix well.
2. Pour in all the milk and mix to a soft, sticky consistency.
3. Turn into tin and scrape bowl with spatula, keeping the top of the tin clean. Flatten the top and wet well with the back of your knuckles.
4. Sprinkle the top with pinhead oatmeal or flaked oats.
5. Bake for 40-45 minutes until nicely browned. Cover for last 20 minutes if getting too brown.
6. Remove from tin using oven mitts. Test by tapping the bottom of loaf. It will sound hollow if it is cooked. See page 159.
7. Cool on a wire rack and cover with a tea towel. Bread is best cut when cold.

Serve for breakfast, with soup or salads or for a snack.

Variation Mixed Seed Soda Bread: Various seeds or chopped nuts can be added to the dry mix at Step 2. Seeds give texture and provide extra nutrition to breads. Try adding a variety of the following, e.g. 50g sunflower seeds, 50g pumpkin seeds, 50g sesame seeds and/or 50g mixed, chopped nuts.

Chef's Tips! Modifications

If modifying a soda bread recipe, do not change the proportions of flour and raising agent. Bread soda is a raising agent (alkali/base) and when mixed with an acid (buttermilk/vinegar/lemon juice/yoghurt), and a liquid CO_2 gas is formed. When the mixture is heated it causes the dough to rise.

No buttermilk	Use fresh milk or water and add 1 tablespoon of white vinegar.
Low salt	Leave it out! Replace with 2 teaspoons of cinnamon for flavour.
High fibre	Replace white flour with wholemeal brown flour and add 2 tablespoons of oat bran.
Diabetic	Omit the sugar and replace with 2 teaspoons of Xylitol or 1 mashed banana at Step 2.
Vegan	Use water or non-dairy milk and add 1 tablespoon of white vinegar.
Gluten-free	Replace flour and oats with gluten-free flour mixed with Xanthan gum and use as directed.
Dairy-free	Use water or non-dairy milk and add 1 tablespoon of white vinegar.

Irish Brown Soda Bread

Ingredients

- 250g wholemeal flour
- 100g plain white flour
- 60g porridge oats
- 1 level teaspoon salt
- 2 rounded teaspoons sugar
- 1 heaped teaspoon bread soda
- 200-250ml buttermilk
- Butter or oil and kitchen paper for greasing

Equipment

baking tray or bread tin, flour dredger, pastry brush, mixing bowl, sieve, spatula, wooden spoon, measuring jug, teaspoon, knife, wire rack, serving board or plate.

Chef's Tip!
Replace the sugar in brown bread with 1 tablespoon molasses softened in 1 tablespoon hot water.

Steps — Method

Preheat oven to 210°C/Fan 200°C/Gas Mark 7.

1 Grease bread tin if using. Put wholemeal flour, oats and sugar into bowl. Sieve in white flour, salt and bread soda and mix well.

2 Gradually add enough milk to form a dough that is soft but not too sticky. Gather into a ball, flour table, knead lightly (8-10 times only).

3 Put the dough on the floured tray, flatten the top just a little. Brush with milk, cut a cross right through.

4 Bake for 40 minutes. Bread should be well risen and a good colour. It should sound hollow when tapped gently on the bottom.

5 Cool on a wire rack.

Serve on a bread board with a bread knife for cutting.

Modify the recipe for dietary needs – see page 162.

Chef's Tips! Modifications

Lower fat	Use skimmed milk or water. Add vinegar, lemon juice or cream of tartar. Omit butter.
Lower salt	The salt is used for flavour, just leave it out or use a low-salt alternative.
High fibre	To make a higher-fibre health loaf, at Step 3 add any combination of the following: (a) 1-2 tablespoons bran and/or (b) 1-2 tablespoons oatbran to the basic ingredients.
Diabetic	The sugar can be omitted altogether or use fructose or an artificial sweetener or 50g raisins if allowed by the diet.
Wheat allergy	Replace all wheat flour with 'spelt' flour – it works just as well.

Practise the basic recipe first and then modify it to suit your needs. Do not change the proportions of flour and raising agent in the basic recipe. The bread soda (ALKALI/BASE) and some form of ACID, (buttermilk, vinegar, lemon juice, yoghurt or cream of tartar) must be added to raise the dough.

Plain White Soda Scones

TRADITIONAL IRISH

Cooking Time: 20 minutes

Serves: 12-16 scones

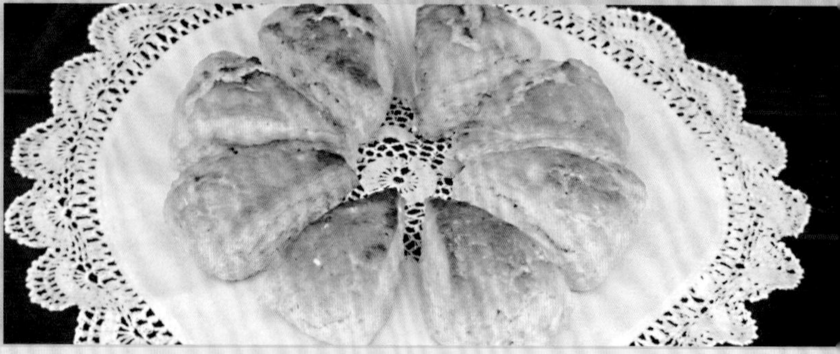

Ingredients

400g plain flour
1 level teaspoon salt
1 level teaspoon bread soda
2 rounded teaspoons sugar
50g butter
300ml buttermilk
1 egg
Butter or white fat and kitchen paper for greasing

Equipment

baking tray, teaspoon, mixing bowl, sieve, knife, spatula, wooden spoon, measuring jug, pot stand, wire rack, serving plate.

Steps — Method

Preheat oven to 180°C/Fan 170°C/Gas Mark 5.

1 Flour baking tray. Beat egg and milk together.
2 Sieve flour, salt and bread soda into a bowl and lightly rub in butter. Add sugar and mix well.
3 Gradually add enough milk to form a dough that is soft in consistency but not too sticky. Lightly dust the countertop with flour.
4 Gather the dough into a ball, knead lightly 4 or 5 times. Divide the dough into two pieces.
5 Knead each one lightly and flatten with your hand into 2 small circles, 2cm in thickness. Cut each circle into 6 or 8 even-sized triangles.
6 Place on floured tray and bake for 15-20 minutes. Cool on a wire rack.

Serve hot or cold with butter and jam for breakfast or with soups and salads. A fresh scone with a filling makes a tasty lunchtime snack.

Variation Sweet: Add 75g raisins or dried cranberries or blueberries at Step 2.

Savoury: Add 50g of crumbled feta cheese and a handful or 15g of chopped fresh or frozen spinach.

Plain Brown Soda Scones

TRADITIONAL IRISH

Serves: 12-16 scones

Ingredients

1 x Irish Brown Soda Bread (page 163) but use only 200ml-250ml buttermilk.

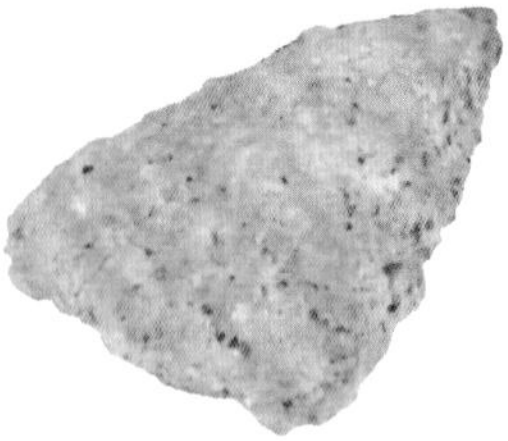

Steps — Method

Preheat oven to 180°C/Fan 170°C/Gas Mark 5.

1 Flour baking tray. Beat egg and milk together Sieve flour, salt and bread soda into a bowl and lightly rub in butter. Add sugar and mix well.
2 Gradually add enough milk to form a dough that is soft in consistency but not too sticky. Lightly dust the countertop with flour.
3 Gather the dough into a ball and knead lightly 4 or 5 times. Divide the dough into two pieces. Knead each one lightly and flatten out with your hand into 2 small circles, 2cm in thickness.
4 Cut each circle into 6 or 8 even-sized triangles. Place on floured tray and bake for 15-20 minutes.

Serve hot or cold with soups and salads or butter and jam for breakfast

Four Seed Bread

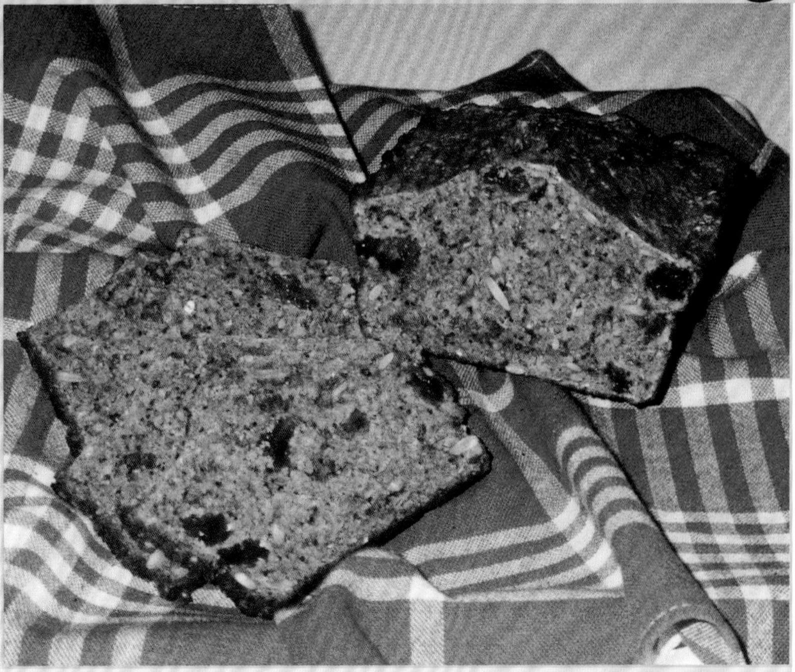

Cooking Time:
40 minutes round tin;
45 minutes loaf tin

Ingredients

- 300g self-raising white flour
- 100g wholemeal flour
- 1 level teaspoon salt
- 1 level teaspoon baking powder
- 1 tablespoon sesame seeds
- 1 tablespoon poppy seeds
- 1 tablespoon sunflower seeds
- 1 tablespoon pumpkin seeds
- 25g dried apricots or sultanas
- 1 tablespoon treacle
- 350ml–375ml warm water
- Margarine or white fat and kitchen paper for greasing
- **Topping:** Sesame seeds

Equipment

500g/2lb loaf tin (or sandwich tin 18cm-20cm), wooden spoon, mixing bowl and sieve, 1 teaspoon, 1 tablespoon, spatula, measuring jug, pot stand, wire rack, serving plate, doyley.

Spatula

Look Up!
Treacle.

Resource Management:
Use a spatula to remove all the mixture from a bowl. Never waste any resources.

Steps — Method

Preheat oven to 200°C/Fan 190°C/Gas Mark 6.

Gather equipment, collect/weigh ingredients, set worktop.

1. Grease tin. Sieve white flour, salt and baking powder into a bowl. Add wholemeal flour, all the seeds and chopped apricots or sultanas.
2. Measure the warm water and heat a tablespoon in this. Using this warm spoon add treacle to the warm water and stir to dissolve. Mix into the dry ingredients all at once. Mix to a soft consistency.
3. Spoon into the tin, wet the top very well with lots of water and sprinkle with some sesame seeds.
4. Bake for 45-50 minutes until nicely browned.
5. Remove from tin using oven mitts. Test by tapping the bottom of the loaf. It will sound hollow if it is cooked.
6. Cool on a wire rack. Do not cut until it is cold.

Serve sliced with butter or toasted for breakfast. It is delicious with cheese. Four seed bread goes well with soups or salad lunches.

Food Fact!
Spelt flour is made from spelt, an ancestor to modern wheat. It is more easily digested than the modern variety due to its low gluten content. It can replace white flour in most recipes but it must not be beaten for longer than 3 minutes. It is particularly good in the Wet Mix White and Brown Bread recipes (page 160 and 162) and the batter recipes in Chapter 4.

Pastry

Shortcrust pastry is the easiest pastry to make. It is used for sweet and savoury dishes.

Oven temperature: 220°C/Fan 210°C/Gas Mark 7 for the first 10 minutes only, then lower the heat to 190°C/Fan 180°C/Gas Mark 5 until cooked through.

Chef's Tip!
Guidelines for best results.

1. Always add a good pinch of salt to bring out the flavour of pastry.
2. Keep everything cold and use very cold butter and water.
3. Do not make the dough too moist.
4. Handle lightly and as little as possible.
5. Allow pastry to 'relax' in the fridge before rolling and cooking.

Healthy Hint!
If using margarine for pastry making, buy one with no trans fatty acids and use it straight from the fridge. If using butter, use hard butter straight from the fridge.

Idea!
See pastry leaves, page 121. See pastry tassels, page 131.

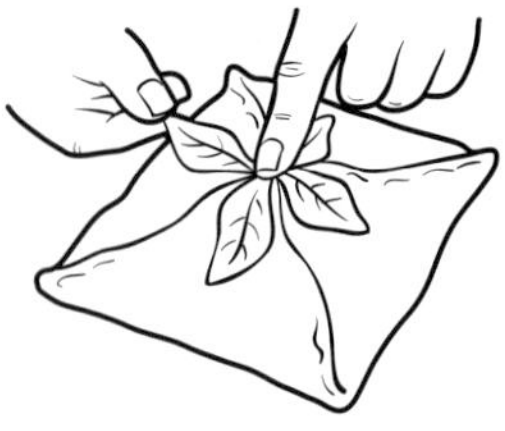

Making pastry leaves

When things go wrong!

Pale in colour or uncooked underneath – Oven set too low or not preheated. Oven shelf too low.

Dark on top and scorched at the edges – Oven set too high or overbaked. Shelf too high in oven.

Hard texture – Too much water used. Over handling. Overbaking at too low a temperature.

Soggy texture inside pie – Insufficiently cooked. Too much liquid. Filling not cooled before use.

Shrinking – Pastry was stretched when rolled or lifted. Insufficient 'relaxing' of pastry.

Blisters on top – Uneven mixing of water.

Making pastry

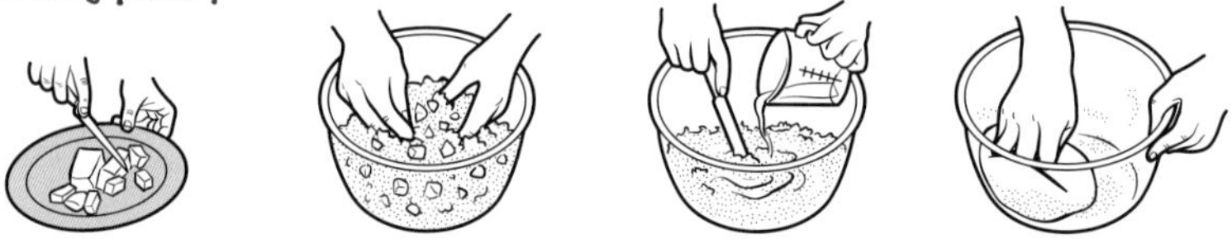

Cutting fat into chunks | *Rubbing in fat and flour* | *Adding water* | *Forming into dough*

Decorative edges

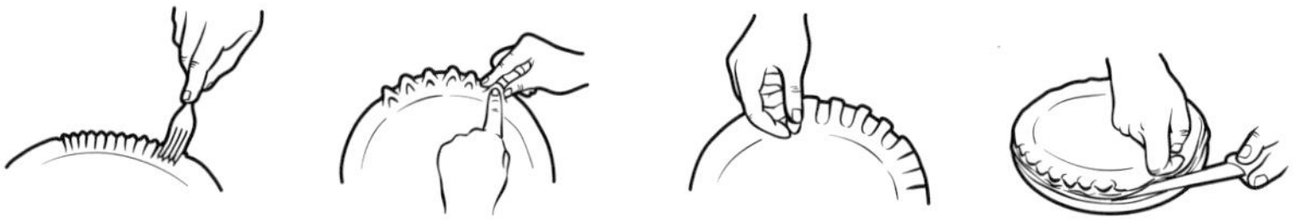

Forked edge | *Fluted edge* | *Cut edge* | *Flaking the edge*

Decorating a lattice tart

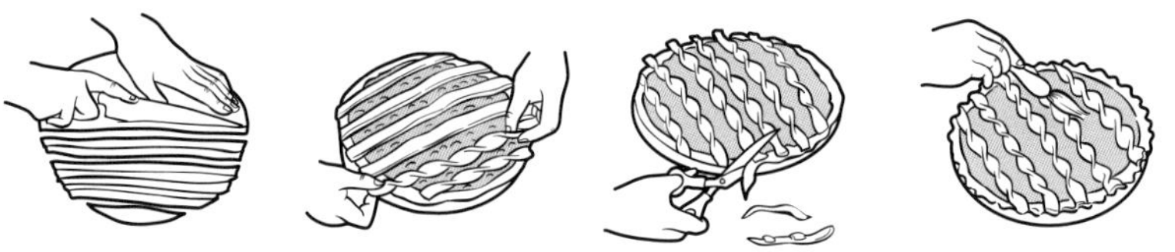

Shortcrust Pastry

THIS RECIPE MAKES 200g PASTRY

Cooking Time:
This depends on the filling used.

Serves: 1 x 24cm tart or 2 x 18cm open jam/mince tarts

Ingredients

200g plain flour
¼ teaspoon salt
100g margarine or hard butter
3-4 tablespoons cold water
Beaten egg to glaze

Equipment

mixing bowl, sieve, rolling pin, small jug, flour dredger, fork, table knife, tablespoon, pastry brush, pot stand.

Chef's Tip!
Shortcrust pastry is used for apple tarts, mince pies, sausage rolls and for tops of pies.

Idea!
Preheat a baking sheet in the oven and place a flan, large tart dish or Pyrex or earthenware dish on this when cooking - it helps to crisp the bottom of large tarts.

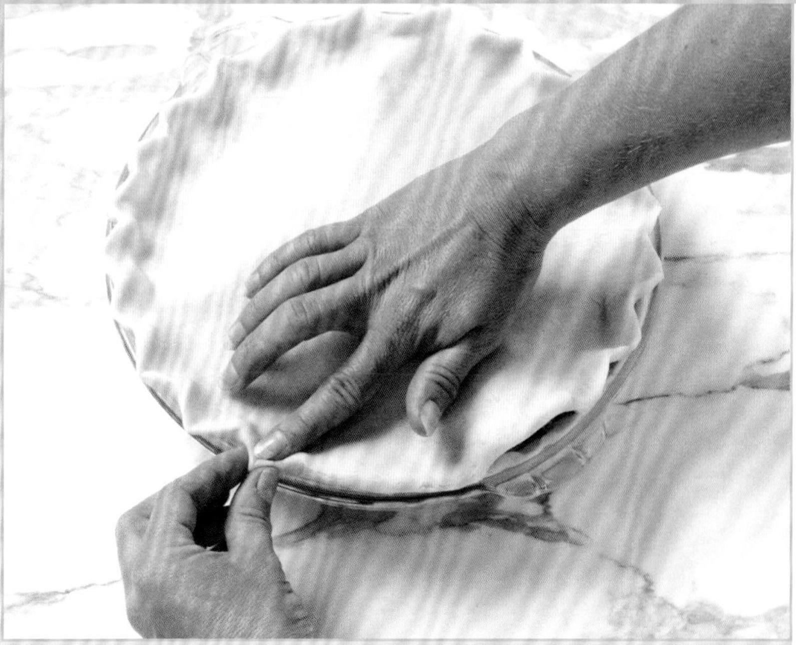

Technique: To decorate the edge of a tart

Steps **Method**

Preheat oven to 220°C/Fan 210°C/Gas Mark 7.

Gather equipment, collect/weigh ingredients, set worktop.

1 Grease baking tin/pie plate.
2 Sieve flour and salt. Cut the margarine or butter into the flour with a knife then rub in lightly. The mixture should look like dry crumbs.
3 Gradually add the water, 2 tablespoons at a time. Use a table knife to mix to a firm dough – 'mix around and around and cut through' to distribute the water.
4 Knead very lightly on a floured surface until just smooth. Leave to 'relax' in refrigerator before rolling.
5 Roll out and shape as required. Relax dough if time permits.
6 **Glaze*** with egg if required.
7 Bake in a hot oven according to recipe.

How much pastry to use?
When a recipe requires a certain quantity of pastry, the amount of flour should equal the amount of pastry required, e.g. for 200g Shortcrust Pastry use:
200g plain flour
¼ teaspoon salt
100g margarine/butter
3-4 tablespoons cold water

***GLAZE** **TECHNIQUE**

Beat an egg with a pinch of salt and use to brush over the top of pastry and scones. It gives a nice shine and a golden brown finish. This is sometimes called an **egg wash**.

Sausage Rolls

Cooking Time: 20-25 minutes

Serves: 3-4

Ingredients

200g **Shortcrust pastry** (page 167)

200g sausage meat

(8 sausages can be used in place of sausage meat – the sausages are laid in a line across the pastry instead of forming the long 'sausage' with the sausage meat)

1 egg (beaten to glaze)

Garnish: fresh parsley

Equipment

pastry brush, baking tray, knife, plate with serviette, small bowl/cup, mixing bowl, sieve, rolling pin, small jug, flour dredger, fork, table knife, tablespoon, wire tray.

Chef's Tip!
To remove skin from a sausage, slit the skin lengthways with a sharp knife or scissors and pull away from the meat.

Idea!
Vary sausage rolls by adding a pinch of mixed herbs or a few drops of Worcestershire sauce or finely-chopped rosemary.

Steps — Method

Preheat oven to 200°C/Fan 190°C/Gas Mark 6.

Gather equipment, collect/weigh ingredients, set worktop.

1 **Pastry:** Make as for Shortcrust Pastry (page 167) and then roll into a square about 30cm x 30cm (just larger than long side of A4 sheet).

2 If using sausage meat, divide the sausage meat in two and, using flour, roll into two long sausages the width of the pastry.

3 Place one sausage (or a row of sausages) across the width of the pastry and roll the pastry around the sausage(s) until the pastry meets again. Dampen the edge of the pastry and continue to roll for another ¼ turn so that the pastry overlaps (page 166).

4 Cut the long 'sausage roll' from the pastry, roll on seam to seal.

5 Repeat the process with the remaining sausage(s).

6 **Glaze** with egg (see technique on page 167). Cut into even-sized pieces of 6cm each or 3cm for bite-sized ones. Cut 2 or 3 slits on the top of each.

7 Bake for 10 minutes in a hot oven, lower the heat a little and continue cooking for 10-15 minutes depending on size.

Garnish with fresh parsley.
Serve hot or cold on a plate with a doyley or serviette.

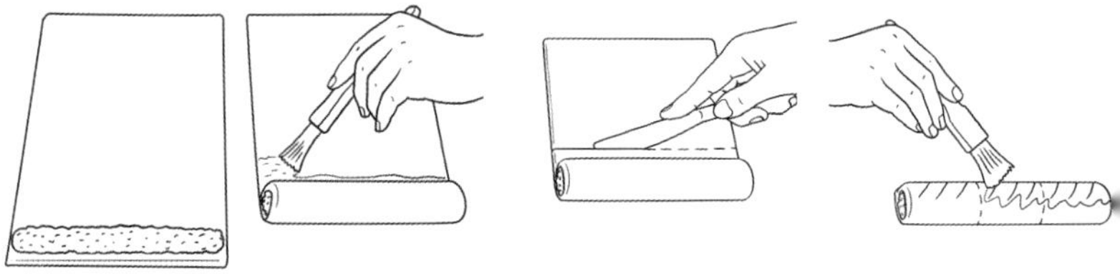

Forming sausage rolls

CROSTATA FRUIT PIE

ITALIAN

Cooking Time: 25 minutes

Serves: 6

Ingredients

Shortcrust pastry (page 167)
150g plain flour
75g butter
2-3 tablespoons cold water

Filling
2 eating apples
25g raisins
1 lemon
20g sugar

Crumble topping
50g plain flour
25g porridge oats
40g butter
40g soft brown sugar
1 teaspoon cinnamon
1 teaspoon nutmeg
Pinch salt
50g walnuts (optional)

Decoration: 1 teaspoon icing sugar

Equipment

sharp knife, board, tablespoon, table knife, teaspoon, wooden spoon, rolling pin, flour dredger, board, 2 bowls, sieve, mixing bowl, 20cm deep round sandwich baking tin.

In a hurry!
Make using 150g thawed, frozen Shortcrust Pastry.

Steps — Method

Preheat oven to 210°C/Fan 200°C/Gas Mark 6.

Gather equipment, collect/weigh ingredients, set worktop.

1 **Pastry:** Make as for Shortcrust Pastry on page 167, chill in a plastic bag in the fridge. Grease the baking tin.

2 **Filling:** Zest lemon. Wash, peel, quarter and core the apples, slice thinly and mix in a bowl with sugar, raisins and zest.

3 **Crumble topping:** Chop walnuts. Sieve flour and rub in butter until it resembles breadcrumbs. Add the oats, sugar, spices and walnuts.

4 **Assembly:** Roll pastry into a 34cm-diameter circle. Fold the pastry circle into quarters (see picture below). Place the centre point of pastry into the centre of the tin, and open out the pastry. Put the apple mix on top of the pastry. Spoon the crumble over the apples. Fold in the pastry and allow to overlap the crumble slightly.

5 **Bake** for 10 minutes and reduce the oven temperature to 180°C/Fan 170°C/Gas Mark 5. Cook for a further 20 minutes, until the apples are just soft and the pastry golden in colour.

Decorate with 1 teaspoon of icing sugar sieved over the top.

Serve warm with whipped cream, crème fraîche or custard (page 155).

Crumble Variations

Nut Crumble: Replace walnuts with pecan, almond or pistachio nuts.

Fruit Variations

See fruit variations on page 151.

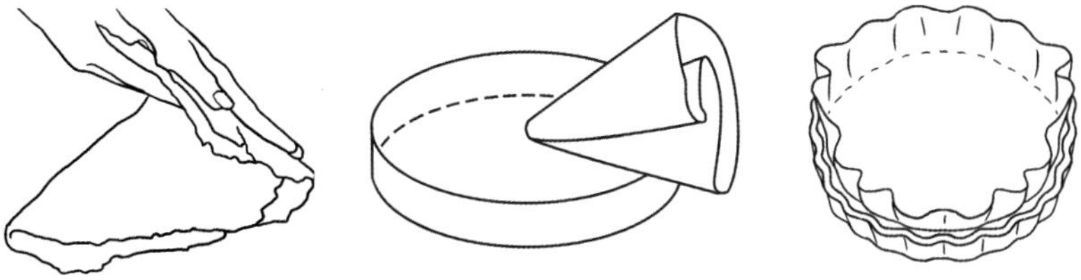

Apple or Rhubarb Tart

Lovely tarts can be made from fresh fruits in season, e.g. blackberry and apple, rhubarb and banana, or with dried fruits, e.g. apple and sultana with ½ teaspoon cinnamon.

Cooking Time: 30 minutes

Serves: 4-5

Ingredients

1 x **Shortcrust pastry** (page 167)

2-3 cooking apples or 4 sticks rhubarb

2-3 tablespoons sugar to sweeten

6 cloves (optional)

Caster sugar to sprinkle

Equipment

pie plate, sharp knife, table knife, peeler, board, small bowl, pastry brush, baking tray, mixing bowl, sieve, rolling pin, small jug, flour dredger, fork, tablespoon, pot stand.

Slicing apple

Steps	Method

Preheat oven to 200°C/Fan 190°C/Gas Mark 6.

Gather equipment, collect/weigh ingredients, set worktop.

1. **Pastry:** Make as for Shortcrust Pastry on page 167. Divide in two, knead each piece. Chill in fridge.
2. **Filling:** Prepare according to chosen fruit tart, e.g. peel, quarter, core and slice apples or wash and chop rhubarb into 2cm pieces. Place apples into a bowl of cold water to prevent enzymic browning, see page 18.
3. Grease pie plate. Roll a circle from one half of pastry, place it on the greased plate.
4. Moisten the edges with water.
5. Pile fruit onto the pastry. Sweeten with sugar, add cloves if using.
6. Roll a circle from remaining dough and place over the pie. Press edges together with fingers.
7. Trim and decorate edges (see page 166). Egg wash or glaze (see page 167), prick with a fork.
8. Bake on baking tray in preheated oven for 10 minutes, then reduce heat and continue cooking for a further 20-25 minutes. Remove from oven and sprinkle with caster sugar.

Serve hot or cold with cream, ice cream, crème fraîche or custard.

Lemon Apple Tart

VARIATION

Ingredients

1 x Apple Tart

1 lemon, zest only

Steps	Method

Add zest (rind) of 1 lemon (page 150) to the fruit in Step 5 above.

> **Resource Management:** Do not be wasteful when preparing apples. Wash, peel, half and quarter the apple and remove core from the centre of each quarter. Place in a bowl of cold water to prevent enzymic browning, see page 18. Slice thinly. Compost all fruit peelings and trimmings.

Mince Pies (Method for Tartlets)

SHORTCRUST PASTRY

Cooking Time: 20 minutes

Serves: 12 pies

Ingredients

200g **Shortcrust pastry** (page 167)

350g Christmas mincemeat – sweet Icing sugar to sprinkle

Equipment

12 patty tins (greased), 5cm and 6cm cutters, plate with doyley, pastry brush, small bowl/cup, mixing bowl, sieve, rolling pin, small jug, flour dredger, fork, table knife, tablespoon, pot stand, wire rack, teaspoon.

Chef's Tip! A grated cooking apple mixed into mince makes it nicer.

Idea! To make luxury mince pies, use biscuit pastry (page 178).

Mince Pies *Lattice Tart*

Steps **Method**

Preheat oven to 200°C/Fan 190°C/Gas Mark 6 for both recipes.

1 Make pastry as for basic Shortcrust recipe (page 167).

2 Roll ⅔ of the dough thinly. Stamp out 12 circles using the larger cutter. They should be a little larger than the wells in the tins. Line each tartlet tin neatly and brush edges with water.

3 Place 1 teaspoon of mincemeat into each.

4 Roll out remaining pastry, cut out rounds with 5cm cutter. Place a top on each pie and seal with fork.

5 Egg wash and prick each with a fork.

6 Bake in a preheated oven for 10 minutes, reduce heat and cook for a further 6-8 minutes. Cool on a wire tray.

Serve dredged with icing sugar. Place on a plate with a doyley.

Lattice Tart (Method for Open Tarts)

SHORTCRUST PASTRY

Cooking Time: 20 minutes

Serves: 4

Ingredients

100g **Shortcrust pastry** (page 167)

2-3 tablespoons jam **or** lemon curd **or** Christmas mincemeat

Egg to glaze

A little icing sugar

Equipment

18cm pie plate or foil, (plus equipment from page 167).

Steps **Method**

1 Make as for Shortcrust Pastry on page 167.

2 Roll pastry into a circle bigger than plate, line plate with pastry.

3 Trim edges (keep trimmings aside).

4 Flake and decorate the edges of the tart. Spread with jam, curd or mince.

5 Roll the trimmings into an oblong, cut into strips 1cm-2cm wide. Twist strips of pastry to give a nicer effect, and lay them across tart to form a lattice (page 166). Egg wash or glaze.

6 Bake for 10 minutes in hot oven and then lower the heat for 5-10 minutes until the pastry is just golden.

Serve hot or cold. Dredge with icing sugar pushed through a sieve.

Idea!
Decorate the tart with leaves made with leftover pastry (page 121).

PASTRY CASES

Ingredients

150g flour
75g butter
2-3 tablespoons water

Equipment

mixing bowl, sieve, rolling pin, small jug, flour dredger, fork, table knife, tablespoon, pastry brush, pot stand.

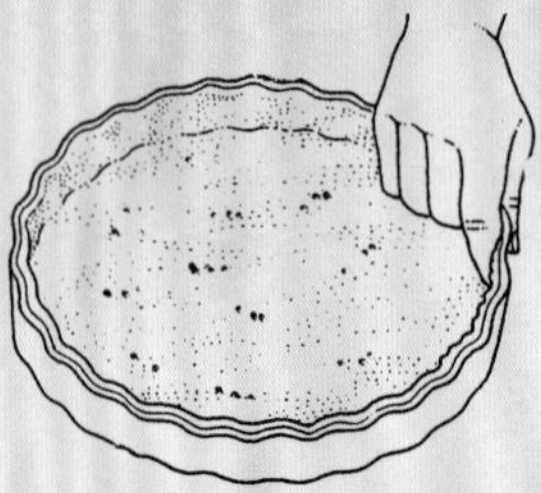

Moulding Pastry

Equipment for Baking Blind

26cm circle baking parchment, 2 tablespoons dried beans/peas to weigh down the pastry and prevent it rising.

Dingle Quiche *Salmon and Broccoli Quiche*

Use uncooked pastry cases for quiche and open tarts.

Steps **Method**

1 Make pastry as for Shortcrust Pastry recipe (page 167) use quantities given here.
2 Roll pastry into a circle 3cm larger than the tin or dish.
3 Line tin evenly with pastry, moulding it into the corners and up the sides to exclude air – **do not stretch the pastry**.
4 Trim excess pastry, mould up the top of pastry to form a small ridge above the rim of the dish or tray as pastry will shrink in the oven. Chill.
5 Wrap and store any leftover pastry for use later as a quiche or tart base.
6 **TO BAKE BLIND*:** Prick the pastry all over with a fork and cover the base with a circle of parchment. Place dried beans on top.
7 Let it relax in fridge for 10-15 minutes.
8 Bake in hot oven for 10 minutes at 180°C/Fan 170°C/Gas Mark 5.
9 Remove beans and paper. Reduce oven temperature by 20°C. Return to oven for 10 minutes to dry out or for 15 minutes to cook through. Use cooked pastry cases for baked raspberry cheese cake (page 173) and open fresh fruit tart (page 178).

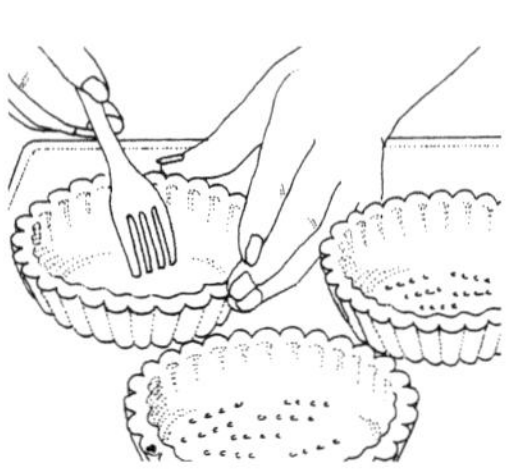

Pastry shells

To bake blind

Chef's Tip!
Cooking an empty pastry case first ensures the pastry base will not be soggy when filled. Before cooking, brush the inside of the pastry case with egg white to ensure further crispness.

*TO BAKE BLIND — TECHNIQUE

Baking blind means to bake an empty pastry case or shell without a filling in it. These pastry cases can be large or small size tartlets. They can be filled with a sweet or savoury filling and served hot or cold.

Baked Raspberry Cheese Cake

Cooking Time: 35 minutes

Serves: 6-8

Ingredients

Shortcrust pastry
150g plain flour
Pinch salt
75g butter
2-3 tablespoons cold water

Filling
200g cream cheese or cottage cheese
4 drops vanilla extract
2 teaspoons cornflour
1 tablespoon sugar
2 eggs
50g caster sugar
125g fresh raspberries

To Decorate
3 raspberries
1 teaspoon icing sugar

Equipment

electric beater, wooden spoon, tablespoon, knife, spatula, flour dredger, 2 medium bowls, rolling pin, 25cm circle parchment paper, baking beans, 20cm deep sandwich tin or quiche dish.

In a hurry!
Biscuit base. Mix 75g melted butter and 150g crushed biscuits of choice. Press into a loose-bottomed tin or quiche dish. Chill in fridge. Pour filling into base. Cook as above.

Idea!
Add 25g white chocolate chips to the filling for a special treat.

Steps — Method

Preheat oven to 200°C/Fan 190°C/Gas Mark 6.

Gather equipment, collect/weigh ingredients, set worktop.

1 **Pastry base:** Make as for Shortcrust Pastry on page 167, but use quantities given here. Roll out pastry into a 25cm circle and line the tin, see page 172.
Bake blind: Cover pastry base with parchment paper and place dried beans on top. Bake in hot oven for 10 minutes. Remove beans and paper and allow to cool. Reduce oven temperature to 170°C/Fan 160°C/Gas Mark 4, see Steps 3 and 4 on page 172.

2 **Filling:** Separate the egg whites from the yolk (page 149) and place in 2 clean bowls. Whisk egg whites (page 175) and beat in 1 tablespoon of the measured sugar to make a stiff meringue.

3 Beat cheese, egg yolks, cornflour, vanilla extract and remaining sugar to a thick, creamy consistency. Gently fold meringue into the cheese mixture.

4 **Assemble:** Pour the filling into the pastry case, using a spatula to clean out the bowl. Place the raspberries evenly on top. Reserve 3 raspberries for decoration.

5 Bake for 15 minutes. Reduce heat to 160°C/Fan 150°C/Gas Mark 3. Continue cooking for a further 20 minutes until the cheese is just set and the pastry nicely browned. Cover the top with parchment paper if getting too brown. Turn off oven. Allow to cool in oven if time permits.

Decorate with sieved icing sugar and raspberries.

Serve warm or cold with whipped cream or fresh berry coulis, page 156.

Food Fact!
Cream cheese is higher in fat content than cottage cheese – choose wisely to suit your diet.

Resource Management: Never waste pastry trimmings. Roll out pastry and make into a small, open jam tart or jam turnover. Bake on a piece of tinfoil until nicely brown. Allow to cool before eating. Be careful as hot jam can burn badly.

Bakewell Tartlets or Tart

Cooking Time: 20 minutes

Makes: 12

Ingredients

150g plain flour
75g butter
Pinch salt
2-3 tablespoons water

Filling

3 tablespoons jam

Madeira Topping

100g soft butter
100g caster sugar
2 large eggs
2 tablespoons milk
100g self-raising flour
50g ground almonds
2 drops almond essence
Icing sugar to dredge
25g flaked almonds (optional)

Equipment

mixing bowl, sieve, rolling pin, measuring jug, flour dredger, wire rack, spatula, table knife, tablespoon, electric beater (optional), 8cm round cutter, patty/bun tin or 21cm sandwich tin, 1 teaspoon, wooden spoon, baking tray.

In a hurry!
Use commercial shortcrust pastry and an electric beater for the Madeira mixture.

Stamping into rounds

Steps — Method

Preheat oven to 180°C/Fan 170°C/Gas Mark 4.

Gather equipment, collect/weigh ingredients, set worktop.

1 **Pastry:** Make as for Shortcrust Pastry on page 167 but use quantities given here. Roll out and stamp into rounds using cutter. Let chill.

2 **Topping:** Cream all the topping ingredients together, beating with a wooden spoon for 3 minutes or with electric beater for 1 minute.

3 Spoon ½ teaspoon of jam into the base of each tartlet.

4 Spoon 2 teaspoons of Madeira mixture over the jam – no need to spread. Scatter a few flaked almonds over the top of each tart.

5 Bake for 20-25 minutes, remove from oven and cool for 5 minutes. Before removing from the tin, allow cool on a wire rack.

Decorate with a little sieved icing sugar when cold.

Variation

Raspberry Bakewell Tartlets: Scatter 75g of fresh raspberries on top of the jam base and continue as above.

Bakewell Tart: Make an uncooked pastry case in a round 21cm tin, as on page 172. Chill. Spread with jam. Cover with Madeira mixture and scatter with almonds. Bake for 40-45 minutes.

TO CRISP A PASTRY BASE — TECHNIQUE

Preheat a baking tray in hot oven. Place the pastry dish to be cooked on this hot tin so that the base will cook quickly and crisp well.

Apple Amber Tart

Cooking Time: 35-40 minutes

Serves: 6

Ingredients

150g Shortcrust Pastry (see pages 167 and 172)

Filling

4 medium cooking apples

13g butter

½ lemon, zest

25g sugar

2 egg yolks

2 tablespoons water

Meringue: 2 egg whites

100g sugar

Equipment

small bowl, knife, sieve, rolling pin, tablespoon, sharp knife, peeler, flour dredger, spatula, whisk or electric whisk, 21cm sandwich tin, saucepan, grater, wooden spoon.

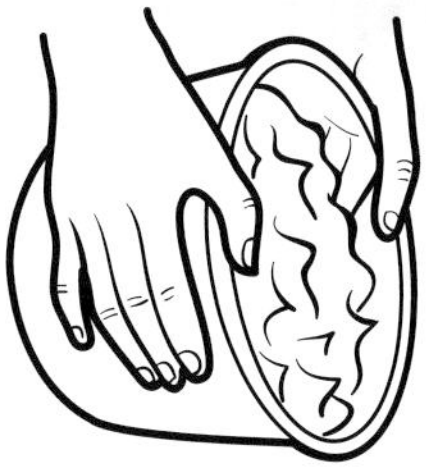

Whisking egg whites until stiff

Steps **Method**

Preheat oven to 180°C/Fan 170°C/Gas Mark 4. Place baking tray on shelf second from top.

Gather equipment, collect/weigh ingredients, set worktop.

1 **Pastry:** Make as for basic Shortcrust Pastry (page 167), line sandwich tin (page 172) and decorate the edges.
2 **Filling:** Wash, quarter, peel, core and slice apples. Stew with water, lemon zest (see page 150) and butter gently until soft. Beat to a pulp with a whisk.
3 Separate yolks from whites of eggs. See Chef's Tip below.
4 Using whisk, beat egg yolks and sugar, mix with apples, pour into case. Bake for 30 minutes.
5 Wash whisk in hot, soapy water. Rinse and dry well.
6 **Meringue:** Beat egg whites stiffly, gently fold in sugar, pile on to apple, lower oven to 100°C and cook until firm to touch.

Serve with freshly whipped cream, ice cream or custard.

Chef's Tip!

To beat egg whites successfully, the eggs must be separated properly – there must be no yolk whatsoever in the white (see page 149). The bowl and the whisk must also be free from grease. Wash in hot soapy water, rinse and dry. To ensure that the meringue is stiff enough, whisk the whites until in peaks. Tilt the bowl and shake gently – the whites will stay put if stiff enough. If the whites come away from the bowl, whisk a little longer.

Quiche Lorraine

A QUICHE IS A SAVOURY FRENCH TAR

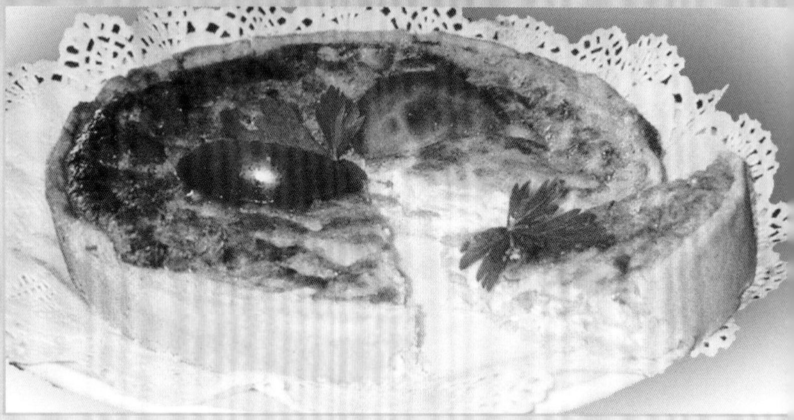

Cooking Time: 30-40 minutes

Serves: 6

Ingredients

150g Shortcrust Pastry (page 167)

Filling

25g butter

4 rashers, cut into strips

1 small onion, diced

75g grated Cheddar cheese

150ml milk or cream

3 eggs

Salt and pepper

Sprig fresh parsley

Garnish: 1 tomato, parsley

Equipment

rolling pin, 25cm pastry tin or deep dish, baking tray, whisk, medium bowl, saucepan, sharp knife, board, grater with large holes, scissors, wooden spoon, flour dredger, serving dish.

Chef's Tip!
Add 100g sliced mushrooms with the bacon for a change.

Idea!
Vegetarian Quiche:
Use vegetarian cheese.

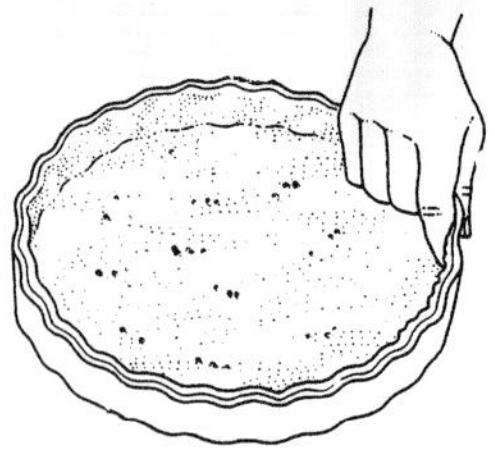

Moulding pastry

Steps — Method

Preheat the oven to 190°C/Fan 180°C/Gas Mark 5.

Gather equipment, collect/weigh ingredients/set worktop.

1 **Pastry:** Make as for Shortcrust Pastry (page 167). Line pastry tin (see basic instructions for Pastry Cases page 172). Chill.

2 **Filling:** Dice onion, derind rasher and cut into strips. Grate cheese. Wash and chop parsley finely.

3 Heat butter, sauté bacon and onion until beginning to go golden. Turn onto a plate to cool.

4 Beat eggs, milk or cream, salt and pepper together and add the onion, bacon, cheese and 1 teaspoon parsley.

5 Place pastry case on a baking tray, pour the mixture into the pastry case.

6 Bake on a baking tray for 30-35 minutes until the mixture is set and nicely browned.

7 Cool a little then remove from pastry tin as necessary, or just clean the top of the dish and serve in the dish.

Serve on a hot dish, cut into wedges.

Garnish with sliced tomato and parsley.

Variations

Replace rashers with the following:

Salmon and Dill Quiche: 400g salmon, 1 tablespoon fresh chopped dill and 2 tablespoons of peas.

Spinach and Goats Cheese Quiche: 1 onion, 100g or ½ bag spinach and 50g feta or goats cheese instead of Cheddar.

Broccoli and Sweetcorn Quiche: 1 small head of broccoli, 1 red pepper and 75g sweetcorn.

Cheese Pastry

USE FOR QUICHE OR CHEESE STRAWS

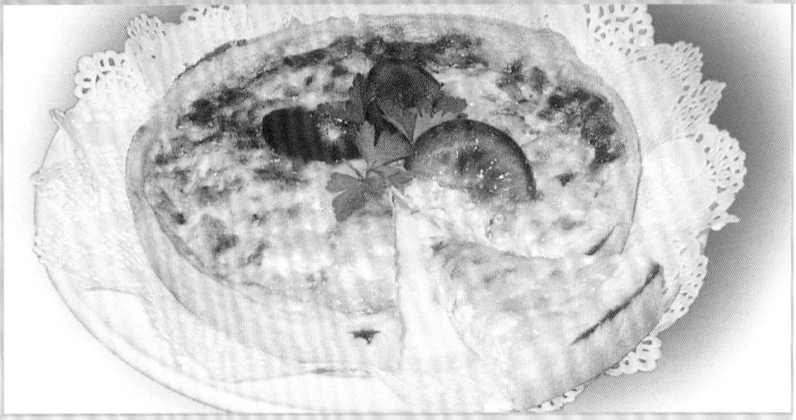

Ingredients

- 200g flour
- ¼ teaspoon salt
- ¼ teaspoon mustard powder
- Pinch of cayenne pepper
- 100g butter/margarine
- 50g hard cheese, grated
- 1 egg yolk mixed with 3 tablespoons cold water

Equipment

mixing bowl, sieve, rolling pin, small jug, flour dredger, fork, table knife, tablespoon, pastry board (optional), pot stand, wire rack, grater.

Steps **Method**

1. Sieve flour and add mustard, cayenne pepper and salt.
2. Rub in the butter evenly and lightly. Add grated cheese and mix.
3. Combine egg and water and use to bind the dough as in basic shortcrust pastry recipe (page 167). Knead lightly. Relax pastry in fridge.

Use: for savoury tarts, biscuits or for any savoury dish or quiche.

Cheese Straws

VARIATION

Ingredients

- ½ the quantity of Cheese Pastry (above)

Steps **Method**

1. Roll cheese pastry to ½cm thick, cut into strips 1cm wide x 10cm long.
2. Twist straws for a nicer look and top with poppy seeds.
3. Bake for 10-15 minutes at 180°C/Fan 170°C/Gas Mark 5 until golden.

Serve as a 'nibble' or with a dip.

Wholemeal Pastry

Ingredients

- 100g self-raising flour
- 100g wholemeal flour
- ¼ teaspoon salt
- 1 teaspoon sugar
- 100g butter/margarine
- 3-4 tablespoons cold water to mix

Steps **Method**

1. Sieve self-raising flour into the bowl and add wholemeal flour, sugar and salt.
2. Rub in the butter or margarine until it resembles breadcrumbs.
3. Gradually add the water and mix with a knife to a firm dough.
4. Knead lightly. Relax in fridge before rolling. Rolling can be a little more difficult with wholemeal pastry.
5. Bake for 35-40 minutes.

Idea!
Use instead of plain Shortcrust pastry to vary the texture and colour and to improve the fibre content.

Chef's Tip!
Use cold ingredients for making pastry. Add water gradually to make a dry dough and knead lightly. Do not overhandle.

Biscuit Pastry

Cooking Time: 15 minutes

Serves: 1 x 24cm tart or 2 x 18cm open jam/mince tarts

Ingredients

200g plain flour
Pinch salt
100g hard butter or margarine
50g icing sugar
1 egg yolk
1 tablespoon cold water
½ teaspoon lemon juice

Equipment

baking tin or pie plate, mixing bowl, sieve, rolling pin, small jug, flour dredger, teaspoon, table knife, fork, tablespoon, polythene bag, pastry brush, board, pot stand, wire rack.

Idea!
Use this sweet, rich pastry for sweet tarts and sweet cakes. It must be chilled before rolling.

Chef's Tip!
When a recipe asks for 200g pastry, it means the quantity of pastry that is made from a recipe using 200g flour and not the sum total of all the ingredients.

Use biscuit pastry for sweet flans

Steps	Method
	Preheat oven to 200°C/Fan 190°C/Gas Mark 6.
	Gather equipment, collect/weigh ingredients, set worktop.
1	Grease baking tin/pie plate.
2	Beat the egg, water and lemon juice.
3	Sieve flour and salt. Cut the butter or margarine into the flour with a knife, rub in lightly – the mixture should look like fine crumbs. Sieve in sugar, mix.
4	Gradually add the egg mixture, 1 tablespoon at a time.
5	Use a table knife to mix to a firm dough – mix around and around and cut through to distribute water.
6	Knead very lightly on a floured surface, until just smooth. Leave to 'relax' in a refrigerator in a polythene bag before rolling.
7	Roll out and shape as required or line a tin (see page 172). Relax dough in fridge if time permits.
8	Glaze/egg wash and bake in preheated oven for 25-30 minutes. **BAKE BLIND** (see page 172), cool and fill with sweetened cream and fruit. Finish tarts as required (see page 166).

Resource Management: Pastry freezes well. Consider making double quantities and freezing unused pastry and leftover trimmings for use later Remember to defrost pastry in the fridge up to 12 hours prior to use.

German Slices – Tray Bake

Cooking Time: 35-40 minutes

Serves: 18 squares

Ingredients

Pastry Base

250g plain flour
125g hard butter
25g caster sugar
2 egg yolks
¼ teaspoon vanilla or lemon essence
2-3 tablespoons water

Filling

3 tablespoons lemon curd or raspberry jam
2 medium cooking apples

Meringue Topping

2 egg whites
100g caster sugar
100g coconut or ground almonds

Equipment

mixing bowl, sieve, knife, pastry brush, fork, spatula, rolling pin, small knife, small bowl, Swiss roll tin, flour dredger, electric whisk, tablespoon.

Idea!
Scatter 50g flaked almonds over the meringue before baking.

Tray bake

Steps — Method

Preheat oven to 170°C/Fan 160°C/Gas Mark 4.

Gather equipment, collect/weigh ingredients, set worktop.

1 **Pastry Base:** Separate yolks from whites of eggs very carefully (see page 149). Beat egg yolks with 2 tablespoons cold water using a fork. Leave aside the whites for the topping. Grease tin.

2 Sieve flour, cut in the butter with a knife and rub in lightly. The mixture should look like dry crumbs. Add 25g sugar and 2 tablespoons egg mixture. Mix around and around and cut through with a knife to distribute the liquid. Continue adding 1 tablespoon egg mix at a time until a dough is formed. Add a little more water if necessary to form the dough.

3 Knead very lightly on a floured surface. Roll out to fit the base of the tin only. Lift the pastry on the rolling pin and mould to fit. Dip the pastry brush into the egg white once and brush the base of the pastry case to seal it.

4 Spread lemon curd or jam over pastry. Wash, peel, quarter and core the apples. Cut them into very thin slices and place on top of the jam.

5 **Meringue Topping:** Beat egg white until stiff (see page 175), add 1 tablespoon sugar and beat until it stiffens. Add 1 more tablespoon sugar and beat again until it stiffens. Stop beating now. **Fold** in remaining sugar, almonds or coconut very gently. Do not stir.

6 Put spoonfuls of the topping all over the fruit. Use a spatula to scrape out bowl. Spread gently with a fork to cover fruit.

7 Bake for 35-40 minutes until golden brown. When cool, cut into 18 squares with a knife dipped in cold water.

Serve as a dessert treat.

Store in an airtight tin.

In a hurry!
Use shop-bought pastry, fresh or frozen and thawed.

Chapter 11

Scones, Buns, Cakes, Icings and Muffins

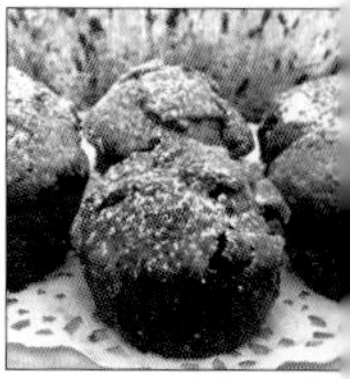

Key Words and Skills

- breadcrumbs
- stamp out
- hygroscopic
- cream
- melt
- dredge

Best Results for Baking

For the best results when baking, always weigh and measure ingredients accurately and preheat the oven to the correct temperature. As **ovens can vary** get to know if your oven needs to be set to a slightly higher or lower temperature. Set the **minute minder** to time correctly. **Avoid opening the oven door.** Turn off oven immediately after use to save fuel. Tidy up as you go along and wash up in hot, soapy water as soon as possible. See page 158 for baking. Irish butter is ideal for baking: it gives the best flavour and has excellent keeping qualities. Avoid hard margarines as they can contain trans fats which are very bad for heart health. Use olive, sunflower or coconut oil as a substitute for butter.

Reduce sugar by adding dried fruits, e.g. dates, sultanas, raisins, currants or dried apricots. See Food Fact on page 201. Try adding chopped, grated or mashed fresh fruits, e.g. eating apple, banana, pineapple, mango or peach. Choose to bake low sugar content recipes, e.g. Beetroot and Walnut Tray Bake (page 142) or Speedy Banana Walnut Tray Bake (page 201). Use Stevia or Xylitol or other natural suger alternatives.

Cakes are classified according to the method of making:

1. **Rubbing in:** Cold fat is cut or grated into the flour and then rubbed in using the tips of the fingers until the mix resembles breadcrumbs, see diagram on page 208.
2. **Melting:** Fat, sugar and/or syrup are gently melted in a saucepan or microwave (page 134) before it is combined with the recipe's dry ingredients.
3. **Whisking:** Eggs and sugar are whisked together using an electric beater until a very thick and creamy mixture is formed. Flour is then gently folded in. This method contains no added fats and is dairy free.
4. **All-in-one:** All the ingredients are placed in a bowl and mixed together using an electric beater.
5. **Creaming:** Fat and sugar are beaten together using an electric beater until smooth and creamy in texture and pale in colour, see curdling on page 198. Then, eggs and some flour are beaten in alternately. The remaining flour is gently folded in.
6. **Muffin method or wet into dry mix:** When using oil instead of butter, the wet mix is simply added to the dry ingredients and lightly mixed.

Evaluation! See pages 223 and 224.

- Did you meet the brief and did you refer to the specific requirements of the task or dish/dishes?
- Discuss the results of your finished dish/dishes including the presentation, colour, taste and texture.
- What aspects were done well and what aspects could be improved?
- Did you correctly cost and budget for all ingredients?

TEA SCONES OR SULTANA SCONES

RUBBING IN METHOD

Cooking Time: 18 minutes

Serves: 8-10 scones

Ingredients

225g self-raising flour
¼ teaspoon salt
50g hard butter
25g caster sugar
1 egg
5-6 tablespoons milk
Dried fruits (optional)
50g sultanas, raisins, cranberries or blueberries

Equipment

baking tray, sieve, mixing bowl, teaspoon, tablespoon, fork, table knife, rolling pin, flour dredger, spatula, small bowl/jug/cup, scone cutter 4cm or 6cm, pastry brush, pot stand, wire rack, plate and doyley.

Chef's Tip!
Work quickly.
Add almost all liquid at once. Knead only until smooth. For evenly risen scones, stamp straight down with the cutter. Do not twist at all.

In a hurry!
Cut dough into 2 pieces. Roll into 2 circles x 2cm thick and cut each into 6 triangles.

Idea!
Put sunflower seeds, pinhead oatmeal, sesame seeds or poppy seeds on saucers for dipping glazed scone tops.

Sultana Scones and Tea Scones with various toppings

Steps — Method

Preheat oven to 200°C/Fan 190°C/Gas Mark 6.

Gather equipment, collect/weigh ingredients, set worktop.

1 Grease or flour baking tin if not non-stick.
2 Beat egg and milk together in a jug/small bowl with fork.
3 Sieve flour, add salt, rub in butter lightly until it looks like fine crumbs. Add caster sugar and sultanas if using.
4 Make a well in the centre, add almost all egg mixture but keep back a little for glazing. Mix with fork or a wooden spoon – 'round about and cut through the mix'- to form a soft dough.
5 Turn onto a floured surface and knead very lightly, 6 to 8 times only, and turn over. Roll to 2cm thickness, not less!
6 Stamp into rounds without twisting the cutter. Glaze with remainder of the egg mix. Dip scone tops into toppings if using (see Idea). Place on baking tray.
7 Bake on top shelf of hot oven for 18 minutes until golden.
8 Remove from tin and cool on a wire rack.

Serve hot or cold on a plate with a doyley, with butter, jam or cream.

Well-made scones should be well-risen, even-sized, nicely browned and a good shape.

Making pastry

Cutting fat into chunks — *Rubbing in fat and flour* — *Adding liquid*

Brown Tea Scones

Ingredients

1 x basic Tea Scone ingredients but replace ½ the amount of white flour with wholemeal flour, and add ½ teaspoon baking powder.

Idea!
Dip glazed tops of scones in pinhead oatmeal, sunflower seeds, sesame or poppy seeds for crunchy tops.

Idea!
Keep back a little grated cheese to dip the tops of the scones into after glazing with egg.

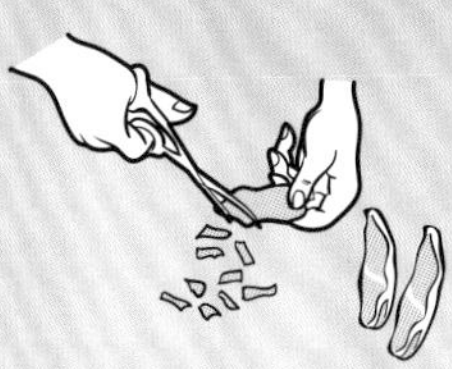

Snipping rashers

Resource Management:
Scones freeze really well and defrost quickly. Place extra scones in sealed freezer bags, take out as required and reseal the bag. Ideal for school lunches.

Cheese Scones and Brown Scones with various toppings

Steps	Method

Preheat oven to 200°C/Fan 180°C/Gas Mark 6.

Make brown scones following the steps and method for Tea Scones (page 182). There is no need to sieve the wholemeal flour.

Serve hot or cold for breakfast, lunch or for snacks with soup or salads.

Sweet Variations:

Follow the basic Tea Scone recipe on page 182 and add variation at the end of Step 3.

Cranberry and Orange: Add 50g cranberries and the zest and juice of 1 orange.

Apple and Cinnamon: Add 1 finely diced eating apple, 1 teaspoon cinnamon and a handful of chopped walnuts.

Banana and Coconut: Add 1 mashed banana and 25g desiccated coconut. See Food Fact on page 186.

Chocolate Chip: Add 50g chocolate chips.

Savoury Variations:

Follow the basic Tea Scone recipe on page 182 and add variation at the end of Step 3.

Cheese and Chive: Add 75g grated Cheddar cheese, 1 tablespoon snipped chives, ½ teaspoon mustard and ½ teaspoon cayenne pepper.

Cheese and Bacon: Add 75g Cheddar cheese and 2 finely snipped, grilled rashers.

When things go wrong with scones:

- **Too rough and shapeless** – under kneading.
- **Small volume** – not enough raising agent or oven too cool.
- **Tough and leathery or too smooth and shiny** – over kneading or overhandling.
- **Hard and close in texture** – not enough liquid used when mixing, oven temperature too cool.
- **Pale and doughy** – oven too cool or baked on too low a shelf or insufficient baking time.

Savoury Scone Rolls

Cooking Time: 20-25 minutes

Serves: 10

Ingredients

- 225g self-raising flour
- 50g butter
- 1 egg
- 5-6 tablespoons milk
- 4 teaspoons green pesto
- 50g sundried tomatoes
- 50g feta or grated Cheddar cheese

Equipment

22cm loose-bottomed cake tin, sieve, mixing bowl, teaspoon, tablespoon, fork, table knife, rolling pin, flour dredger, scissors, spatula, small bowl, pastry brush, wire rack, pot stand, serving plate.

Healthy Hint!
These savoury scones are a great way to curb a sweet tooth and are a lovely addition to any lunchbox. Store in a plastic bag for 3-4 days in a fridge or freeze in a freezer bag where they will last for up to 4 months.

Snipping rashers

Steps — Method

Preheat oven to 190°C/Fan 180°C/Gas Mark 5.

Gather equipment, collect/weigh ingredients, set worktop.

Follow Steps 1 to 4 of the Tea Scone recipe on page 182.

5 Turn dough onto a floured surface and knead lightly 6 to 8 times. Using a rolling pin, roll into a 25cm x 28cm rectangle shape.

6 Spread with pesto. Crumble the feta cheese and snip the sundried tomatoes. Spread the cheese and tomatoes evenly over the pesto.

7 Roll up from the longer side like a Swiss roll. Halve the roll and divide each half into 5 even pieces.

8 Place in a circle on tin with the cut side facing upwards. **Glaze*** (page 167) with the remaining beaten egg.

9 **Bake*** for 20-25 minutes until nicely browned.

Use as a snack, for lunch or in a picnic box.

Variations

Feta and Spinach: Use 50g feta cheese and 100g chopped spinach at Step 6.

Bacon, Onion and Tomato: At Step 6, add 3 grilled, snipped rashers and ½ finely chopped red onion.

BAKING — COOKING METHOD

Baking means cooking food in hot air in a ventilated oven. If food is covered, it partially cooks in its own steam and stays moist.

Raspberry Buns

Cooking Time: 15-20 minutes

Serves: 8-10 buns

Ingredients

- 225g self-raising flour
- ¼ teaspoon salt
- 50g hard butter
- 1 dessertspoon sugar
- 1 egg
- 5-6 tablespoons milk
- 3 teaspoons raspberry jam
- 4 teaspoons granulated sugar

Equipment

baking tray, dessertspoon, sieve, mixing bowl, teaspoon, tablespoon, spatula, table knife, flour dredger, small bowl/jug, wooden spoon, fork, pastry brush, pot stand, wire rack, plate and doyley.

Watch Out!
Hot jam can burn your fingers. BE CAREFUL!

Rubbing in fat and flour

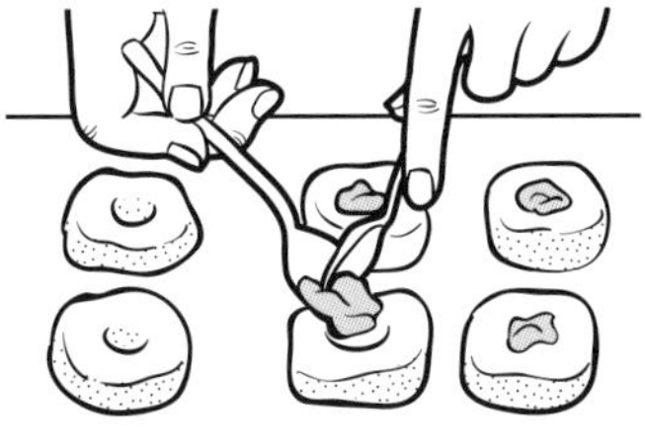

Preparing raspberry buns

Steps — Method

Preheat oven to 200°C/Fan 190°C/Gas Mark 6.

Gather equipment, collect/weigh ingredients, set worktop.

1. Flour baking tin/tray if not non-stick.
2. Beat egg and milk with fork.
3. Sieve flour, add salt, rub in butter lightly until it looks like fine crumbs. Add caster sugar.
4. Make a well in the centre, add almost all egg mixture (keep back a little for glazing).
5. Mix with fork or wooden spoon – 'round about and cut through the mix' – to form a soft dough.
6. Turn onto a floured surface and knead very lightly 6 to 8 times only. Form dough into a roll and divide evenly into 8 or 10 pieces.
7. With floured thumb, make a hole in the centre of each and drop ¼ teaspoon jam into centres. Draw edges together to cover jam.
8. Egg wash or **glaze** (see page 167), sprinkle with sugar and put on baking tray.
9. Bake on top shelf of hot oven for 15-20 minutes until golden. Remove from tin and cool on a wire rack.

Serve hot or cold on a plate with a doyley.

Resource Management: Using a spatula, remove all excess mixture from the mixing bowl. Do not allow any to go to waste. Freeze buns in sealed freezer bags and defrost as required.

Coconut Buns

Cooking Time: 20 minutes

Serves: 8-10 buns

Ingredients

- 225g self-raising flour
- ¼ teaspoon salt
- 50g hard butter
- 25g caster sugar
- 1 egg
- 5-6 tablespoons milk
- 50g desiccated coconut (see Food Fact below)
- 2 tablespoons jam

Equipment

patty tin, sieve, spatula, mixing bowl, 2 saucers, teaspoon, tablespoon, 2 forks, small jug/bowl, pot stand, wooden spoon, wire rack, plate and doyley.

Dipping bun in jam

Dipping bun in coconut

Steps — Method

Preheat oven to 200°C/Fan 190°C/Gas Mark 6.

Gather equipment, collect/weigh ingredients, set worktop.

1 Grease patty tin if not non-stick.

2 Beat egg and milk in a jug/small bowl with fork.

3 Sieve flour, add salt, rub in butter lightly until it looks like fine crumbs. Add caster sugar and half the coconut. Place remaining coconut on a saucer.

4 Add egg to flour. Mix with fork or wooden spoon – 'round about and cut through the mix' – to form a soft dough.

5 Using two forks, pile mixture into patty tin making 8-10 cakes. Do not smooth out the mixture, leave them rough on top.

6 Bake on top shelf of oven for 20-25 minutes until golden.

7 Meanwhile soften jam by beating it in a small bowl and warming it if necessary.

8 When cooked, turn out buns, dip tops into jam and then dip in remaining coconut. Cool on a wire rack.

Serve warm or cold on a plate with a doyley.

Food Fact!
Desiccated coconut means the dried, shredded coconut that you buy for use in cookery, e.g. in cakes and curries.

Healthy Hint!
These homemade buns are great for packed lunches or snacks as they are made with fresh ingredients and are free from artificial additives.

Rock Buns

Cooking Time: 20 minutes

Makes: 8-10 buns

Ingredients

225g self-raising flour
¼ teaspoon salt
50g cold butter
1 dessertspoon sugar
1 egg
5-6 tablespoons milk
¼ teaspoon mixed spice
50g dried fruit
25g mixed peel
2 tablespoons granulated sugar to sprinkle

Equipment

patty tin, sieve, spatula, mixing bowl, teaspoon, tablespoon, 2 forks, knife, wooden spoon, small jug/cup, pot stand, wire rack, plate and doyley.

Healthy Hint!
For those who dislike dried fruit or who wish to add extra protein to their diet, replace fruit with 75g mixed seeds (e.g. sesame, flax, sunflower, pumpkin or poppy) or nuts (e.g. almonds).

Rubbing in fat and flour

Steps **Method**

Preheat oven to 200°C/Fan 190°C/Gas Mark 6.

Gather equipment, collect/weigh ingredients, set worktop.

1 Grease patty tin if not non-stick.

2 Beat egg and milk in a jug/small bowl with fork.

3 Sieve flour, add salt, rub in butter lightly until it looks like fine crumbs. Add caster sugar, spice and fruit.

4 Add egg to flour. Mix with fork or wooden spoon – 'round about and cut through the mix' – to form a soft dough.

5 Using two forks, pile into patty tin making 8-10 cakes. Do not smooth over the tops. Sprinkle with sugar.

6 Bake on top shelf of oven for 20-25 minutes until golden. When cooked, turn out and cool on a wire rack.

Serve warm or cold on a plate with a doyley.

Food Fact!
Nuts and seeds are high in protein, Vitamins (A, B, C and E) and minerals (calcium, iron and other trace elements). One teaspoon added to a balanced diet per day is all you need. Use them in cereals and salads, as toppings for desserts and scones or eat as a snack.

Watch Out!
If your fingers get burned, hold under a cold running tap or use Aloe Vera gel to soothe.

GINGERBREAD

Cooking Time: 30-35 minutes in a round sandwich tin; 35-40 minutes in a loaf tin.

Ingredients

- 250g flour
- 2 teaspoons ground ginger
- ½ teaspoon bread soda
- 50g sultanas (optional)
- 50g mixed peel (optional)
- 50g crystallised ginger (optional)
- 100g butter
- 100g brown sugar
- 2 tablespoons treacle
- 1 egg, beaten
- 150ml milk

Equipment

1 x 18cm deep sandwich tin or medium loaf tin, sieve, small saucepan, teaspoon, wooden spoon, mixing bowl, spatula, table knife, fork, tablespoon, small bowl/jug, pot stand, wire rack, plate with doyley.

Chef's Tip!
Melting does not mean boiling! Before measuring syrup or treacle, dip the spoon in boiling water for a runny syrup.

Watch Out!
Always use oven gloves to prevent burns.

Spatula

Steps — Method

Preheat oven to 190°C/Fan 180°C/Gas Mark 5.

Gather equipment, collect/weigh ingredients, set worktop.

1 Grease tin well if not non-stick.

2 Sieve flour, bread soda and ginger into a bowl. Add fruit if using.

3 Melt butter, sugar and treacle over a low heat or microwave for 1 minute. **Warm only; do not boil.**

4 Pour into the dry ingredients. Add egg and milk together and mix to give a soft consistency.

5 Put into the greased tin. Clean out bowl with spatula, see diagram on left.

6 Bake for about 30-40 minutes. It cooks quicker in a deep round sandwich tin rather than a loaf tin.

7 Cool in tin for 5-10 minutes before turning out.

Serve on a plate with a doyley.

Use for picnics, lunchboxes and parties as well as snacks.

Variation

Add 50g chopped crystallised ginger at Step 2.

When things go wrong with melted mixtures:

- **Mixture sank in the middle** – door was opened too soon, too much raising agent used.
- **Cake dark and hard on the outside** – too much syrup, oven too hot, cooked for too long.
- **Cake overcooked and doughy in the centre** – too much liquid used, oven too hot.

Wholemeal Carrot Cake

Cooking Time: 35-40 minutes in a round sandwich tin; 40-45 minutes in a loaf tin.

Serves: 6-8

Ingredients

- 100g butter
- 100g brown sugar
- 200g carrot (2 medium carrots)
- 2 eggs
- 125g self-raising flour
- 125g wholemeal flour
- 2 teaspoons mixed spice
- 50g sultanas
- 25g walnuts (optional)
- Juice of 1 orange

Icing

- 100g cream cheese
- 25g icing sugar
- Zest of 1 orange
- ¼ teaspoon cinnamon

Equipment

18cm-20cm round sandwich tin or loaf tin (2lbs), mixing bowl, sieve, spatula, wooden spoon, tablespoon, table knife, teaspoon, fork, coarse grater, plate, small bowl/jug, saucepan, juicer, grater, pot stand, skewer, wire rack, plate with doyley.

Wholemeal Carrot Cake with Orange Cream Cheese Icing

Steps **Method**

Preheat oven to 180°C/Fan 170°C/Gas Mark 4-5.

Gather equipment, collect/weigh ingredients, set worktop.

1. Grease tin if not non-stick, zest and juice the orange.
2. Mix flours, spice, fruit and nuts in bowl.
3. Wash and grate carrot. Melt butter (see Chef's Tip) and remove from heat. Stir in sugar, carrot, add the orange juice and finally the eggs.
4. Add carrot mixture to flour mix to make a soft dough. If the mixture is too stiff, add 1-2 tablespoons water. Turn mixture into greased tin.
5. Bake in oven for 35-45 minutes until nicely browned, well risen and cooked through; check by piercing with a skewer, it should come out moist but clean.
6. Cool for 5-10 minutes in the tin. Turn onto a wire rack and cool completely.
7. **Icing:** Sieve icing sugar into bowl, add cream cheese, orange zest and cinnamon. Beat until smooth and spread on cold cake. Decorate with orange zest and walnuts. See cream cheese icing, page 203.

Serve on a plate with a doyley.

Store in an airtight tin or box.

Chef's Tip!
When recipes say 'melt,' do not boil. Just melt over a gentle heat or in the microwave for 20 seconds.

Food Fact!
Carrots are good for your sight as they contain beta-carotene, which converts to Vitamin A in the body. This is great for healthy eyes. Carrots are low in calories and can be eaten as a snack or a vegetable, in a salad or a cake.

Watch Out!
Some people may be allergic to all nuts.

Resource Management:
Always use a spatula to scrape the mixture out of the mixing bowl, so nothing is wasted and the wash up is easier.

Swiss Roll

Cooking Time: 10 minutes

Makes: 8 slices approximately

Ingredients

Basic Whisked Sponge

4 medium eggs
100g caster sugar
100g plain flour

Topping

3 teaspoons caster sugar to dredge

Filling

2 tablespoons jam
or lemon curd
or chocolate spread

(For method of filling Swiss roll when cold see page 191)

Equipment

1 Swiss roll tin, 2 sheets baking parchment, mixing bowl, sieve, electric beater, spatula, metal tablespoon, knife, pot stand, wire rack, plate, doyley.

Chef's Tip!
Use an electric whisk. Be patient, wait for the mixture to look thick and creamy. Fold lightly to incorporate the flour - do not stir!

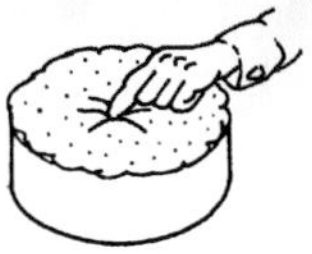

Testing a sponge: it should spring back when cooked.

Steps — Method

Preheat oven to 190°C/Fan 180°C/Gas Mark 5.

Gather equipment, collect/weigh ingredients, set worktop.

1 Grease and line baking tin with parchment paper (see diagram).

2 Using electric beater, whisk eggs and sugar until the mixture is **THICK AND CREAMY AND HOLDS THE IMPRINT OF THE BEATER OR THE FIGURE '8'.**

3 Sieve the flour onto the mixture and fold in very gently using a metal tablespoon. Pour into the prepared tin.

4 Bake in top or centre of oven for 10-12 minutes.

5 Meanwhile place second sheet of paper on a clean, damp tea towel. Sprinkle with caster sugar. Prepare filling – beat jam or choice of spread in a cup to soften (add a drop of hot water if necessary).

6 When sponge is cooked, turn out onto the sugared paper (see diagram on page 191) and gently peel off the lining paper. Trim any hard edges.

7 Spread warm sponge with softened jam, roll up tightly taking care not to include paper. Cool on a wire rack.

Serve on a plate with a doyley.

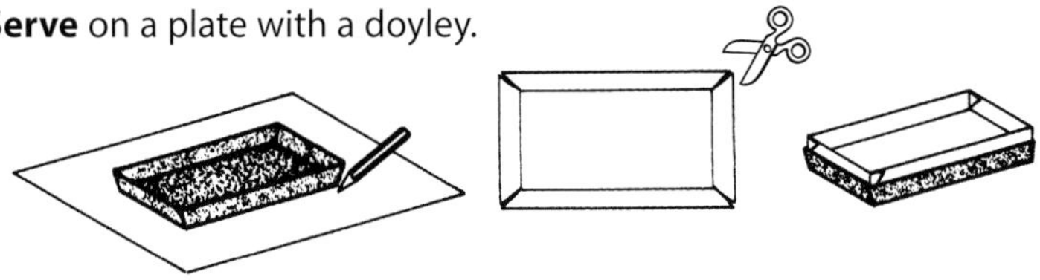

Lining a Swiss Roll Tin with Baking Parchment.

THE WHISKING METHOD — TECHNIQUE

Sponges made by this method contain no fat and so are often suitable for low-fat diets. The eggs and sugar are whisked together until thick and creamy and then the flour is lightly folded into the mixture. For best results, always use free-range eggs as they have the best emulsifying and foaming properties. For baking, keep eggs at room temperature.

Chocolate Swiss Roll

NO ADDED FAT
WHISKING METHOD

ngredients

Instead of 100g flour, use
75g plain flour
25g cocoa powder.

To decorate:

1 teaspoon cocoa powder

1 teaspoon icing sugar

Idea!
A Swiss roll makes a lovely dessert when filled with fresh strawberries and cream.

Chef's Tip!
A Christmas log is a white or chocolate Swiss roll filled and covered with chocolate butter icing, see page 203.

Steps **Method**

1 Make as for Swiss Roll (page 190).

2 Roll sponge without filling but include the parchment paper.

3 Allow to cool, then unroll, remove paper and fill with jam, cream, fruit and cream, butter icing (page 203) or cold filling, see below.

4 Roll up again, sieve the icing sugar and cocoa powder over the top.

Filling a Swiss Roll with a Cold Filling

TECHNIQUE

ngredients

250ml whipped cream
or cream and sliced fruit
or butter filling or icing
(page 203)

Steps **Method**

1 Roll sponge without filling but include the parchment paper. Allow to cool, then unroll, remove paper and spread with filling. Roll up again.

2 Dredge with icing sugar.

This makes a lovely dessert when filled with strawberries and cream.

How To Fill And Roll A Warm Swiss Roll

TECHNIQUE

This method is used when rolling a hot Swiss roll with a filling that does not melt in the heat, e.g. jam, curd, cold filling. See above for cream or buttercream filling.

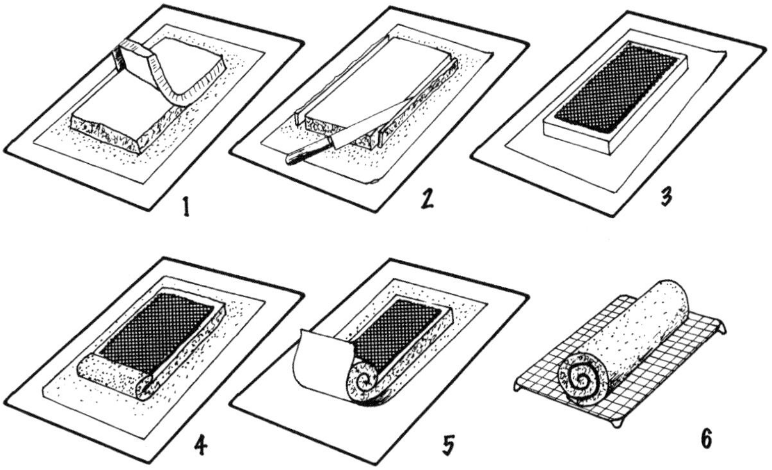

nice Swiss roll should have a ponge that:

- is a nice golden colour,
- is evenly rolled,
- is not over or under filled,
- is light and airy with an even texture.

SPONGE SANDWICH

NO ADDED FA
WHISKING METHO

Cooking Time: 15 minutes

Ingredients

Basic Whisked Sponge

4 medium eggs

100g caster sugar

100g self-raising flour or plain flour and ½ teaspoon baking powder

Filling of choice

Equipment

baking parchment, mixing bowl, sieve, electric beater, spatula, metal tablespoon, knife, pot stand, wire rack, plate, doyley, 2 x 18cm sandwich tins.

Chef's Tip!
For a pretty pattern, place a doyley on top of cake, sieve icing sugar over it, carefully lift off the doyley.

Sponge Sandwich *Chocolate Sponge*

Steps **Method**

Preheat oven to 190°C/Fan 180°C/Gas Mark 5.

Gather equipment, collect/weigh ingredients, set worktop.

1 Grease tins generously, line bottoms only. See page 159.

2 Using electric beater, whisk eggs and sugar until the mixture is **THICK AND CREAMY AND HOLDS THE IMPRINT OF THE BEATER OR THE FIGURE '8'.**

3 Sieve the flour onto the mixture and fold in very gently using a meta tablespoon. Divide the mixture between the tins.

4 Bake for 12-15 minutes. To test, see page 159. Turn onto wire rack. Gently remove paper.

5 When cool, fill with filling of your choice. Dredge with icing sugar.

CHOCOLATE SPONGE

VARIATIO

Ingredients

Basic Whisked Sponge

4 eggs

100g caster sugar

75g self-raising flour

25g cocoa powder

3 teaspoons caster sugar or icing sugar to dredge

Filling of choice or butter icing (page 202, 203)

Equipment

baking parchment, mixing bowl, sieve, electric beater, spatula, metal tablespoon, knife, pot stand, wire rack, plate, doyley, two 18cm sandwich tins.

Steps **Method**

Preheat oven to 190°C/Fan 180°C/Gas Mark 5.

1 Grease tins generously, line bottoms only.

2 Using electric beater, whisk eggs and sugar until the mixture is **THICK AND CREAMY AND HOLDS THE IMPRINT OF THE BEATER OR THE FIGURE '8'.**

3 Sieve the flour and cocoa onto the mixture. Fold in very gently using a metal tablespoon. Divide mixture between the two tins.

4 Bake for 12-15 minutes. To test, see page 159. Turn onto wire rack. Gently remove paper. When cold, fill as for Chocolate Swiss Roll (page 191).

When things go wrong with the whisking method:

- **Small volume** – too small a size of eggs used; not beaten enough; oven was too cool.
- **Hard lumps in the cake** – flour was not evenly folded into the mixture.
- **Tough and leathery** – flour stirred or beaten in instead of folded.
- **Cracks badly when rolled** – overcooked; not rolled quickly enough; hard edges not trimmed from Swiss roll.

Fresh Fruit Celebration Sponge

NO ADDED FAT
WHISKING METHOD

Cooking Time: 12-15 minutes

Ingredients

Basic Whisked Sponge

3 eggs
75g plain flour
75g caster sugar
2 teaspoons flour
2 teaspoons caster sugar

Filling

1 punnet fresh fruit– berries, nectarines, peaches, apricots, grapes, mango, passionfruit
125ml cream
Juice of 1 orange

To decorate

Fresh mint leaves

Equipment

20cm cake tin, kitchen paper, juicer, mixing bowl, sieve, electric beater, spatula, metal tablespoon, knife, pot stand, wire rack, 1 plate, doyley, piping bag and nozzle, saucepan, wooden spoon, tin opener, skewer.

Filling a piping bag with cream

Piping whipped cream

Steps — Method

Preheat oven to 190°C/Fan 180°C/Gas Mark 5.

Gather equipment, collect/weigh ingredients, set worktop.

1 Grease cake tin generously, dust with 2 teaspoons caster sugar and 2 teaspoons flour mixed. Juice the orange.

2 **Basic Whisked Sponge:** Follow Steps 2, 3 and 4 of Sponge Sandwich (page 192). Pour the mixture into the cake tin. Bake for 12 minutes and cool on a wire rack.

3 **Prepare Fruit:** Wash, drain and dry fresh fruit with kitchen paper. De-stone and slice fruits.

4 Whip cream until it stands in soft peaks, but do not whip too much as cream can quickly turn into butter!

5 **Assembly:** Place cold sponge on serving plate. Pierce all over with a skewer. Drizzle the sides and base with juice. Do not saturate.

6 Put 2 tablespoons of cream onto the sponge, spread lightly. Arrange the fruit nicely in circles or create the shape of a number for a birthday celebration.

7 Place nozzle in the piping bag, fill with cream (see diagrams). Pipe cream carefully around the edges. Decorate with fresh mint leaves.

Store in fridge. **Serve** within a few hours.

Food Fact!
Butter is made by churning cream or milk until the fat separates from the liquid. The liquid whey/buttermilk is used in bread making while butter is available as a salted or unsalted product.

Victoria Sandwich

ALL-IN-ONE METHOD

Cooking Time: 25-35 minutes

Ingredients

Basic Victoria Sponge

175g caster sugar

175g butter at room temperature

3 large eggs or 4 small eggs

200g self-raising flour **or** 200g plain flour plus 1 teaspoon baking powder

Filling

2 tablespoons jam or lemon curd

Topping

1 tablespoon caster sugar

Equipment

2 x sandwich tins (19cm-21cm), baking parchment, scissors, electric beater or wooden spoon, mixing bowl, sieve, metal tablespoon, spatula, small bowl/jug, 2 pot stands, wire rack, serving plate, doyley.

Chef's Tip!
Butter gives a much better flavour to both cakes and icing. Always line the bottom of tins with parchment paper.

This is a quick method for making large cakes, with different finishes, for festive occasions.

Steps **Method**

Preheat oven to 170°C/Fan 160°C/Gas Mark 3-4.

Gather equipment, collect/weigh ingredients, set worktop.

1. Grease tins, line the bottoms with baking parchment, cut the circles just smaller than the tins.
2. Beat the first four ingredients together with an electric beater at slow speed until well blended for 2 minutes or beat with a wooden spoon for 4 minutes.
3. Using the spatula, divide the mix between the two tins.
4. Smooth the tops with the back of a wet tablespoon.
5. Bake for 25-35 minutes until just golden.
6. When cooked, turn out onto a wire rack, remove paper and cool. Warm and beat jam or curd to soften it.
7. Spread each half with softened jam and then sandwich together.
8. Sprinkle a little caster sugar over the top.

Serve on a plate with a doyley.

Lemon Cake

VARIATION

Ingredients

1 x Basic Victoria Sandwich ingredients

1 lemon

Filling

3 tablespoons lemon curd

Steps **Method**

1. Wash, zest and juice the lemon (see page 150).
2. Make Victoria Sandwich, adding the zest and juice at Step 2 with all the other ingredients.
3. When cool, fill with lemon curd or lemon buttercream (page 203).
4. Dredge with icing sugar pushed through sieve or ice top for special occasions.

Chocolate Cake

🗝 *VARIATION*

Ingredients

1 x Basic Victoria Sandwich ingredients

3 tablespoons cocoa blended with 5 tablespoons boiling water

Filling and Icing

1 quantity buttercream (page 203)

Topping

Icing sugar if required or chocolate flake bar

Chef's Tip!
For a pretty pattern, place a doyley on top of cake, sieve icing sugar over it, carefully lift off the doyley.

Steps | **Method**

1 Follow the method for making Victoria Sandwich (page 194), adding cooled chocolate mixture at Step 2 with all other ingredients and continue as for basic recipe. Bake and allow to cool.

2 Sandwich together with chocolate buttercream filling or icing.

Decorate with icing and a crumbled chocolate flake or sieved icing sugar.

Coffee Cake

🗝 *VARIATION*

Ingredients

1 x Basic Victoria Sandwich ingredients

2 teaspoons instant coffee dissolved in 1 tablespoon boiling water or use Irel or Camp coffee

Filling and Icing

1 x quantity buttercream (page 203)

To decorate: 8 walnuts

Testing cake

Steps | **Method**

1 Follow the method for making the Victoria Sandwich, adding the cooled coffee mixture or Irel coffee at Step 2 with all other ingredients. Continue as for basic recipe. Bake and allow to cool.

2 Sandwich together with coffee butter icing (see page 203). Ice the top with remaining icing.

Decorate with 8 walnuts.

Spiced Fruity Tray Bake

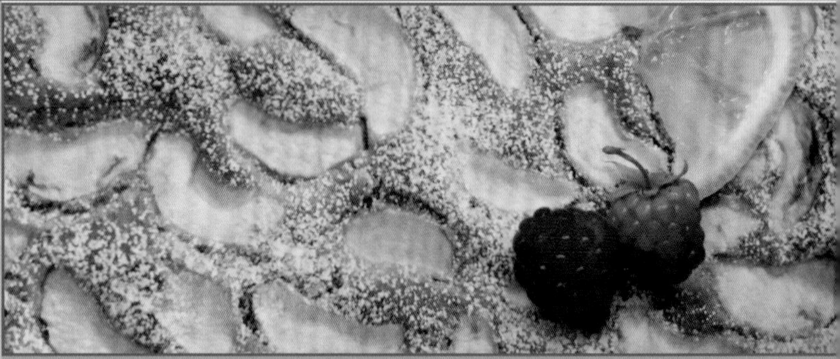

Cooking Time: 40 minutes

Slices: 8-10

Ingredients

300g self-raising flour
200g butter
25g butter for greasing
2 medium cooking apples
200g light brown sugar
3 large eggs
Juice of ½ lemon
2 teaspoons ground cinnamon
1 tablespoon milk
Serve: 1 dessertspoon icing sugar

Equipment

mixing bowl, electric beater, wooden spoon, sieve, bowl, teaspoon, tablespoon, spatula, juicer, peeler, chopping board, sharp knife, deep ovenproof dish or 18cm x 28cm tin.

Idea!
Scatter 25g almonds or sunflower seeds over the apple on top.

Resource Management: Always use a spatula to scrape the mixture out of the mixing bowl, so nothing is wasted and the wash up is easier.

Steps — Method

Preheat oven to 180°C/Fan 170°C/Gas Mark 5.

Gather equipment, collect/weigh ingredients, set worktop.

1 Generously grease tin with butter. Juice the lemon. Peel, quarter, core and slice apples very thinly, place in bowl and toss with lemon juice to prevent **enzymic browning** (see page 18).

2 Put butter, sugar, flour, eggs, milk and 1 teaspoon of cinnamon into a mixing bowl and beat using an electric mixer for 2 minutes.

3 Spoon half the mixture into the tin and spread evenly over the base using a spatula. Place half the apples on top and sprinkle with the remaining cinnamon. Spoon blobs of the remaining mixture evenly on top of the apples and level out the surface. Scatter remaining apples evenly on top and press lightly onto the surface.

4 Bake for 40 minutes until golden on top and the apples are soft and the cake is cooked through. Leave in the tin to cool, dust with icing sugar and cut into squares.

Serve with bio live yoghurt, frozen yoghurt, whipped cream or custard sauce, see page 155.

Variations

Apple and Blueberry: Add 125g of washed blueberries to middle layer.

Chocolate and Pear: Replace apples with 4 pears and scatter 100g chopped chocolate on top of the pears in the middle layer only.

Rhubarb and Ginger: Take 5 sticks of rhubarb, top, tail, wash, chop and stew for 2 minutes in 1 tablespoon water and 2 tablespoons sugar and 2 teaspoons of ground ginger. Use as the middle layer.

When things go wrong with the all-in-one method:

- **Close heavy texture** – insufficient creaming; mixture curdled; oven not preheated sufficiently; cakes under-cooked.
- **Streaky appearance** – bowl not scraped down with spatula during mixing; flour not evenly folded into mixture.
- **Mixture sank in the middle** – over creaming; oven not preheated or set at too low a setting; door opened too soon and/or slammed; cake was moved before it was set; cake underdone.
- **Cake risen to a peak in the middle** – oven set too hot; cake put on too high a shelf in the oven.

Lemon Polenta Cake

Cooking Time: 50 minutes

Slices: 10-12

Ingredients

- 150g fine polenta
- 2 teaspoon gluten-free baking powder
- 150g butter
- 25g butter for greasing
- 125g caster sugar
- 150g ground almonds
- 3 eggs
- 2 unwaxed lemons
- 1 dessertspoon fresh rosemary

Syrup

- 2 lemons, juice only
- 50g caster sugar
- 1 sprig rosemary

Equipment

mixing bowl, electric beater, parchment paper, wooden spoon, sieve, 2 bowls, teaspoon, dessertspoon, spatula, skewer or cocktail stick, juicer, grater, board, sharp knife, saucepan, 19cm round tin.

Chef's Tip!
Serve with coffee or as a dessert docorated with cream and fresh fruit.

In a hurry!
Bake in a square 18cm x 18cm sandwich tin. The cake's height will be reduced, but it will cook quicker.

Steps — Method

Preheat oven to 170°C/Fan 160°C/Gas Mark 4.

Gather equipment, collect/weigh ingredients, set worktop.

1. Grease tin with butter and line with parchment paper, see page 159. Wash, zest and juice the lemons. Finely chop the rosemary.
2. Whisk the eggs until thick and creamy.
3. Cream the butter, sugar, lemon zest and rosemary together until pale and fluffy. Stir in the ground almonds and gradually beat in the egg mixture.
4. With a spatula, fold in the polenta and baking powder. Pour the mixture into the tin. Bake for 15 minutes. Reduce heat to 160°C/Fan 150°C/Gas Mark 3 for 30-35 minutes until a skewer or cocktail stick comes out clean, see page 159.
5. **Syrup:** Put all the syrup ingredients into a saucepan with 1 tablespoon water, boil for 2-3 minutes. Remove from heat, cool slightly and remove the rosemary using a strainer.
6. Remove cake from oven, cool for 10 minutes then remove from tin. Transfer to a plate, prick top with skewer or cocktail stick and spoon the warm syrup over the top. Cool before serving.

Serve on a plate with no doyley.

Food Fact!
Polenta is gluten-free when made from corn. Coeliacs must use gluten-free baking powder as some baking powders contain gluten.

Queen Cakes/Cup Cakes (Madeira Mixture)

Cooking Time: 15-20 minutes

Makes: 12 cakes

Ingredients

Basic Madeira

100g caster sugar

100g butter

2 medium eggs

150g plain flour and
½ teaspoon baking powder
or 150g self-raising flour

Flavouring: few drops vanilla or lemon essence

Equipment

patty/bun tin, bowl, fork, 12 paper cases, sieve, electric beater or wooden spoon, teaspoon, pot stand, small bowl/cup, spatula, 2 dessert-spoons, wire rack, plate with doyley.

Chef's Tip!
Have all the ingredients at room temperature; this helps to stop the mixture curdling. Do not overbeat when using an electric mixer.

Idea!
Use Irish butter as it gives the best flavour.

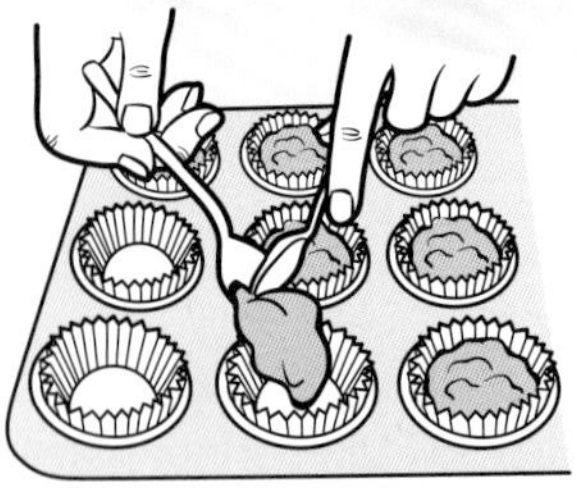

Filling paper cases with mixture

Steps / Method

Preheat oven to 190°C/Fan180°C/Gas Mark 5-6.

Gather equipment, collect/weigh ingredients, set worktop.

1. Put paper cases into the bun tin. Beat eggs with a fork in small bowl/cup.
2. Cream butter and sugar for 5 minutes until pale and fluffy.
3. Add half the egg and half the flour and beat.
4. Add flavouring (vanilla or lemon) to remaining egg. Beat for 1 minute.
5. Sieve the remaining flour and baking powder directly into mixture. Fold in the flour very gently.
6. Using 2 dessertspoons, fill ⅔ of each of the paper cases with mixture.
7. Use spatula to scrape out the bowl well.
8. Bake on middle or top shelf for 15 minutes or until golden.
9. Remove cakes from tins. Cool on a wire rack.

Serve on a plate with a doyley.

Decorate as required. Cup cakes are decorated with a large swirl of buttercream icing, see page 203.

When things go wrong with the creaming method:

- **Close heavy texture** – insufficient creaming; mixture curdled; oven not preheated sufficiently; cakes under-cooked.
- **Mixture sank in the middle** – over creaming; oven not preheated or set too low; door opened too soon and/or slammed; cake was moved before it was set; cake underdone.
- **Cake risen to a peak in the middle** – oven set too hot; cake put on too high a shelf in the oven.

CREAMING METHOD — TECHNIQUE

Fat and sugar are creamed together until pale and fluffy, egg is added a little at a time and finally flour is folded into the mixture.

CURDLING — COOKING TERM

A mixture curdles when it separates from a smooth to a grainy texture. It can happen when making Madeira mixture, when the butter and eggs are cold or at different temperatures, making it difficult to form an emulsion. Keep beating and don't worry – everything will be alright when baked.

BUTTERFLY CAKES

CREAMING METHOD
VARIATION

Ingredients

1 x Basic Madeira ingredients (page 198)

2 tablespoons jam or lemon curd

150ml-200ml whipped cream

Equipment

1 sharp knife plus equipment from page 198.

Steps — Method

1 Make as for basic Madeira recipe, page 198.

2 When cakes are cold, cut off a 'top' from each cake in a thick slice and leave aside. Spread ½ teaspoon jam and spread or pipe 1 teaspoon whipped cream on each cake.

3 Cut each top in half across the middle. Stand the 'middle cut' of each into the centre of the cream to resemble wings.

4 Sieve some icing sugar over each to finish.

SULTANA CAKES OR CHERRY CAKES

VARIATION

Ingredients

1 x Basic Madeira ingredients (page 198)

50g sultanas or glacé cherries

2-3 drops lemon essence

Steps — Method

1 Wash cherries, dry in kitchen paper, quarter and toss in flour.

2 Make as for basic recipe (page 198) but add cherries or sultanas at Step 5 with the flour.

3 When cold, ice with water icing (page 202) and top with ½ cherry.

CHOC-CHIP CAKES

VARIATION

Ingredients

1 x Basic Madeira ingredients (page 198)

50g chocolate, chopped (or chocolate drops)

Steps — Method

1 Make as for basic recipe but at Step 5 add chopped chocolate or drops and fold in with the flour.

2 If desired, sieve a little icing sugar mixed with cocoa over the top.

CHOCOLATE CAKES

VARIATION

Ingredients

1 x Basic Madeira ingredients (page 198)

Substitute 25g cocoa for 25g of the flour

1 quantity butter or water icing (pages 202 and 203)

Steps — Method

1 Make as for basic recipe but at Step 5 sieve cocoa with flour and continue to end.

2 Ice tops with chocolate butter icing (page 203) or water/glacé icing (page 202).

ICED SMARTIE CAKE

Cooking Time: 20 minutes

Ingredients

Madeira Mixture

175g caster sugar

175g butter at room temperature

3 large eggs

175g self-raising flour and ½ teaspoon baking powder

Flavouring: 3 drops vanilla extract or lemon essence

Icing and Filling

1 x quantity butter icing/filling (page 201)

Flavouring of choice

½ packet Smarties

Equipment

2 x 19cm-21cm sandwich tins, bowl, fork, sieve, scissors, baking parchment, mixing bowl, electric beater or wooden spoon, teaspoon, pot stand, small bowl/jug, spatula, 1 dessertspoon, wire rack, plate with doyley.

Chef's Tip!
Use natural essences or flavourings rather than synthetic ones.

Decorating iced smartie cake

Steps	Method

Preheat oven to 190°C/Fan 180°C/Gas Mark 4-5.

Gather equipment, collect/weigh ingredients, set worktop.

1 Grease tins, line with baking parchment, cut the circles just smaller than the tins, page 159.
2 Cream butter and sugar until pale and fluffy – 5 minutes.
3 Add half the egg and half the flour and beat.
4 Add flavouring, vanilla extract or lemon essence with remaining egg. Beat for 1 minute.
5 Sieve the remaining flour and baking powder directly into mixture. Fold in the flour very gently.
6 Divide the mixture between tins.
7 Use spatula to scrape out the bowl well.
8 Bake on middle or top shelf for 20-25 minutes or until golden.
9 Remove cakes from tins. Cool on a wire rack.
10 When cold, spread with water or butter icing (you could use a piping bag for butter icing). See Icings (page 203).

Decorate with Smarties.

In a hurry!
Beat all of the Maderia mixture and flavouring ingredients together with an electric beater for 1 minute or beat using a wooden spoon for 3 minutes, then resume recipe at Step 6.

Speedy Banana and Walnut Tray Bake

WET TO DRY METHOD
HIGH FIBRE, LOW SUGAR

Cooking Time: 30 minutes

Makes: 15-16 slices

ngredients

- 4 eggs
- 150ml olive oil
- 3 ripe bananas
- 50g walnuts
- 50g brown sugar
- 120g self-raising flour
- 120g wholemeal flour
- ¼ teaspoon salt
- 2 teaspoons cinnamon
- 1 teaspoon nutmeg
- 1 teaspoon bread soda
- Oil for greasing

quipment

sharp knife, board, mixing bowl, wooden spoon, spatula, fork, teaspoon, measuring jug, electric beater or stick blender, 24cm x 18cm x 4cm brownie tin, wire rack.

Food Fact!
Fruit contains fibre and the natural sugars: glucose, fructose and sucrose. These sugars combine with the fruit's fibre and are slowly released into the bloodstream. Fibre slows down the body's absorption of sugar, regulating the sugar surge in the bloodstream and its impact on the body. See sugar on pages 181 and 209.

Steps **Method**

Preheat oven to 190°C/Fan 180°C/Gas Mark 5.

Gather equipment, collect/weigh ingredients, set worktop.

1. Grease tin. Mash the bananas, but not too much. Chop the walnuts.
2. Beat the oil and eggs in a bowl using an electric beater, until pale and creamy. Add the sugar, mashed banana and walnuts.
3. Sieve in the white flour, cinnamon, nutmeg, salt, bread soda and add the wholemeal flour. Fold together using a wooden spoon.
4. Pour the mixture into the tin, use a spatula to clean the bowl. Bake for 30-35 minutes until a skewer pushed into the centre comes out clean.
5. Remove from the oven and cool for 15 minutes before turning onto a wire rack.
6. When cold, lightly dust with icing sugar and divide into 15-16 slices

Serve as a lunchbox treat or as an after-school snack.

Store in an airtight container in the fridge.

Variations

Banana and Ginger Tray Bake: Add 50g of chopped, crystallised ginger in place of the walnuts.

High-Fibre Tray Bake: Substitute 1 banana for 1 unpeeled, grated, dessert apple and add 50g extra walnuts.

No Sugar Tray Bake: Replace the brown sugar with 50g of sultanas.

Resource Management: Unplug the electric beater. Remove the beaters and using a knife, remove excess mixture from the beaters. Use a spatula to clean out the bowl thoroughly and wash the beaters in a bowl of hot, soapy water. Wipe the machine with a well-squeezed, damp cloth.

Water or Glacé Icing

FAT FREE

Ingredients

200g icing sugar, sieved

Boiling water

1 teaspoon flavouring

Colouring if desired
(2-3 drops only)

Flavourings

Lemon – Zest of ½ lemon, 1 teaspoon juice

Orange – Zest of ½ orange, 1 teaspoon juice

Chocolate – 1 tablespoon cocoa powder + 1 teaspoon milk

Coffee – 3 teaspoons instant coffee dissolved in 1 teaspoon hot water

Adding food colouring

Decorated Queen Cakes

Steps **Method**

1 Sieve icing sugar into bowl.

2 Add chosen flavourings and colour if using.

3 Beat in water, adding 1 teaspoon at a time until the correct consistency is reached – be patient!

KEEP ICING FIRM RATHER THAN TOO RUNNY, SEE CHEF'S TIP BELOW.

4 Use immediately or cover with a damp cloth until required.

5 Spread with a clean palette knife dipped in a little hot water.

Chef's Tip!
This quantity will ice the top of a 19cm-21cm cake or 12 queen cakes.

Chocolate Coating

METHOD FOR MELTING CHOCOLATE

Ingredients

125g milk, dark or plain chocolate

Equipment

small Pyrex/delph bowl, saucepan, spatula.

Chef's Tip!
Chocolate can be melted in a microwave but add 2 teaspoons of milk and be very careful not to burn it. If the chocolate gets hard, add 2 teaspoons of milk and beat.

Melting chocolate in bowl over water in saucepan

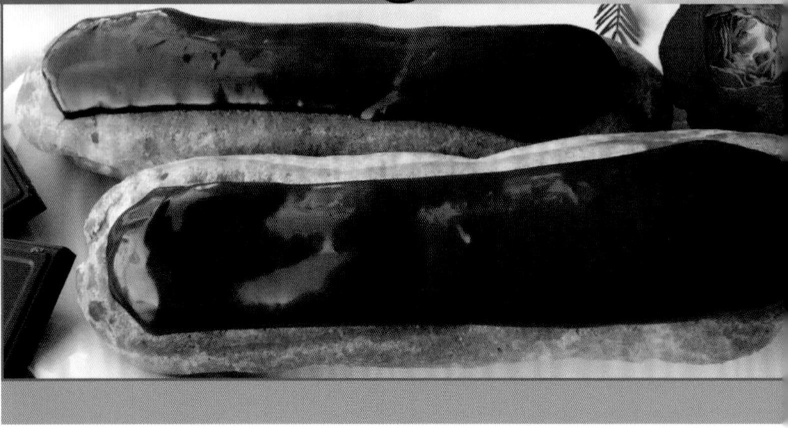

Steps **Method**

1 Break chocolate into a bowl. Place over a saucepan of boiling water.

2 Remove from heat when it begins to melt. Use as required.

Chef's Tip!
Be very careful when adding the liquid so that the icing is firm rather than runny. When adding food colouring, dip the end of a skewer or cocktail stick into the bottle, then shake into the mixture drop by drop and stir to mix.

Cream Cheese Icing (Lemon, Orange or Cinnamon)

ngredients

100g cream cheese

25g icing sugar

Flavourings

1 **lemon** zest
1 **orange** zest **or**
2-3 drops vanilla essence and 1 teaspoon **cinnamon**

Spreading icing on cake

Carrot Cake with Cream Cheese Icing

Steps **Method**

1 Sieve the icing sugar into a bowl, add the cream cheese and half the lemon or orange zest or vanilla and cinnamon. Beat well until smooth.

2 Spread over the cold cake. Score with a fork.

3 Dust with cinnamon and the remaining zest.

When things go wrong!

❖ **If your icing is too hard** – add some liquid, ½ teaspoon at a time. Be patient!

❖ **If your icing is too runny** – sieve in some more icing sugar but it will get very sweet.

Butter Icing or Filling

ngredients

50g butter

100g icing sugar, sieved

1 tablespoon milk to soften

Flavourings

Lemon – Zest of ½ lemon, 1 teaspoon juice

Orange – Zest of ½ orange, 1 teaspoon juice

Chocolate – 1 tablespoon cocoa powder + 1 teaspoon milk

Coffee – 3 teaspoons instant coffee powder dissolved in 1 teaspoon hot water

Idea!
Use Irel or Camp coffee instead of instant coffee.

Steps **Method**

1 Using the electric beater, cream butter and sieved icing sugar together until soft and creamy.

2 Beat in the flavouring ingredients of your choice. Use milk to soften only if necessary. The mixture should hold its shape.

3 Use to fill or decorate cakes that have cooled. Use immediately or cover with a damp cloth until required.

This quantity of icing/filling will fill the centre and ice the top of one cake.

American Muffins

Cooking Time: 25 minutes

Makes: 10 muffins

Ingredients

100g soft margarine or butter
125g caster sugar
2 eggs
100ml natural yoghurt (1 carton)
4 tablespoons milk
225g plain flour
¼ teaspoon bread soda

Equipment

muffin tin/bun tray, sieve, round-topped knife, tablespoon, mixing bowl, pot stand, wire rack, wooden spoon, teaspoon, whisk or electric beater, spatula, serving plate, doyley.

Chef's Tip!
A non-stick muffin tin is essential for good results when making muffins. Don't panic! This mixture looks curdled (page 198) but it works out well.

Healthy Hint!
When buying margarine, look for one that contains little or no trans fatty acids.

In a hurry!
Use queen cake paper cases to make mini muffins – these will cook faster.

Steps — Method

Preheat oven to 200°C/Fan 190°C/Gas Mark 6.

Gather equipment, collect/weigh ingredients, set worktop.

1 Grease tins if not using non-stick tins.
2 Cream margarine/butter and sugar until pale and creamy.
3 Whisk in the eggs, milk and yoghurt. (This will look curdled.)
4 Sieve in the flour and bread soda and fold in gently.
5 Use the tablespoon to ¾ fill the muffin tins.
6 Bake for 20-25 minutes until golden brown.
7 Loosen from tins gently with a round-topped knife.

Serve hot on a plate with a doyley or cold in a lunchbox or for a picnic.

Variations

Oat Muffins: Use 50g oats instead of 50g flour.

Lemon and Poppy Seeds: Add zest and juice of 1 lemon and 1 tablespoon of poppy seeds.

Chocolate Chip: Add 50g chocolate chips.

Double Chocolate: Add 1 tablespoon cocoa powder and 50g chocolate chips.

Bacon, Tomato and Pesto: Reduce sugar to 50g and add 2 grilled, snipped rashers, 4 chopped sundried tomatoes and 2 teaspoons of pesto.

Idea!
Use an ice-cream scoop to fill the muffin tins equally.

Resource Management: Unplug the electric beater. Remove the beaters and using a knife, remove excess mixture from the beaters. Use a spatula to clean out the bowl thoroughly and wash the beaters in hot, soapy water. Wipe the machine with a well-squeezed, damp cloth.

QUICK BLUEBERRY AND APPLE MUFFINS

MUFFIN METHOD
WET TO DRY METHOD

Cooking Time: 20 minutes

Makes: 10 muffins

Ingredients

100g plain flour
100g wholemeal flour
100ml sunflower oil
½ teaspoon bread soda
40g ground almonds
100g caster sugar
2 eggs
100ml natural yoghurt
125g blueberries
1 eating apple

quipment

sharp knife and chopping board, mixing bowl, sieve, wooden spoon, measuring jug, fork, small bowl, teaspoon, kitchen paper, muffin tin, paper cases (optional).

In a hurry!
Use queen cake paper cases to make mini muffins – these will cook faster.

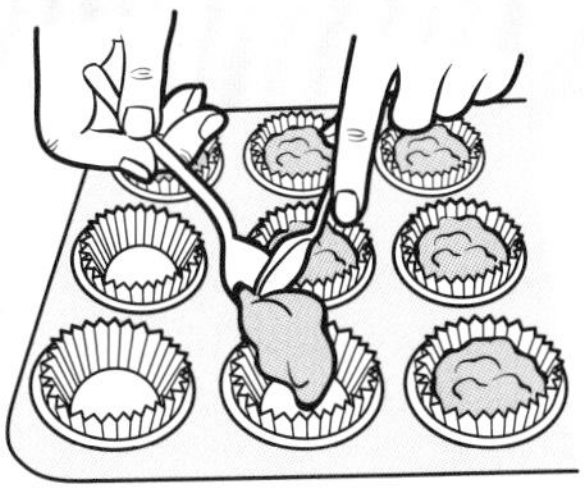

Filling paper cases with mixture

Steps | **Method**

Preheat oven to 200°C/Fan 190°C/Gas Mark 6.

Gather equipment, collect/weigh ingredients, set worktop.

1 Grease muffin tin well with oil or use muffin cases.
2 Peel, quarter, core and dice the apple. Wash the blueberries, dry on kitchen paper.
3 Sieve flour, bread soda and cinnamon into a large bowl, stir in sugar, diced apple, blueberries and almonds.
4 Measure the oil into a small bowl, add the eggs and yoghurt, beat well with a fork. Stir into the dry mix.
5 Spoon mixture into 10 muffin cases. **Bake*** for 20 minutes until risen and golden in colour. Dust with icing sugar.

Serve on a plate with a doyley.

Store in an airtight container and use as a lunchbox treat.

Variations

Cranberry and Orange: Add 50g dried cranberries and zest of 1 orange.

Banana and Pecan: Add 1 mashed, ripe banana and 50g chopped pecans.

Rosemary and Feta: Add 1 teaspoon of finely chopped rosemary, zest of 1 lemon and 50g crumbled feta.

BAKING — COOKING METHOD

Baking means cooking food in hot air in a ventilated oven. If food is covered, it partially cooks in its own steam and stays moist.

HONEY MUFFINS

Cooking Time: 20 minutes

Makes: 8

Ingredients

- 250g almond flour
- ½ teaspoon bread soda
- ¼ teaspoon salt
- 1 teaspoon cinnamon
- 2 eggs
- ½ teaspoon vanilla extract
- 6 tablespoons honey
- 125g blueberries or cranberries
- 1 tablespoon chia seeds

Equipment

mixing bowl, sieve, metal spoon, measuring jug, fork, teaspoon, kitchen paper, muffin tin, paper cases (optional), spatula, wire rack.

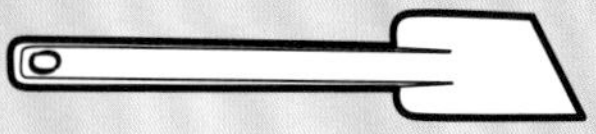

Spatula

Food Fact!
Honey is a sugar. It can contain trace elements, which have great health benefits. Irish heather honey has powerful healing qualities to ease sore throats and help with digestive issues, see page 14.

Steps — Method

Preheat oven to 190°C/Fan 180°C/Gas Mark 6.

Gather equipment, collect/weigh ingredients, set worktop.

1. Wash blueberries and dry on kitchen paper. Put the paper cases into the muffin tin.
2. Sieve flour, bread soda, salt and spices into a bowl. Mix in half of the chia seeds.
3. Beat the eggs, honey and vanilla extract together.
4. Add the wet mix to the dry ingredients. Mix lightly, then **fold in*** the fruit using a metal spoon, see below.
5. Divide into 8 muffin cases and use the spatula to clean out the bowl. Sprinkle remaining chia seeds on top.
6. Bake for 20 minutes, reduce heat to 170°C/Fan 160°C/Gas Mark 3 and bake for a further 10 minutes. Cool on a wire rack.

Store in an airtight container.

Resource Management: Remove all excess mixture from the bowl using a spatula. Do not allow any to go to waste. Freeze buns in freezer bags or containers and defrost as required.

FOLDING IN — TECHNIQUE

Folding is the term given to mixing ingredients lightly together so air and volume are not lost. Using a large metal spoon, cut through the mixture right to the bottom of the bowl and gently lift the mixture from the bottom to the top. Turn the bowl and repeat. Avoid overmixing as this will result in a heavy texture.

Chapter 12

Biscuits

 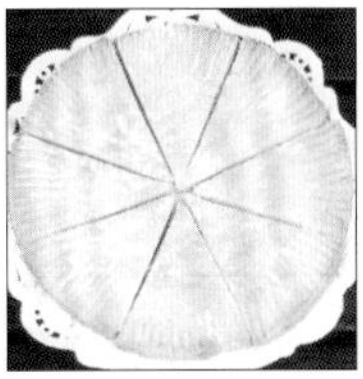 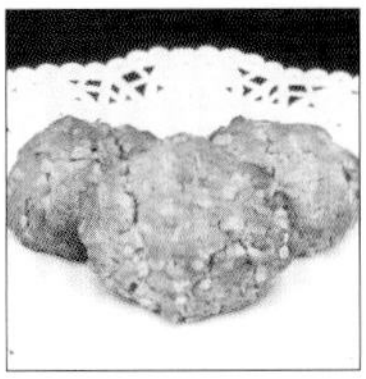  

Making biscuits at home can be fun as they are easy to make and taste delicious. Biscuits are ideal for home bakes, cake sales and enterprise projects. When comparing home-baked biscuits with commercial biscuits, it is important to read the labels on packets and note the hidden sugars, see pages 135 and 181. Biscuits may contain a lot of sugar and fat and eating too many can lead to obesity and heart disease.
1 teaspoon sugar = 4g sugar = 4 kcalories/17kJ of energy.

Baking Biscuits

1. Biscuits have to be timed carefully as they burn easily. They should be slightly pale in colour when removed from the oven.
2. Biscuit mixtures often spread when in the oven, so allow space between each biscuit when placing on a baking tray.
3. Biscuits should be the same size.
4. Biscuits can be soft when baked. They will harden a little when cooling.
5. When cold, store biscuits in an airtight container. Do not store biscuits in the same container as cake because the biscuits will absorb the moisture and become soft.

See page 181 for the best results when baking.

Key Words and Skills

- rub in
- fold in
- creaming
- bake
- simmer
- roll out
- beat
- melt
- blend
- zest
- knead
- sieve

Evaluation! See pages 223 and 224.

- Did you meet the brief and did you refer to the specific requirements of the task or dish/dishes?
- Discuss the results of your finished dish/dishes including the presentation, colour, taste and texture.
- What aspects were done well and what aspects could be improved?
- Did you correctly cost and budget for all ingredients?

Scottish Shortbread

Cooking Time: 20-25 minutes

Serves: 8-12 biscuits

Ingredients

125g flour
25g cornflour
50g caster sugar
100g hard butter
Caster sugar to sprinkle

Equipment

20cm sandwich tin, fork, mixing bowl, sieve, knife, pot stand, tablespoon, wire rack, plate, doyley.

Scottish Shortbread

Rubbing in method

Chef's Tip!
Irish butter gives the best flavour when making biscuits. Turn the tin once during baking for even cooking. When cooked, biscuits should be soft to touch but will harden on cooling.

Steps — Method

Preheat oven to 180°C/Fan 170°C/Gas Mark 4.

Gather equipment, collect/weigh ingredients, set worktop.

1. Grease tin if not non-stick.
2. Sieve flour and cornflour, add caster sugar.
3. Rub in butter until it comes together, kneading everything to a ball.
4. Press mixture into tin with knuckles and smooth gently with the back of a wet tablespoon. Mark the edges with a fork and prick all over.
5. **Bake*** for 20-25 minutes until pale golden. Cut into 8 or 12 triangles with a sharp knife. Dust with caster sugar. Cool in the tin, then transfer to a wire rack to cool completely.

Serve on a plate with a doyley.

Store in an airtight tin.

Variations

Orange Shortbread: Add the zest of 1 orange to the flour mixture.
Chopped Nut Shortbread: Add 25-30g of chopped nuts to the flour mixture.
Chocolate Chip Shortbread: Add 25-30g chopped chocolate or drops to the flour mixture.
Lemony Kale Shortbread: Add 1 very finely chopped kale leaf and the zest of ½ lemon to the flour mixture.
Rosemary Shortbread: Add 1 teaspoon very finely snipped rosemary to the flour mixture.

BAKING — COOKING METHOD

Baking means cooking food in hot air in a ventilated oven. If food is covered, it partially cooks in its own steam and stays moist.

Oatmeal Biscuits for Cheese

RUBBING IN METHOD

Cooking Time: 15 minutes

Makes: 18 biscuits

Ingredients

- 100g wholemeal flour
- 50g porridge oats
- 75g butter
- 2 teaspoons soft brown sugar
- 1 dessertspoon milk
- ½ teaspoon baking powder
- ¼ teaspoon salt

Equipment

bowl, teaspoon, dessertspoon, rolling pin, flour dredger, wooden spoon, spatula, 6cm cutter, baking tray, parchment paper, wire rack.

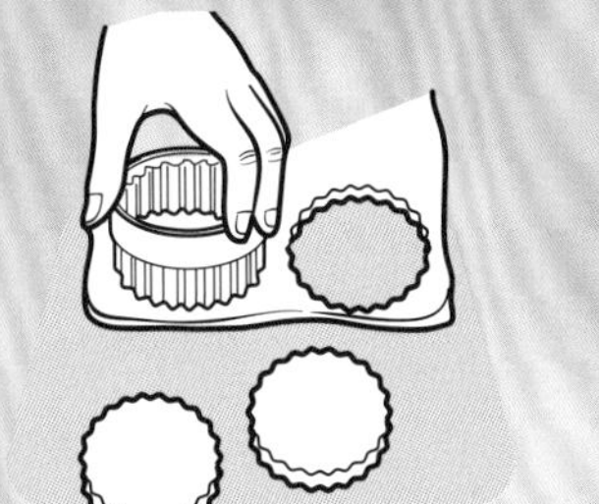

Stamping into rounds

Buy Local, Buy Irish!
Buy Irish cheese for these biscuits.

Look Up!
Fructose, dextrose and corn syrup.

Steps — Method

Preheat oven to 180°C/Fan 170°C/Gas Mark 4.

Gather equipment, collect/weigh ingredients, set worktop.

1. Grease the baking tray or line with parchment paper.
2. Mix the dry ingredients in a bowl. **Rub*** in the butter, see technique below.
3. Add the milk and work the dough until it comes together like pastry. Knead lightly on a floured surface 6 times. Roll out using a rolling pin until 3mm thick. Stamp into rounds using a cutter or cut into squares.
4. Place on the baking tray, bake for 15-20 minutes until lightly browned. Cool on a wire rack.

Serve with cheese, hummus (page 21) or smashed avocado (page 19).

Store in an airtight container.

Healthy Hint!
'Sugar free' or 'low sugar' labels can be misleading. There are many different names for sugar, so it can appear many times on food labels. Look out for the following on packets: agave, fructose, dextrose, lactose, sucrose, corn syrup, concentrated fruit juice, honey, molasses, sorbitol, glucose and treacle.

*RUBBING IN — TECHNIQUE

Cold fat is cut or grated into the flour and then rubbed in using the tips of the fingers until the mix resembles breadcrumbs, see diagram on page 208.

German Christmas Biscuits

Cooking Time: 10-12 minutes

Makes: 20-24 biscuits

Ingredients

100g plain flour
½ teaspoon baking powder
50g light brown sugar
25g ground almonds
1 rounded teaspoon of mixed spice
50g hard butter
1 egg, beaten
Icing sugar to roll

Equipment

baking tray, mixing bowl, wooden spoon, tablespoon, sieve, table knife, rolling pin, pot stand, wire rack, fancy cutter.

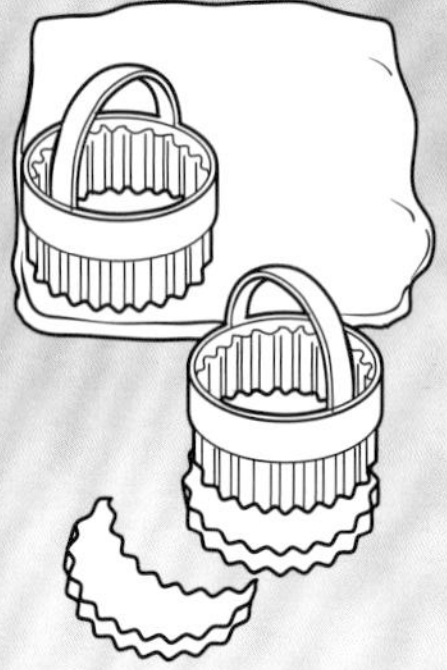

Making crescents

Making gingerbread people

German Christmas Biscuits and Gingerbread Person

Steps — Method

Preheat oven to 190°C/Fan 180°C/Gas Mark 5.

Gather equipment, collect/weigh ingredients, set worktop.

1. Grease baking tray if not non-stick. Sieve flour, sugar, almonds and spice together and rub in butter, see page 209.
2. Using a knife, mix in only enough egg to form a stiff, dry dough. Knead lightly on icing sugar and roll out thinly.
3. Stamp into crescents (see diagram) or fancy shapes, e.g. stars. Place on tin and bake for 10-12 minutes. Cool on a wire rack.
4. Ice with white or flavoured water or glacé icing (page 202). Allow to dry.

Store in a tin or airtight box.

Idea!
Serve these without icing with Fruit Fool (page 146).

Variations

Gingerbread People: Replace the mixed spice with 1 heaped teaspoon of ground ginger, and use a gingerbread person cutter in Step 3. Decorate with a thick water or glacé icing (page 202) using a fine piping set.

In a hurry!
Buy piping or writing icing from your local shop or dust with vanilla sugar.

Healthy Granola Soft Bake Bars

Cooking Time: 20 minutes

Makes: 12-14 bars

Ingredients

- 150g pitted dates
- ¼ teaspoon bread soda
- 200ml water
- 1 banana
- 50g dried apricots
- 50g mixed nuts
- 55g coconut oil
- 250g porridge oats
- 1 teaspoon vanilla extract
- 1 teaspoon cinnamon
- 50g seeds

Equipment

sharp knife, board, small saucepan, mixing bowl, wooden spoon, measuring jug, teaspoon, spatula, hand or stick blender, parchment paper, 18cm x 28cm baking tray, wire rack.

Chef's Tip!
Look for medjool dates as they have a rich caramel-like taste and a soft, chewy texture.

Look Up!
Compare the ingredients of commercial energy bars with your home bake.

Steps **Method**

Preheat oven to 190°C/Fan 180°C/Gas Mark 5.

Gather equipment, collect/weigh ingredients, set worktop.

1. Gently simmer dates in the water with bread soda for 15-20 minutes until soft. Allow to cool.
2. Line tin with parchment paper. Peel and slice banana. Finely chop the apricots and roughly chop the mixed nuts.
3. Blend dates, oil, banana and vanilla in electric blender until smooth, transfer to a bowl.
4. Add the oats, apricots, nuts, seeds and cinnamon to the bowl and mix well.
5. Turn mixture into tin. Press down using wet hands. Bake for 20-25 minutes until golden brown.
6. Cool in the tin then cut into 12-14 bars. Transfer to a wire rack to cool completely.

Store in an airtight container. Use as a lunchbox treat or as a healthy snack.

In a hurry!
Replace the oats, apricots, nuts and seeds with 400g sugar-free muesli.

Watch Out!
1 teaspoon of sugar = 4g of sugar = 4 kilocalories = 17kJ.

Idea!
These bars could be individually wrapped and used for bake sales or enterprise projects. Be careful to label each bar correctly.

Resource Management:
Always use a spatula to scrape the mixture out of the mixing bowl, so nothing is wasted and the wash up is easier.

FLAPJACKS

Cooking Time: 25 minutes

Makes: 16-18 biscuits

Ingredients

75g brown sugar
125g butter
2 tablespoons golden syrup
250g porridge oats
Butter or oil for greasing

Equipment

18cm x 24cm tin, saucepan, sharp knife, tablespoon, wooden spoon, wire rack, pot stand.

Cutting flapjacks into squares or oblong bars

Buy Local, Buy Irish!
Oats are grown and milled in Ireland. They are high in fibre and have a low Glycemic Index.

Look Up!
Glycemic Index (GI).
Why is it bad to use palm oil?

Steps — Method

Preheat oven to 180°C/Fan 170°C/Gas Mark 4.

Gather equipment, collect/weigh ingredients, set worktop.

1. Grease the baking tin if not non-stick.
2. Heat tablespoon in hot water and then measure the golden syrup into the saucepan. Melt with butter and sugar over low heat; do not boil. Remove from heat, see melting method page 181.
3. Add the oatmeal and mix thoroughly. Turn mixture into tin and smooth with the back of a wet tablespoon.
4. Bake for 20-25 minutes until golden.
5. Cool for five minutes and then cut into squares or oblong bars. Cool in the tin. Remove using a knife. Transfer to a wire rack to cool completely.

Serve the biscuits in lunchboxes, for picnics or as a snack.

Store in an airtight container.

Use as a lunchbox treat and cut into squares.

Variations

Apricot and Lemon Flapjacks: Add 50g finely chopped, dried apricots and the zest of 1 lemon at Step 3.

Low Sugar Flapjacks: Replace the brown sugar with 1 mashed, ripe banana and 50g chopped apricots at Step 3.

Mixed Seed Flapjacks: Add 3 tablespoons of mixed seeds, e.g. pumpkin, sunflower, sesame or flax.

Food Fact!
Oats are gluten-free, however if they are grown in a field in close proximity to where wheat is being produced, this results in the production of gluten contaminated oats.

GINGER SNAPS

MELTING METHOD

Cooking Time: 15 minutes

Serves: 14 biscuits

Ingredients

- 100g self-raising flour
- 1 rounded teaspoon ground ginger
- 50g butter
- 50g granulated sugar
- 1 tablespoon golden syrup

Equipment

baking tray, saucepan, mixing bowl, tablespoon, wire rack, pot stand.

Steps **Method**

Preheat oven to 180°C/Fan 170°C/Gas Mark 4.

Gather equipment, collect/weigh ingredients, set worktop.

1 Sieve flour and ginger into bowl.

2 Melt with butter, syrup and sugar over low heat; **do not boil**. Mix into flour and stir well. See melting method on page 181.

3 Shape into 14-15 small balls. Place on tin, leaving space to spread, and flatten with the back of a wet tablespoon.

4 Bake for 15 minutes until brown. Cool a little and lift onto wire rack.

CHOCOLATE NUT CRUNCHIES

MELTING METHOD

Cooking Time: 15 minutes

Serves: 18

Ingredients

- 50g dark chocolate
- 100g butter
- 75g brown sugar
- 1 dessertspoon golden syrup
- 50g nuts of choice (e.g. almonds)
- 100g flour
- ¼ teaspoon baking powder
- 100g porridge oats
- Pinch salt

Watch Out!
Some people can be allergic to nuts. Use raisins or chopped dried apricots instead.

Steps **Method**

Preheat oven to 170°C/Fan 160°C/Gas Mark 3.

1 Grease trays with oil. Chop chocolate and nuts finely. Sieve flour into bowl, add salt, oats, ½ the chocolate and nuts. Mix well.

2 Melt butter, sugar and syrup gently in saucepan. Do not boil.

3 Mix the melted mix into the flour, add baking powder and stir well to form a dough. Divide the dough into 18 small balls. Flatten out, dip tops into remaining chocolate and nuts to decorate and place on the trays.

4 Bake for 15 minutes. Cool on tray for 15 minutes, then lift out onto wire rack to finish cooling.

Store in an airtight tin.

Coconut Jumbles

MELTING METHOD

Cooking Time: 15-20 minutes

Serves: 14 biscuits

Ingredients

100g flour
¼ teaspoon bread soda
50g caster sugar
50g coconut
50g flakemeal/porridge oats
90g butter
1 tablespoon golden syrup

Equipment

baking tray, saucepan, bowl, wooden spoon, wire rack, tablespoon, pot stand.

Chef's Tip!
For Chocolate Jumbles brush with melted chocolate (page 202).

Steps **Method**

Preheat oven to 180°C/Fan 170°C/Gas Mark 4.

Gather equipment, collect/weigh ingredients, set worktop.

1 Grease tray. Sieve flour and soda. Add sugar, coconut and flakemeal or oats.
2 Gently melt the butter and syrup with 2 teaspoons of water. Turn into the flour mixture and mix together. See melting method page 181.
3 With wet hands, form into 14 balls. Place on tray and flatten well.
4 Bake for 15-20 minutes until just golden. Cool on wire rack.

No Bake Chocolate Slices

MELTING METHOD

Ingredients

125g butter
25g cocoa
1 tablespoon golden syrup
225g digestive biscuits or gluten-free digestives

Topping

50g milk chocolate
2 teaspoons milk

Equipment

19cm-21cm sandwich tin, saucepan, tablespoon, wooden spoon, pot stand, plastic bag, rolling pin, spatula, small pyrex bowl.

Chef's Tip!
Stir in 50g raisins for a nice change.

Steps **Method**

Gather equipment, collect/weigh ingredients, set worktop.

1 Grease tin. Put biscuits into plastic bag and crush with rolling pin.
2 Heat butter, cocoa and golden syrup over a gentle heat. Stir until butter has melted. Add the crushed biscuits.
3 Turn into the greased tin, smooth over and chill.
4 **Topping**: Melt chocolate and milk in a bowl over a saucepan of hot water or in the microwave as in Chocolate Coating (page 202). Spread over the top.
5 Chill until set. Remove from tin and cut into 8-12 slices.

Melting Moments

Cooking Time: 20 minutes

Serves: 20

Ingredients

- 100g butter at room temperature
- 75g caster sugar
- Zest ½ lemon or ¼ teaspoon vanilla
- 1 egg yolk
- 125g flour
- 25g cornflakes

Equipment

baking tray, mixing bowl, sieve, electric beater/wooden spoon, pot stand, wire rack, small freezer bag, grater with small holes.

Chef's Tip!
Butter gives the best flavour when making biscuits. Keep all the ingredients at room temperature as this helps to stop curdling (page 198). Do not overbeat when using an electric mixer.

Idea!
Use the zest of one orange instead of the lemon.

Zesting a lemon

Steps **Method**

Preheat oven to 180°C/Fan 170°C/Gas Mark 4.

Gather equipment, collect/weigh ingredients, set worktop.

1. Grease tray if not non-stick.
2. Crush cornflakes in freezer bag.
3. Cream butter and sugar using wooden spoon or mixer, see page 216.
4. Beat in lemon zest or vanilla and egg. Sieve in flour and mix to a smooth dough.
5. Shape into small balls and roll in cornflakes. Place on tray, leaving space to spread. Bake for 20 minutes.
6. Cool on a wire rack.

Serve on a plate with a doyley.

Store in an airtight tin.

Resource Management: Egg whites can be stored in a clean, covered container in the fridge and used in any other egg dish, e.g. cakes, batters, omelettes, etc.

***ZEST** **TECHNIQUE**

To zest a lemon, lime or orange. Wash fruit, then grate the coloured outer skin only with a wet grater. Do not go into the white pith beneath as it is bitter. The zest or coloured part contains the beautifully flavoured citrus fruit oils. Use the small or medium holes on the grater and use a pastry brush to remove all the zest.

Chocolate Chip Cookies

CREAMING METHOD

Cooking Time: 8-10 minutes

Makes: 12-15

Ingredients

100g butter
50g caster sugar
150g flour
50g or 1 bar chocolate, chopped
½ teaspoon baking powder
Pinch salt
4 drops vanilla extract
50g chopped nuts (optional)

Equipment

electric beater/wooden spoon, 2 baking trays, mixing bowl, tablespoon, pot stand, wire rack, parchment paper (optional).

Rolling into balls

Flatten out biscuits. Leave a space between each for spreading

Buy Local, Buy Irish! Choose Irish chocolate when making this recipe.

Steps **Method**

Preheat oven to 170°C/Fan 160°C/Gas Mark 4.

Gather equipment, collect/weigh ingredients, set worktop.

1 Grease baking tins if not non-stick or line with parchment paper.
2 Beat butter, sugar and vanilla extract until fluffy. Stir in flour, baking powder, salt and nuts (if using) and chocolate. Knead with the hands to form a smooth dough.
3 Divide mixture into even-sized balls. Place apart on baking trays and flatten well with the back of a tablespoon or fork, see diagram.
4 Cook for 12-15 minutes until evenly browned. Cool a little and then lift off and cool on a wire rack.

Serve on a plate with a doyley.

Store in an airtight tin or box.

Food Fact!
Refined sugar offers no nutritional value to our diet and gives no feeling of fullness. It is a major contributory factor to obesity and diabetes. Sugar gives a quick burst of energy and the excess is stored as fat. **See Healthy Hint, page 209.**

***CREAMING** TECHNIQUE

Fat and sugar are beaten together using an electric mixer until smooth and creamy in texture and pale in colour, see curdling on page 198. Then, eggs and some flour are beaten in alternately. The remaining flour is gently folded in.

Budget
€
€
Notes
Time Plan
9:30
9:40
9:50
10:00
10:20
Smart Cooking 1
Smart Exam Material
Design Brief
Research R
Research R
Research R
Shopping List
Evaluation
Presentation
Colour
Flavour
Texture
Exam Folder
Home Ec.
Culinary Skills
Costing
@€
@€
@€

Smart Checklist

When you get your Brief for CBA 2 Follow the Design Brief

A. Do Some SMART Research, see page 220.

1 **Analyse the brief** – What exactly do I have to do? ☐

2 **Research** every aspect of the brief. ☐

3 Outline the **factors** to be considered. ☐

4 Develop **possible solutions**. ☐

5 Present **your ideas** for feedback from others. ☐

6 **Make notes** using the feedback given. ☐

B. After Feedback, Make SMART Decisions – Be Creative.

1 Decide on a **solution for each aspect** of the task. ☐

2 **Give reasons** for choosing each task. ☐

3 **Name the dishes** you intend to prepare. ☐

4 Prepare a **shopping list and cost** the dishes. ☐

5 List the **ingredients** for each dish. ☐

6 List the **equipment**, include apron, pencil, etc. ☐

7 List what you will do in the 30 minute **preparation time, see page 222.** ☐

8 Make a **time plan** for the exam. ☐

9 Make a **MENU** on page 12. ☐

10 Make a **word bank**. ☐

11 **Practise your dishes and Evaluation**. ☐

C. Exam Day – see page 222.

1 Follow your **preparation time plan**. ☐

2 **Prepare, cook and serve** your dishes. ☐

3 **Evaluate** the presentation colour, texture, and flavour of your dish/dishes, see pages 223 and 224. ☐

4 **Wash up,** clear and tidy everything. ☐

FOOD LITERACY SKILLS BRIEF – CLASSROOM-BASED ASSESSMENT 2

Advice for Students

- You will be helped by your teacher to prepare for your Classroom-Based Assessment (CBA 2).
- From year to year there may be changes to what is expected in the exam. Your teacher will advise you of any changes.
- Get to know the descriptions/descriptors for the **4 Features of Quality** used for assessment:

  A. ***Is the work – Exceptional?***
  B. ***Is the work – Above expectations?***
  C. ***Is the work – In line with expectations?***
  D. ***Is the work – Yet to meet expectations?***

Statement of Brief

The briefs, issued by the State Examinations Commission, may include but not be exclusive to options from the following broad areas:

- Healthy family meals to reflect the current healthy eating guidelines,
- A special dietary consideration or a diet-related disease,
- A particular stage of the life cycle,
- Healthy school lunches,
- A healthy homemade alternative of a commercial/takeaway meal,
- Resourceful cookery,
- A food enterprise/farmers' market product/s,
- Ethnic cookery.

Examples

1 Certain people have special dietary needs.
Design and set out a two-course menu suitable for either (i) a coeliac or (ii) an anaemic young adult.
Prepare and serve the complete main course of the meal.
Prepare and serve the starter or dessert to complete the evening meal.
Calculate the cost of the main dish.

2 Bake sales are popular fund-raising activities.
List a variety of sweet and savoury goods that could be sold at a fund-raising event.
Demonstrate your baking skills by preparing, baking and serving one sweet and one savoury product listed.
Calculate the cost of both products and compare them to commercially sold products.

3 It is important to make healthy lunchtime choices.
Suggest some healthy snacks and savoury dishes that could be served in a school canteen.
Demonstrate your culinary skills by preparing, cooking and serving one healthy savoury dish.
Prepare a healthy snack to serve in a school canteen.
Calculate the cost of both dishes.

The Design Brief Process in 8 Smart Steps

1 **Read and analyse your Brief**
2 **Research the factors**
3 **Generate ideas/solutions**
4 **Present your ideas for feedback**
5 **Final solution**
6 **Write your report**
7 **Plan, prepare and produce product/s**
8 **Evaluate the product**

1. Read and Analyse your Brief carefully

- **Underline** and/or highlight all the **key words** in your brief. Look up words you do not understand.
- Identify clearly the **problems to be solved**.
- Is there a **theme**?
- Write the brief out again in your own words saying **what exactly you are being asked to do**.

2. Research the Factors

As part of the Classroom-Based Assessment, you will use technology, where appropriate, in researching, analysing, planning and presenting your results.

- Plan the areas you need to **research**.
- Research **ALL aspects** of the brief and **show evidence** of your research.
- Find the information you need for every aspect of your Brief, e.g. **books, internet, magazines, family, teacher, apps, etc.**
- To generate ideas. Make notes of the **facts** you discovered and keep good records of exactly where you found them.
- **Human factors** could be: nutritional needs, age, health, diseases, responsible family living, etc. Make notes and a bibliography.
- **Material factors** include: time, methods of cooking, availability of ingredients, costs, resources available, equipment and technology, environment and sustainability (seasonal foods, local ingredients, free foods, Fairtrade products). Make notes and a bibliography.

3. Generate Ideas/Solutions to satisfy your Brief

- **List three factors** to be considered, choosing possible solutions for **each part** of your Brief. Say why each one fulfils/satisfies the Brief in every way. You will need this to present your research and ideas to justify your choices to others for/during feedback.
- **Give two possible solutions** for **each part** of the Brief.
- **Give two** sources of information for each solution given.
- **Select** a solution that can be completed within the time allocated for the exam.
- **Timing:** Preparation 30 minutes, examination time including Evaluation 1 hour 30 minutes.
- Choose **your best solution** which is within your **level of ability and best shows your skills**.
- Give **two** good reasons for your choice for all aspects of the Brief. Your choice and reasons must always refer back to the theme of your brief.
- **List** and **show the evidence** of all your research. **(Bibliography)**

Take Note:

- Menus must be presented in **Menu form**, see page 12.
- Ensure your menu can be made and presented in the time allocated.
- Choose a solution which is within your level of ability and best shows your skills.
- All your answers and solutions must be specific to your theme.

4. Presenting Your Ideas to Others for Feedback **and justify your decisions**

I have chosen this menu because… Listen carefully to the feedback and note the following in your report folder as evidence of learning:

- What you did well.
- What needs improvement.
- Any weak areas identified by your teacher and peers.
- Reflect on what you aim to achieve.
- Use peer discussion to reflect on your own work and provide feedback to your peers. The opportunity to share one's reflections and findings is beneficial.

5. Final Solution **after feedback make decisions**

- **Upon reflection** take on board what your classmates and teacher advised and finalise your dishes to satisfy each aspect of your brief and make your final choice.
- When giving reasons for choosing a solution (dishes) develop answer with reference to your specific brief.

6. Write Your Report **This will be evidence of learning for assessment**

Present it as **fact sheets, a poster, computer presentation or in a folder.** Be clear and creative.

1. Statement of brief. *What exactly am I being asked to do?*
2. **Three factors** to be considered when choosing a possible solution for each aspect of your task.
3. **Two possible solutions** for **each** aspect of your task.
4. **Two** sources of information.
5. Your **chosen solutions**.
6. **Two reasons** for your choices. Develop your answer and make reference to your Brief.
7. Evidence of the research you carried out, presented as a bibliography.

- Write out your **Menu**, see page 12 for format.
- Write out your **shopping list** with costs/prices.
- List the **Equipment** you will need.
- Make a **Word Bank** for evaluation.
- **Practise** the Dishes and **Evaluation**. See pages 223 and 224.

7. A. Plan, Prepare and Produce the Product/s on Exam Day

1 Make sure you know the date, day and time of your exam.
2 Make sure you have your folder with your recipes, lists of ingredients, plan, etc.
3 The day before the exam, check you have all the ingredients you will need.
4 Shop for any fresh foods you will use on the day before the exam. Store them correctly.
5 Weigh, pack and label all the ingredients carefully. Store perishables in a fridge.
6 Check with your teacher what equipment you will need to bring from home, e.g. serving dishes, sharp knives, etc.

B. Exam Day Preparation: 30 minutes

1 **Prepare self**
Remove nail polish, jewellery and jumper. Roll up sleeves and tie back hair. Cover cuts. Put on apron and number, wash hands. (Comfortable, flat shoes are safest.)

2 **Prepare your equipment and utensils**
Gather everything that you will need. (Wash and polish if necessary.) Put out dish cloths and tea towels. Place a plate beside the hob for spoons and oven gloves for hot dishes. Have a bowl/glass, serviette and cutlery ready for examiner. Oven may be turned on very low but not set to correct temperature until exam begins. Open cans/tins, grease and line baking trays and/or tins.

3 **Prepare your ingredients**
Measure and weigh accurately. Prepare ingredients for different dishes on separate plates. Wash fruit and vegetables but do not peel, chop or mix anything. Make stock.

4 **Put your exam number, task number and name of your dish/es in large lettering on an A4 sheet and hang it on the front of your table or unit.** Make sure that you have your work sheets and a biro or pencil for your evaluation. (Make sure to use the toilet before the exam begins!)

C. Exam: 1 hour 30 minutes

- Listen to the examiner's instructions. Have Time Plan opened.
- If using an oven, set the temperature.
- Work methodically, paying attention to Good Practices while Cooking (pages 3 and 4).
- Do not waste resources, food, water or energy. Separate waste correctly, e.g. compost peelings, general waste, etc.
- Use the dish cloth to clean down the table. Use the tea towel for drying dishes only.
- If you make a mistake, work out a rescue plan – don't panic!
- Work quickly, watch the time (do not talk during exam).
- Garnish and serve the dish/es as soon as it is ready. Make sure you serve the complete dish. Do not leave any food in the saucepan or wok. There is no need to portion food. Call the examiner immediately.
- Start washing up. Do not wash equipment under a running tap.
- As soon as the examiner has tested your dish, taste (serve yourself a little on a plate; do not eat from dish) and evaluate your brief and dish/es.
- Finish washing up, dry all dishes and leave out for examiner to check.
- Show contents of your waste bins to examiner.
- Wipe sink, cooker and unit/table and sweep floor.

8. Evaluate the Product

Evaluate your work and the dishes you made under the following headings:

- Describe what went well.
- Explain what you were unhappy with and say why.
- What do you think you could do better next time?

1 Meeting the Brief

Think! What were you asked to do? Explain. Did you achieve your aim?

2 Specifics:

Think! What are the specific requirements of the brief? Write out the key points of your brief, include: dietary requirements, restrictions, age groups, costings, sustainability, nutritional guidelines, ethnic dish/dishes, specific menu, etc.

3 Critical appraisal of end result/results (each dish)

Think of the overall result of your cooking.

Describe the various aspects of your dish/dishes (see below) and give reasons for your comments, e.g. *'the pastry was a nice golden colour because it was brushed with egg and cooked at the right temperature and for the right amount of time.'*

Presentation, e.g. garnish/decoration (attractive, clean, neat, colourful, edible, fresh, suitable, even)

Colour (pale, light, golden, underdone, bright, dark, burnt, etc.)

Consistency/texture (thick, chewy, tough, smooth, creamy, hard, soft, crispy, dry, etc.)

Shape (even, uneven, lopsided, shapeless, good, bad, etc.)

Taste and flavour (bitter, sweet, salty, oily, cold, hot, spicy, savoury, mild, etc.

Undercooked or overcooked (white, pale, dark, burnt, etc.)

4 Evaluation of implementation

Think efficiency, skills, proposed modifications, etc.

Planning and preparation (Did you have all your ingredients, equipment, Time Plan, etc.)

Skills (dicing, rubbing in, sautéing, simmering, folding, kneading, etc.)

Cooking (preheated oven, temperature, timing, correct cooking methods, etc.)

Hygiene (clean, tidy work area, wash up, utensils and equipment properly cleaned, etc.)

Safety (oven mitts, pot handles, pot stands, hot liquids, cross-contamination, etc.)

Resources (peeling vegetables thinly, no waste of ingredients, water, fuel, time, etc.)

5 Proposed Modifications

Think! What do you need to improve in the future and what would you change? (Weigh and measure ingredients more accurately, check timing and temperature more carefully, practise more often, follow the Time Plan in sequence, etc.)

FOUR SMART EVALUATIONS

Evaluate your work! Complete one of the following assessments after your culinary skills class.

A. Do Some SMART Research, see page 220.

1 Explain what you researched and learned before class. What did you already know?
2 How did you prepare (i) yourself and (ii) the worktop for food preparation?
3 List the following that you learned today:
  (a) skills
  (b) cooking methods
  (c) technology
4 Give the cost of three ingredients you used? Look up one food on the internet.

B. Management and Cookery, see page 223.

1 Did you follow each step of your recipe correctly? What did you learn from this?
2 Explain how the following are important when preparing food:
  (a) safety
  (b) hygiene
  (c) tidiness
3 Describe how you saved the following resources:
  (a) food
  (b) hot water
  (c) fuel
  (d) time
4 Give three examples of how you recycle correctly. What have you learned?

C. Finished Dish. See page 223 for Ideas.

1 Explain how you **presented** or would present your dish for an exam.
2 Describe the **colour** of your finished dish and explain if it could be improved.
3 Did you like the **flavour**? Explain why. Describe how you might modify it next time.
4 Describe the **texture**. Was it cooked properly? What have you learned?

D. Knowledge, Learning and Modifying Fun.

1 Did you already know how to make what did you in class today? Did you do it well?
2 What did you learn? Was there anything you could have improved?
3 Are there any changes (modifications) you would include if making the dish again?
4 List **three** useful things you learned in class today. Did you enjoy it?
5 Decide if your learning was one of the following, and explain why:
  (a) Exceptional,
  (b) Above expectations,
  (c) In line with expectations,
  (d) Yet to meet expectations.

Notes

Glossary of Cookery Terms

Accompaniment: a food served with another, e.g. Yorkshire Pudding served with Roast Beef.
A la crème: served with cream or a cream-based sauce.
Al dente: an Italian expression meaning with a 'bite', e.g. pasta is cooked 'al dente'. See page 84.
Au gratin: food covered in sauce sprinkled with crumbs or cheese, browned under the grill.
Baking blind: a method of baking a pastry case without a filling. See page 172.
Bap: a soft bread roll used to accompany soups or used for a sandwich.
Blanch: to place food briefly in boiling water (a) to remove the skin, e.g. from tomatoes or almonds, (b) to remove strong flavours, e.g. onions or (c) to inactivate enzymes before freezing vegetables.
Blend: to mix ingredients smoothly together to prevent lumps, e.g. custard powder and milk.
Bouquet garni: a small bunch of herbs and spices, e.g. parsley, thyme and peppercorns, placed in muslin and tied with string or made into a sachet. Used to flavour soups, sauces, etc. See page 24.
Brine: a salt and water solution used for preserving.
Buffet: when food is placed on a table and people help themselves.
Casserole: to cook food slowly in a heatproof dish in an oven or an ovenproof dish with lid.
Chill: to place foods in the refrigerator or on ice.
Chowder: a thick soup usually made with seafood. See page 29.
Colander: a perforated metal or plastic container used for draining away liquids.
Consistency: the thickness of a mixture.
Creaming: beating butter and sugar together until pale and fluffy, e.g. Madeira cake. See pages 181, 198.
Crème fraîche: cream that has been allowed to mature with special bacteria but not allowed to sour.
Croûtons: small cubes of fried (or oven toasted) bread served with soups and salads. See page 34.
Crudités: raw vegetables, cut into batons and served with dips or as a hors d'oeuvre. See page 20.
Curdle: when milk or sauce separates into solids and liquids by overheating or by adding acid. See pages 155, 198.
Dice: to cut into small cubes. See page 34.
Doyley: small lace-effect paper mat used on plates (named after a London draper c.1712). See page 10.
Dredge: to coat food by sprinkling with icing or caster sugar.
Dumpling: small balls of dough which are cooked and used to garnish soup and stews. See page 117.
Essence: concentrated liquid flavourings for food, e.g. vanilla or almond. See page 155.
Folding: gently mixing ingredients together using a large metal spoon and a light cutting action. See page 206.
Fool: a cold dessert made from a mixture of fruit purée and whipped cream or custard. See page 146.
Garnish: enhancing a savoury dish with edible decoration, e.g. parsley, chives, tomato, etc.
Glaze: a glossy finish given to food by brushing with egg or milk before baking, e.g. pastry.
Goujon: small pieces of fried fish or chicken.
Herbs: aromatic plants. They can be fresh, frozen or dried, e.g. parsley, thyme and basil.
Hors d'oeuvres: hot or cold appetisers served at the start of a meal.
Infuse: to heat herbs or spices slowly in liquid, e.g. bay leaves, vanilla pod, to draw out flavour. See page 42.
Knead: to work dough with the hands to develop elasticity and to make it smooth.
Liaison: a thickening agent, e.g. flour, cornflour, arrowroot. Used for stews, soups, etc.
Marinade: a blend of oil, acid and herbs or spices used to tenderise and flavour meat or fish. See page 57.
Menu: a list of foods available for a meal. It should be written in menu form. See page 12.
Offal: edible internal organs, e.g. liver, heart and kidney.
Panard or **panada**: a very thick sauce used to bind ingredients together.
Parboil: to partially cook by boiling.
Pectin: a natural substance found in the walls of fruit and used to set jams and jellies.
Pith: the inner white part under the outer coloured skin of citrus fruit. It has a bitter taste.
Poach: to cook gently in water that is well below boiling point. See page 75.
Pulses: peas, beans and lentils (also called legumes). They are the seeds of these plants.
Purée: a soft smooth mixture of fruit or vegetables, usually liquidised, processed or sieved.

Quiche: a pastry case filled with a savoury filling/mixture of egg vegetables, meat or seafood.
Raising agent: a substance used to produce CO2 gas in a mix, e.g. bread soda (alkali/base) + buttermilk (acid), baking powder or yeast. When heated CO2 expands and raises a dough.
Ratatouille: stew made of aubergines, courgettes, onions, peppers and tomatoes cooked in olive oil. See page 60.
Roux: equal quantities of flour and fat cooked together. Used to thicken sauces, soups, etc. See page 41.
Rubbing in: to crumble fat into flour using the fingertips until it resembles breadcrumbs. See pages 181, 209.
Sauté: to fry food rapidly in hot fat. It is sometimes browned; sometimes not. See pages 28, 44, 46, 60, 70.
Searing: browning meat rapidly with high heat to seal in the juices. See page 128.
Seasoning: adding salt, pepper, herbs or spices to foods to improve the flavour.
Shortening: any fat used in baking which produces a brittle effect, e.g. butter, margarine, lard.
Simmering: cooking in a liquid just below boiling point; the water is barely moving. See pages 25, 29, 86.
Skimming: to remove froth, scum or fat from the surface of a liquid.
Smash garlic: give the unpeeled clove of garlic a sharp bash with a wide blade of a knife – this allows the skin to come off easier. Avoid the white tip as it is bitter. See page 39.
Stewing: to simmer food slowly or very gently in a casserole or saucepan. See page 115.
Stir-fry: cooking in a wok/pan with very little oil while stirring with two spoons or chopsticks. See page 132.
Suet: fat from around the liver and kidney.
Syrup: a thick sweet liquid made by boiling sugar and water and/or fruit juice.
Vinaigrette: a salad dressing made with oil, vinegar, salt and pepper and sometimes herbs.
Zest: the coloured outer skin of citrus fruit (oranges, lemons, limes and grapefruit) which has a wonderful flavour. Grated or peeled, it is used to flavour foods. Avoid the white pith. See pages 150, 215.

STORE CUPBOARD

White flour: plain, self-raising, cornflour.
Brown flour: brown, wholemeal.
White sugar: granulated, caster, icing.
Brown sugar: Demerara – larger crystals, soft brown sugar – smaller crystals.
Raising agents: baking powder, bread soda.
Rice: long grain, pearl or pudding rice, brown rice, wild rice, basmati.
Pasta: spaghetti, tagliatelle, macaroni, lasagne, shapes, wholewheat, green, red, etc.
Grains: quinoa, fine couscous, bulgur wheat.
Oats: porridge oats, jumbo oats, pinhead oatmeal.
Chocolate: cocoa powder, chocolate bars (plain or milk – 70% cocoa solids is best).
Nuts: walnuts, peanuts, almonds – flaked and ground, cashews.
Dried fruits: raisins, sultanas, apricots, cranberries.
Salt: table salt, sea salt, pink Himalayan salt.
Pepper: white pepper, ground black pepper, black peppercorns.
Oils: extra virgin olive, sunflower, avocado, coconut.
Vinegars: red wine vinegar, white wine vinegar, white vinegar, balsamic, cider vinegar.
Mustards: Dijon, wholegrain, English.
Coconut: desiccated coconut, coconut milk, coconut water, creamed coconut.
Tinned pulses: red kidney beans, butter beans, mixed beans, chick peas, Puy lentils.
Tinned tomatoes: unflavoured, chopped or whole (but chopped are best), cherry tomatoes.
Tinned sweetcorn: choose unsalted vacuum packed.
Tinned fruits: choose only in natural unsweetened juice.
Tomato purée: buy the tube when using small amounts, otherwise buy a small tin.
Pesto: red or green.
Pastes: Thai curry paste, red or green, tahini.
Sauces: Worcestershire sauce, tomato ketchup, soy sauce, fish sauce, miso. Coeliacs use Tamari sauce.
Jam: good-quality fine cut marmalade, strawberry, raspberry, apricot.
Honey: locally produced or Irish honey.
Juices: cartons of natural unsweetened, orange, apple, Jif lemon juice.
Herbs: dried or frozen, parsley, thyme, mint, basil, dill, coriander, oregano, marjoram or tarragon.
Spices: ginger, nutmeg, cinnamon, turmeric, cloves ground and whole, chilli, cayenne pepper, paprika pepper, curry powder – Thai green or red.
Seeds: sesame, poppy, sunflower, pumpkin, flax, chia, goji berries.

Food Pyramid

These are some examples of foods in each of the main food groups. Servings identified are for adults and children per day. It is recommended to drink at least 8 glasses of water a day.

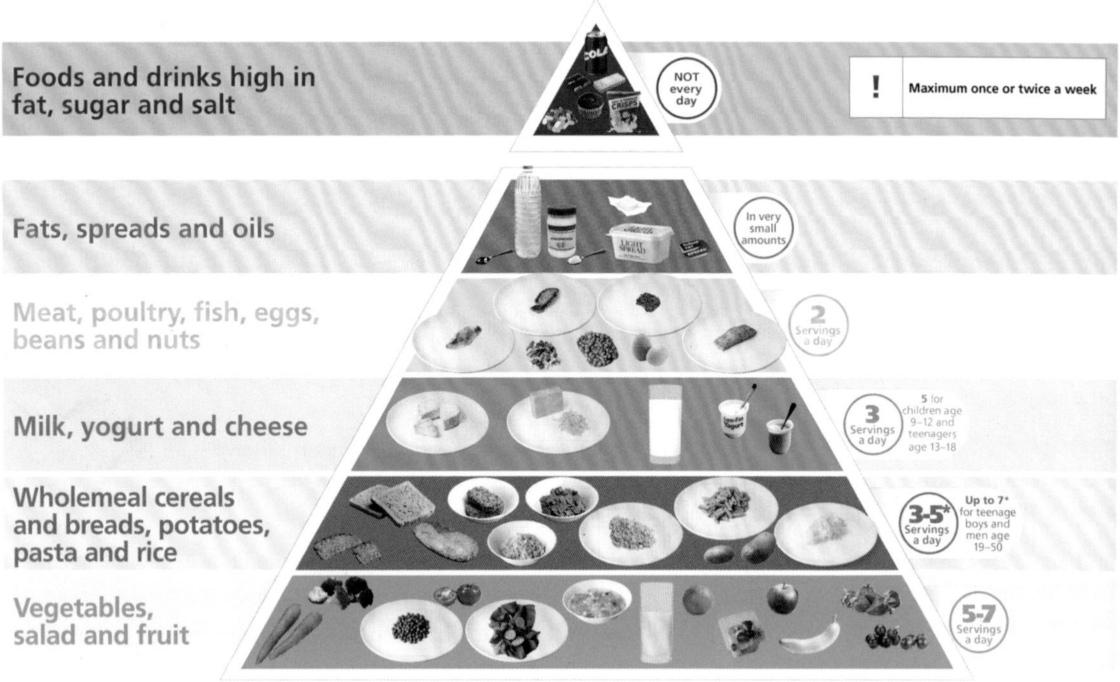